ENTROPY
Into the Greenhouse World

BANTAM NEW AGE BOOKS

This important imprint includes books in a variety of fields and disciplines and deals with the search for meaning, growth and change.

Ask your bookseller for the books you have missed.

ENTROPY
Into the Greenhouse World

Revised Edition

Jeremy Rifkin
with Ted Howard

Afterword by Dr. Nicholas Georgescu-Roegen

BANTAM BOOKS
NEW YORK • TORONTO • LONDON • SYDNEY • AUCKLAND

To Dr. Nicholas Georgescu-Roegen,
who laid the groundwork by persevering
as prophet and teacher.

ENTROPY: INTO THE GREENHOUSE WORLD

A Bantam Book / published by arrangement with
The Viking Press

Printing History
Viking Press edition published September 1980
Originally published as ENTROPY: A NEW WORLD VIEW

Bantam New Age and the accompanying figure design as well as the statement *"the search for meaning, growth and change"* are trademarks of Bantam Books, a division of Bantam Doubleday Dell Publishing Group, Inc.

Grateful acknowledgment is made to Harvard University Press for permission to reprint an excerpt from The Entropy Law and the Economic Process by Nicholas Georgescu-Roegen.

Bantam edition / October 1981
Bantam Revised edition / June 1989

Library of Congress Cataloging-in-Publication Data

Rifkin, Jeremy.
   Entropy : into the greenhouse world / by Jeremy Rifkin, with Ted Howard ; afterword by Nicholas Georgescu-Roegen.—Rev. ed.
      p.   cm.
   Bibliography: p.
   Includes index.
   ISBN 0-553-34717-9
   1. Human ecology—Philosophy. 2. Entropy. 3. Civilization—Philosophy. 4. Nonrenewable natural resources. I. Howard, Ted. II. Title.
GF21.R535   1989
304.2—dc19
                                                              88-39959
                                                                   CIP

Published simultaneously in the United States and Canada

PRINTED IN THE UNITED STATES OF AMERICA

FG   0   9   8   7   6   5   4   3   2   1

Acknowledgments

Special Editorial Contributions:
Noreen Banks
Dan Smith

Our special thanks to Marylin McDonald and Jeffrey Apter for their help in the copy-editing and preparation of the manuscript.

We would also like to acknowledge the contributions of Jenny Speicher and Randy Barber of the People's Business Commission.

We would especially like to thank Alan D. Williams, our editor at The Viking Press; his belief in the importance of this book has been a constant source of encouragement.

We'd also like to thank Leslie Meredith at Bantam Books for shepherding *Entropy* into this revised edition and Elissa Ditrio, Alyce Camille Richardson, and Matt Pawa for their help on this edition.

Contents

Author's Note

The industrial world is fast depleting the stock of nonrenewable fossil fuels that propel and maintain the engines of commerce and our modern way of life. At the same time, the mass burning of those very same fossil fuels has now resulted in the heating up of the earth's atmosphere to a point that now threatens our survival. The emerging energy crisis and the related global greenhouse phenomenon are the price humanity is now being forced to pay for failing to heed the entropic imperative.

To a civilization nurtured on the modernist notion of a future without physical constraints and a world without material boundaries, the truths of the Entropy Law will at first appear sobering, even somber. That is because this law defines the ultimate physical boundaries within which we are constrained to act.

If we continue to ignore the truth of the Entropy Law and its role in defining the broad context in which our physical world unfolds, then we shall do so at the risk of our own extinction.

After finishing this book some will remain unconvinced that there are physical limits that place restraints on human action in the world. Others will be convinced but will conclude with despair that the Entropy Law is a giant cosmic prison from which there is no escape. Finally, there will be those who will see the Entropy Law as the truth that can set us free. The first group will continue to uphold the existing world paradigm. The second group will be without a world view. The third group will be harbingers of the new age.

PART ONE

WORLD VIEWS

Into the Greenhouse World

The year is 2035.

In New York City palm trees line the Hudson River from 125th Street to the midtown exit. Recently, massive dikes have been built around the entire island of Manhattan in a concerted effort to hold back the rising sea water.

Phoenix is in its third week of temperatures over 120 degrees, and the city has begun the process of enclosing the downtown business district in giant air conditioned domes to accommodate the changing climate.

Bangladesh has ceased to exist. Torrential rains and rising flood waters have killed several million people. The remaining population has scattered to higher ground in Pakistan and India where they remain in makeshift refugee camps.

Desertification claims large sections of central Europe and the American midwest. Decades of drought have scorched the earth, turning once fertile agricultural lands into parched deserts.

Tens of millions of people continue to trek northward to higher latitudes in the greatest mass migration of populations in recorded history. Entire nations experience massive depopulation and starvation in the wake of prolonged droughts. Canada has become overrun, its population swelling from 25 million to 80 million in less than four decades.

Forest fires rage out of control over millions of acres of national parks for months on end. A long unremittent dry spell turns the Cascades region of the northwest United States into a giant tinder box.

The once mighty Mississippi River was closed to commercial traffic earlier in the century. In the summer months large sections of the river in Illinois and Missouri evaporate into giant mud flats, allowing people to cross by foot for the first time.

The earth's ozone layer continues to thin, causing a pandemic of cancer deaths. Hundreds of millions of people are exposed to dangerous levels of ultraviolet radiation, compromising their immune systems. Millions more become vulnerable to a range of exotic new diseases that have been spawned by the radical disruption and uprooting of entire ecosystems around the globe.

Welcome to the Greenhouse World of the twenty-first century.

Since the mid-1970s, climatologists and environmental scientists, coming together in small conference centers around the planet, have studied the changing climatic pattern of the earth, tracing shifts in precipitation and wind currents, testing air and water samples, compiling reams of data, and conducting sophisticated computer simulation modeling. Their conclusion? The planet is moving into the early stages of a significant shift in climate, a global warming trend so vast in scope that it could fundamentally affect all life, from microbes to man, in less than a century. Even more disturbing, this basic change in the earth's atmosphere is not the result of natural forces at work, but rather of human experimentation. For the first time, humankind has succeeded in altering the very climate of the planet, changing the dynamics of ecosystems and the prospects of habitation for thousands of years to come.

The greenhouse phenomenon is a simple process that has complex and unfathomable consequences. Carbon dioxide and other atmospheric gases allow solar radiation to enter the earth's atmosphere. The earth's surface absorbs much of the solar energy, converting it to infrared energy or heat. The heat then rises from the earth's surface and bombards the carbon dioxide and other gaseous molecules in the atmosphere, forcing the molecules to vibrate. The gas molecules act as reflectors, sending some of the heat back toward the surface of the earth, creating a warming effect. The greenhouse phenomenon is an essential feature of the earth's atmosphere, providing a warm temperature band conducive to the emergence of life on the planet. The natural greenhouse cover has varied little over eons of history.

With the dawn of the Industrial Age, in the mid-eighteenth century, the burning of massive amounts of fossil fuels caused carbon dioxide (CO_2) in the upper atmosphere to increase dramatically, blocking the release of heat from the planet. The result is a dramatic global warming unparalleled in geological history. In 1750, the earth's atmosphere contained approximately 280 ppm (parts per million) of CO_2. Today, the atmosphere contains 346 ppm.[1] Over the past 128 years, since 1860, the industrial nations have released more than 185 billion tons of carbon into the atmosphere from burning fossil fuels. In the same period carbon dioxide emissions have risen from 93 million tons to nearly 5 billion tons per year.[2] Scientists now project that sometime around A.D. 2030, the CO_2 concentration in the atmosphere will double, with world temperatures rising to unprecedented levels.[3] Carbon dioxide emissions from the burning of coal, oil, and natural gas account for nearly half of the increase in the greenhouse effect.[4]

Chlorofluorocarbons used in refrigerants, fast food containers, and aerosol sprays are also potent greenhouse gases that significantly affect global warming. Concern over CFCs has heightened over the past few years with the startling discovery in 1985 of a hole in the ozone layer above Antarctica. The ozone in the upper atmosphere provides a vital protective shield, preventing excessive amounts of ultraviolet radiation from reaching the earth. CFC gases migrate to the upper atmosphere where they are broken down by the sun's rays, releasing atoms of chlorine, which in turn destroys ozone.

The tear in the Antarctic ozone is worsening each year. Researchers recorded a 50 percent loss in 1985 and a 60 percent loss in 1987, and reported a gaping hole in the ozone layer the size of the continental U.S.[5] More recently, 100 leading atmospheric scientists reported a second tear in the ozone shield over the mid-Northern Hemisphere.[6] Now there are indications that a third tear has opened up in the Arctic, with scientists reporting a hole in the stratosphere the size of Greenland. The U.S. National Aeronautics and Space Administration (NASA) projects a 10 percent depletion of the ozone layer around the earth by the year 2050. The Environmental Protection Agency (EPA) predicts that this dramatic reduction in ozone protection will result in 2 million additional skin cancer cases annually.[7]

The increase in ultraviolet radiation also damages the human immune system, making people all over the planet more vulnerable to a host of infectious diseases. "It is no exaggeration to say that the health and safety of millions of people around the world are at stake," says Donald Douglas of the Natural Resources Defense Council.[8]

Plant and animal species are also vulnerable to the increase in ultraviolet radiation. At the University of Maryland, botanist Alan Teramura found that ultraviolet radiation results in tissue and cell damage in two-thirds of the 200 species tested.[9] According to Richard Adams of Oregon University, a 15 percent reduction in stratosphere ozone by the year 2050 could cause crop losses of $2.6 billion a year in the U.S.[10]

Perhaps the most dangerous finding to date is the effect of ultraviolet radiation on the photosynthesis and metabolism of plankton, the microscopic marine organisms that are the base of the ocean food chain. A recent study has reported serious effects on plankton in Antarctica in 1987, raising questions about the very survivability of aquatic life in the wake of increased ultraviolet radiation exposure.[11]

Increased ultraviolet exposure even affects plastics, paints, and other materials and will likely result in an additional $2 billion annual loss according to the EPA.[12]

While CFCs block ultraviolet rays from penetrating the atmosphere to reach the earth, they also trap heat radiating from the earth. In fact, CFCs are even more powerful blocking agents than CO_2. CFC emissions are climbing at an alarming rate, contributing greatly to the global warming trend.

Nitrous oxide largely from chemical fertilizers also contributes to the greenhouse phenomenon. The massive use of nitrogen-based fertilizers has been instrumental in increasing agricultural yields around the world over the past three decades. Ironically, the very chemical fertilizers that led to unparalleled gains in food production during that Green Revolution are now altering the climate over much of the temperate regions of the world, threatening the future of entire agricultural regions.

Scientists predict that nitrous oxide emissions from heavy use of chemical fertilizer will increase the global warming by the year 2030 by 10 to 20 percent over the level anticipated by carbon dioxide emissions.[13]

The Green Revolution has also increased the amount of methane gas released into the atmosphere, adding to the global warming trend. Methane is produced by bacteria that decompose organic matter in oxygen-deficient environments. Most of the methane emissions are released by rice paddies, the digestive tracts of cows, and landfills. By dramatically increasing rice production and cattle production to feed an ever-expanding human population, the Green Revolution increased the amount of methane released into the atmosphere. A burgeoning population, in turn, has led to an increase in garbage, more landfills, and still more methane emissions. For thousands of years, the amount of methane released into the atmosphere remained relatively constant. In the past 350 years it has nearly doubled and is increasing at 1 to 2 percent annually.[14] Over 140 million tons of methane are being released each year and research scientists predict that by the year 2030 methane emissions could increase the global warming by 20 to 40 percent.[15]

While carbon dioxide, CFCs, nitrous oxide, and methane all block the release of heat from the planet, the greenhouse phenomenon is further exacerbated by massive deforestation around the globe. Trees absorb vast amounts of carbon dioxide. At the present time, the worldwide rate of deforestation is ten times the rate of reforestation. According to the World Resources Institute, the deforestation rate is approximately 27 million acres a year.[16] Much of the deforestation is taking place in Brazil, Indonesia, and Zaire, which contain nearly half of the forests in the tropics.

Pollution from coal-burning power plants is also decimating forests around the world. Coal burning produces sulfur dioxide and nitrogen oxide. When released into the atmosphere, these gases produce acid rain. In 1984, the German government reported that 50 percent of the forests were damaged by acid rain.[17] Overall, 14 percent of European forests have been damaged by acid rain.[18] In Switzerland, Austria, Finland, Luxembourg, the Netherlands, Poland, and Czechoslovakia between 25 and 50 percent of the forests are severely damaged.[19]

Acid rain is also destroying the soil and polluting lakes and streams around the world. As soil acidity increases, nutrients are leached out, ruining the soil for agricultural production. Soil acidity in southwestern Sweden has increased tenfold in the past 60 years.[20] The soil base of countries throughout Europe has been seriously compromised by the increase in acidity.

Acid rain is also decimating aquatic life. In the United States the waters of the Adirondacks have experienced a sizable reduction in fish population because of increased acidity.[21] Scientists at the Freshwater Institute in Canada provided dramatic evidence of the effect of acid rain on aquatic life. Researchers intentionally acidified a small lake in Ontario and found that when the pH fell below 5.4 none of the species was able to reproduce.[22]

The total annual financial losses from acid rains are staggering. In Germany, scientists estimate a loss of $2.4 billion a year for the next several decades.[23] Worldwide, losses already exceed tens of billions of dollars annually.

Just five hundred years ago, much of the planet was covered in dense forest. Today, the globe has been stripped, leaving only isolated patches of trees to absorb overwhelming amounts of CO_2 emissions being spewed into the atmosphere.

Many scientists now predict that if the current trend of carbon dioxide, chlorofluorocarbon, nitrous oxide, and methane emissions continues into the next century, increased industrial activity could subject the entire globe to an increased temperature rise of four to nine degrees Fahrenheit or more in less than sixty years. To understand the enormity of this projected change, consider the fact that in the past 18,000 years during which human civilization has emerged, the average global temperature has varied less than 3.6 degrees Fahrenheit.[24]

A global warming of four to nine degrees in just five or six decades would exceed the entire rise in global temperatures since the end of the last ice age. If the scientific projections are correct, the human species will experience the unfolding of an entire geological epoch in less than one lifetime.

Deluge and Drought

Until 1988, the greenhouse phenomenon had remained a purely scientific issue, a subject of grave concern to climatologists and environmental scientists, but few others. The great farm drought of 1988 has now lifted the issue from academic obscurity to public attention, forcing policy makers to begin to address the problem.

In June of 1988, Dr. James E. Hansen, the director of the NASA Goddard Institute for Space Studies stunned a congressional committee by asserting that we have already entered the Greenhouse World, earlier than anticipated. According to the NASA report, "The earth is warmer in 1988 than at any time in the history of instrumental measurement. The rate of global warming in the past two decades is higher than at any time in the record. The four warmest years in the past century all have occurred in the 1980s. . . . The global warming is now sufficiently large that we can ascribe with a high degree of confidence a cause and effect relationship to the greenhouse effect."[26] According to Hansen, heat waves and drought in the southeastern and midwestern regions of the U.S. will become increasingly frequent in the decades ahead.[27]

While not all climatologists are willing to ascribe the current heat wave to the greenhouse phenomenon, they are virtually united in their belief that we are on the threshold of a fundamental global warming that will disrupt the ecosystems and social systems of this planet in fundamental ways, some of which lie well beyond the human ability to control or direct. A few examples illustrate the magnitude of the crisis ahead.

Global warming will lead to thermal expansion of seawater and melting of land ice in the polar regions. Climatologists now predict a dramatic rise of up to five feet (1.5 meters) in sea level by the year 2050.[28] A one- to five-foot rise in water level in less than sixty-five years could devastate coastal areas where half of the world's population resides, resulting in massive loss of lives and property. It is estimated that the cost of just protecting the shore areas of the east coast of the U.S. will be between $10 and $100 billion in the wake of a three-foot rise in the ocean level.[29]

The rise in sea level will devastate major port facilities throughout the world, and wreak havoc on drainage systems, locks, and canals. Many nations are already concerned over the possibility of salt water intrusion into freshwater rivers and groundwater, contaminating the drinking water of millions of people. The Public Works Department of the Netherlands estimates that a three-foot rise in sea level will necessitate the expenditure of several billion dollars in repair and maintenance to secure its fragile coastal infrastructure.[30] Hundreds of large ports and thousands of smaller ones around the world face a similar threat. Worldwide expenditures to protect vital seaports could exceed hundreds of billions of dollars.

The rise in sea level will likely destroy many smaller island nations like the Marshall Islands of the Pacific, the Caribbean islands, and the Maldives off the coast of India. "You're looking at a potential refugee problem of unprecedented dimensions," says Robert Buddemeier of Lawrence Livermore National Laboratory. "In the past people have run away from famine or oppression, but they've never been physically displaced from a country because a large part of it has disappeared."[31]

Low-lying countries like Egypt will also feel the shock of an increase in sea level. According to a study conducted by James Broadus of the Woods Hole Oceanographic Institute, Egypt could lose 15 percent of its arable land along the Nile Delta, displacing one-seventh of its population. This massive loss of productive land would lower the gross domestic output of Egypt by a staggering 14 percent.[32]

It is expected that the sea level rise will also destroy the remaining coastal wetlands, salt marshes, swamps, and bayous—most of which lie in the southeastern region off the Gulf of Mexico and Atlantic seaboard. An EPA study predicts that a five-foot rise in sea level will destroy upward of 90 percent of America's wetlands, a rich and diverse complex of unique ecosystems that have flourished unmolested since well before the dawn of recorded history until the incursion of Western European settlers.[33] While the financial losses will be extraordinary, the ecological and aesthetic losses are truly incalculable.

The rise in sea temperature and sea level will also increase both the number and intensity of hurricanes worldwide. Hurricane intensity is directly linked to the temperature of the water surface. According to the models of meteorologist Kerry Emanuel of the Massachusetts Institute of Technology, the increase in global warming and sea warming will increase the intensity of hurricanes by 40 to 50 percent.[34] The potential damage to life and property along coastal areas is likely to be unprecedented in human history. Large parts of Miami could be swept away by sixteen-foot walls of water. Cities like Galveston, Atlantic City, and Myrtle Beach could be decimated by the impact of superhurricanes.[35]

Global warming will also fundamentally alter precipitation patterns in every region of the globe. In some areas, lakes, rivers, and aquifers that have nurtured entire ecosystems for years will shrink or dry up altogether. In other regions, new lakes and streams will appear for the first time in human history, radically changing the topography and environment. The flow of the Upper Colorado River Basin will drop by an estimated 40 percent.[36] Some climatologists predict a 40 percent decline in rainfall in the agricultural belts of the U.S., turning parts of the bread basket of the world into a dust bowl.[37]

Retooling the nation's dams and irrigation systems to adjust to the global warming will cost between $7 and $23 billion.[38] Worldwide, 18 percent of the cropland is currently under irrigation and accounts for a third of the agricultural production on the planet. The radical change in climate and precipitation will require an estimated $200 billion outlay to retool and relocate irrigation systems.[39]

As water becomes scarce in many regions of the U.S. and the world, entire communities and populations will be forced to migrate.

The Great Lakes will be free of ice for eleven months of the year. Lower water levels will mean an increase of 30 percent or more in shipping costs for coal, limestone, and grain, because the deep-draft freighters that carry such bulk cargo will no longer be able to navigate the lock systems of the St. Lawrence Seaway that connects to the Atlantic Ocean.[40]

A significant rise in global temperature is likely to melt much of the polar ice in the Arctic, opening up new sea lanes for the first time in human history. "The fabled Northwest Passage would be open," according to Walter Roberts of the National Center for Atmospheric Research. "You could sail from Tokyo to Europe in half the time." On the other hand, shipping companies are worried that losses of cargo and crew would increase as the Northern Atlantic became strewn with dangerous icebergs.[41]

The global warming is going to wreak havoc on the delicate web of chemical balances and flows that regulates the growth and maturation of plants and animals and governs the complex interrelationships in planetary ecosystems. For example, increased levels of CO_2 may result in the deterioration of food quality as plant leaves become richer in carbon and poorer in nitrogen. In an article in *Fortune* magazine in 1988, A. H. Moore graphically illustrated the chain reaction that can be triggered by such an event. Insects would have to ravage many more nitrogen-poor plants to fulfill their nitrogen requirements. "Hungrier pests and damaging diseases might thrive on the greenhouse effect, forcing farmers to buy more pesticides. . . ."[42]

Global warming will also lead to mass extinction of tree species and the loss of millions of acres of forest, especially in the middle latitudes of the planet. According to the Bellagio Report, a detailed study conducted this past year by some of the world's leading climatologists and environmental activists, the greenhouse phenomenon is likely to have major effects on forests by the year 2000. The authors of the report predict a large-scale forest dieback before A.D. 2100.[43] A catastrophic loss of forest cover will accelerate the greenhouse effect, since there will be fewer trees available to absorb the CO_2 emissions.

The rapid destruction of forest habitats will also accelerate the loss of animal life and could lead to the mass extinction of many remaining species. We are already losing one species to extinction every sixty minutes. It is estimated that even without the global warming phenomenon, we might lose up to 17 percent of all the remaining species of life over the next few decades as a result of the ravaging of tropical rain forests for development purposes—timbering, grazing, and cropping.[44]

Forests will not be able to migrate as fast as the climate changes accelerate. Writing in the journal *Science,* Richard A. Kerr points out that "each one degree centigrade of warming pushes climatic zones 100 to 150 kilometers [60 to 95 miles] northward." Within sixty years, the climate that nurtures Yellowstone National Park, for example, will have shifted well to the north into Canada.[45] Trees are not capable of migrating at the speeds set by the greenhouse phenomenon. In every region of the globe, entire ecosystems—trees, insects, microbes, animals—will be trapped by these rapid shifts in climate, left behind to wither and die.

Economic systems, like ecosystems, are going to find it difficult, if not impossible, to adjust in time to the rapid changes in climate. Virtually every nation in the world is currently making future development decisions based on the false assumption that the climatic environment its ancestors have lived within for thousands of years will continue to exist fifty years from now. At the conclusion of the World Climate Program in 1985, scientists from twenty-five industrialized and developing nations warned that "many important economic and social decisions are being made today on long-term projects . . . such as irrigation and hydropower; drought relief; agricultural land use; structural designs and coastal engineering projects; and energy planning—all based on the assumption that past climatic data . . . are a reliable guide to the future. This is no longer a good assumption since the increasing concentrations of greenhouse gases are expected to cause a significant warming of the global climate in the next century."[46]

For example, British Petroleum has invested $11 billion in

Alaska. The roads, housing, and drilling equipment along the trans-Alaska pipeline are built on permafrost, which is likely to thaw within the next three to five decades, seriously affecting billions of dollars of BP infrastructure.[47]

Nor is BP alone. Multinational corporations and nation states around the world may well have to retool trillions of dollars of infrastructure to adapt to the rapidly changing climatic conditions. Present-day buildings, bridges, dams, roads, sewer systems, canals, and machinery of all kinds, are all designed for climatic stress tolerances that will no longer be applicable in fifty to 100 years. Jesse Ausubel, of the National Academy of Engineers, expresses the feeling of deep anxiety emerging within the development community when he asks, "What do you do when the past is no longer a guide to the future?"[48]

In the concluding statement of the Changing Atmosphere Conference held in Toronto in June 1988, government leaders and scientists from forty-eight countries warned the world of the dangers that lie just ahead with the continued global warming brought on by the greenhouse effect:

"Humanity is conducting an uncontrolled, globally pervasive experiment whose ultimate consequences could be second only to a global nuclear war."[49]

Our species now faces its greatest challenge: to awaken the consciousness and conscience of humanity to the perils of a globe that is burning up. Like the creatures that live within its environs, the earth too is an organism that lives within a narrow temperature band. Now the earth is experiencing a runaway fever that threatens to extinguish the life pulse of the planet. The global greenhouse warming is the first truly universal crisis that our species has ever faced. The altered climate of the globe affects every aspect of existence, from the reproductive success of the lowliest plankton on the ocean surface to the survival of the great urban cultures that occupy the coastal land mass of the planet. This is a crisis from which there is no escape, and no place to hide. Its impact will be felt across all geopolitical, ethnic, and class boundaries. The global warming is the first human crisis in which the context is the entire planet.

The first photos of Earth taken from outer space allowed us to see ourselves as a single entity in the universe. The global greenhouse crisis forces us, for the first time, to understand that our personal survival now depends entirely on the collective will of humanity. The greenhouse crisis can only be effectively addressed by a massive mobilization of human effort on a scale never before attempted. It will be necessary to cross language barriers, religious barriers, geographic, political, and ideological barriers, and unite the fragmented and often warring strands of humanity into a unified force with a single mission: to return the globe to equilibrium and breathe life back into the lungs of the earth.

The first crucial stage along the road to restoration is to understand the path that led to the crisis. The global greenhouse phenomenon is not an accident or aberration. Nor is it the inevitable consequence of evolutionary forces at work. The greenhouse crisis is a crisis induced by humans. We are all responsible for the global warming trend. The greenhouse crisis represents the final bill, come due, for the Industrial Age.

The global warming trend is the second phase of an energy crisis now threatening the very existence of industrial civilization. The first phase of that crisis began in the early 1970s with the dramatic rise in worldwide oil prices. Disruption in oil supplies caught the industrial nations and developing countries by surprise. For the first time, the public became aware of the fact that the energy we rely on to maintain our way of life is a diminishing resource. While the energy crisis of the 1970s has temporarily abated, and oil is presently available in sufficient volume to meet world demand, energy experts foresee a dramatic decline in the remaining oil reserves over the next several decades, and steeper prices to offset the rising cost of exploration and increased consumer demand. As oil becomes more scarce and expensive, many nations will shift toward even greater reliance on coal, further exacerbating the global warming trend and the greenhouse crisis.

The energy crisis, then, is a two-fold phenomenon. At the same time as we are running short in our fossil fuel reserves, we are experiencing a global warming produced by the past burning of fossil fuels during the entire Industrial Age.

The energy crisis and the greenhouse global warming trend reflect the values we have chosen to live by during the short reign of the modern era. Over the past several hundred years, western civilization spawned a revolutionary new way of thinking about nature and our relationship to it. That "new way of thinking" cleared the way for the Industrial Age and the present Age of Progress. The new way of thinking gave us urbanization and electrification, automobiles and skyscrapers, processed foods and television, computers and space travel. The new way of thinking also inexorably led to species extinction, soil depletion, poisoned air and water, ozone holes, acid rain, forest destruction, urban blight, the uprooting of traditional cultures, and mass starvation, and now the energy crisis and related greenhouse phenomenon. The short-term benefits of the Industrial Age have been purchased at the expense of the long-term sustainability of the earth which houses us.

To understand the present crisis then, we first need to turn our attention to the world view that gave rise to it, paying particular attention to the underlying ideas that have led us to seriously compromise our obligations to the planet and to future generations who will inhabit it.

In the process of examination, we will begin to explore a radical new world view based on a completely different set of assumptions than the ones that inform our present thinking. The Entropy Law and the laws of thermodynamics provide the context for a postmodern way of thinking about the world and our relationship to it; a way of thinking that can help us arrest the present energy crisis and greenhouse warming and unite us in a new shared vision of the future.

The entropic world view promotes an empathetic science based on reestablishing a sense of relationship and participation with the planet as opposed to the more conventional science which emphasizes a detached exploitation of nature and the environment. In an entropic civilization new tools and technologies would be designed to favor long-term sustainability and durability over short-term hyper-efficiency and expediency. An entropic culture recognizes that all economic activity is merely an extension of the environment. As such, economic production and social consumption would never be allowed to outpace the eco-system's ability to recycle waste and renew the stock of available resources. The entropy paradigm is steeped in a new vision of the planet as a single organism in which all of the myriad relation-ships are nurtured and respected.

The entropic way of thinking provides a context for a post-modern form of consciousness that is far more sophisticated and challenging than the forms of knowing we have relied on in the past. In the pages that follow we will use the entropic paradigm to both reenvision our civilization and lay the foundation for heal-ing the planet. We will explore alternative energy technologies including solar, wind, and hydropower, examine the newest inno-vations in waste treatment and recycling, discuss the new field of ecological agriculture, and discuss the revolutionary changes that are likely to occur in our conception of work and education. We will also focus on alternative lifestyles and new ways of living together that are more compatible with our new ecological consciousness.

The deepening energy crisis and global warming trend are forcing us to reevaluate the very assumptions upon which our civilization is built. The new entropy framework provides a vehi-cle to both effectively critique the existing order and chart a new course for the coming century.

World Views

Throughout history, human beings have felt the need to construct a frame of reference for organizing life's activities. The need to establish an order to explain the how and why of daily existence has been the essential cultural ingredient of every society. The most interesting aspect of a society's world view is that its individual adherents are, for the most part, unconscious of how it affects the way they do things and how they perceive the reality around them. A world view is successful to the extent that it is so internalized, from childhood on, that it goes unquestioned.

Most Americans believe that the world is progressing toward a more valuable state as a result of the steady accumulation of human knowledge and techniques. We also believe that the individual exists as an autonomous entity, that nature has an order to it, that people have always desired private property, and that competition between individuals has always occurred. In fact, all these beliefs are considered to be part of "human nature" and therefore immutable. Of course, they are not, and other societies and civilizations at other periods in history would simply be unable to comprehend some of the notions we ascribe to human nature. That is the power of a world view. Its hold over our perception of reality is so overwhelming that we can't possibly imagine any other way of looking at the world.

Our modern world view took shape some 300 years ago, and while it has been greatly refined and modified in the years since, it has retained much of its early vision. We live under the influence of the seventeenth-century Newtonian world view paradigm. In the next chapter we will explore this paradigm in detail. There probably isn't one person in a hundred who could explain the intricate features of Newtonian mechanics; nonetheless, its shadow is always with us, influencing our every move.

But now, the modern world view is being challenged for the first time in the wake of the long-term energy crisis and the escalating greenhouse crisis. These stark new realities are forcing us to question many of the basic tenets that make up the central operating assumptions of the Age of Progress. At the same time, a new world view is beginning to emerge, one that will eventually replace the Newtonian paradigm as the organizing frame of history: the Entropy Law will preside as the ruling paradigm over the next period of history. Albert Einstein said that it is the premier law of all of science; Sir Arthur Eddington referred to it as the supreme metaphysical law of the entire universe. The Entropy Law is the second law of thermodynamics. The first law states that all matter and energy in the universe is constant, that it cannot be created or destroyed. Only its form can change but never its essence. The second law, the Entropy Law, states that matter and energy can only be changed in one direction, that is, from usable to unusable, or from available to unavailable, or from ordered to disordered. In essence, the second law says that everything in the entire universe began with structure and value and is irrevocably moving in the direction of random chaos and waste. Entropy is a measure of the extent to which available energy in any subsystem of the universe is transformed into an unavailable form. According to the Entropy Law, whenever a semblance of order is created anywhere on earth or in the universe, it is done at the expense of causing an even greater disorder in the surrounding environment. The Entropy Law will be explained in detail in Part Two.

For now a few simple observations are in order, observations that the reader will have to accept on faith, at least until we perform a thorough autopsy on the prevailing world view and explore the hidden dimensions of the new entropy paradigm. The Entropy Law undermines the idea of history as progress. The Entropy Law destroys the notion that science and technology create a more ordered world. In fact, the Entropy Law challenges the modern world view with a force of conviction that is every bit as convincing as was the Newtonian paradigm when it replaced the medieval Christian world view.

Step by step the Entropy Law will provide us with an understanding of exactly why the existing paradigm has broken down. Our generation, caught between the old paradigm that we were nurtured on and the new entropy paradigm just emerging, will begin to marvel at how we could have believed in principles and axioms so obviously false. We will stumble into the new paradigm, ill at ease and groping like a visitor to a foreign land. Unable to completely shed our native world view, we will take on the new entropy paradigm as a second language, never completely comfortable with it and never able to fully articulate it into our daily routines. For our grandchildren's generation the entropic world view will be like second nature: they will not think about it, they will merely live by it, unconscious of its hold over them, as we have for so long been unconscious of the hold Newtonian mechanics has had over us.

Already the outline of the new entropy paradigm is being filled in by scholars around the world. Within a few years every academic discipline will be influenced by the new entropy conception. There will be attempts to graft the Entropy Law onto the existing world view, a task that will ultimately fail. Politicians will proclaim its importance in addressing issues ranging from energy to disarmament. Theologians will construct new interpretations of Biblical authority based on it. Technicians will develop new approaches to problem solving in the misguided belief that it can be quantified and reduced to precise measurement. Economists will scramble to redesign classical economic theory to conform with its central truths. Psychologists and sociologists will reexamine human nature with entropy as a backdrop.

There will also be those who will stubbornly refuse to accept the fact that the Entropy Law reigns supreme over all physical reality in the world. They will insist that the entropy process only applies in selective instances and that any attempt to apply it more broadly to society is to engage in the use of metaphor. Quite simply, they are wrong. The laws of thermodynamics provide the overarching scientific frame for the unfolding of *all physical activity* in this world. In the words of the Nobel Prize-winning chemist Frederick Soddy, the laws of thermodynamics "control, in the last resort, the rise and fall of political systems, the freedom or bondage of Nations, the movements of commerce and industry, the origins of wealth and poverty, and the general physical welfare of the race." Every single physical activity that humankind engages in is subject to the iron clad imperative expressed in the first and second laws of thermodynamics.

It should be emphasized that the Entropy Law deals only with the physical world where everything is finite and where all living things must run their course and eventually cease to be. It is a law governing the horizontal world of time and space. It is mute, however, when it comes to the vertical world of spiritual transcendence. The spiritual plane is not governed by the ironclad dictates of the Entropy Law. The spirit is a nonmaterial dimension where there are no boundaries and no fixed limits to attend to. The relationship of the physical to the spiritual world is the relationship of a small part to the larger unbound whole within which it unfolds. While the Entropy Law helps govern the world of time, space, and matter, it is, in turn, governed by the primordial spiritual force that conceived it.

The way a civilization organizes its physical reality and the importance it attaches to the material plane of existence determines how favorable the conditions are for seeking spiritual enlightenment. The more steeped a world view is in the material side of life, the less conducive it is to the human quest for spiritual transcendence. The less attached a civilization is to the physical world, the freer the human collectivity is to transcend the confines of the material plane and become one with the profound spiritual essence that encompasses all.

The laws of thermodynamics, then, help shape the physical world. The way humanity decides to interact with those laws in establishing a framework for physical existence is of crucial importance in whether humankind's spiritual journey is allowed to flourish or languish. A thorough comprehension of the Entropy Law is crucial for understanding the physical context from which all spiritual sojourns must start.

Historians and anthropologists have long speculated over why a particular world view emerges at a particular time and place in history. This essay will suggest an answer to that question: that the energy condition of the environment sets the broad frame for the world view that emerges. But before attempting to demonstrate that claim, it is important that we remove ourselves from our own world view just long enough to take a hard look at how our own perception of reality has been shaped over the centuries.

The Greeks and the Five Ages of History: Cycles and Decay

How do we account for the fact that the philosophers of antiquity viewed history in a way that is exactly opposite to how we perceive it? Horace, a Roman, mused that "time depreciates the value of the world."[50] Horace didn't know about the second law of thermodynamics, but in this verse he summed up the very essence of the Entropy Law (as we will see in Part Two). For the Greeks, history was a process of continual degradation. In Greek mythology, history is represented by a series of five stages, each more degraded and more harsh than the one preceding it. The Greek historian Hesiod describes these ages as the Golden, Silver, Brass, Heroic, and Iron. The Golden Age was the apex: a period of abundance and fulfillment.

In the beginning, a golden race of mortal men was made by the immortal dwellers on Olympus. . . . They lived like Gods with hearts free from care, without part or lot in labor and sorrow. Pitiful old age did not await them, but ever the same in strength of hand and foot, they took their pleasure in feasting, apart from all evils. When they died it was as though they were overcome by sleep. All good things were theirs and the grain harvest was yielded by bountiful earth of her own accord—abundantly, ungrudgingly—while they in peace and good will lived upon their lands with good things in abundance.[51]

Hesiod's Golden Age would have been dismissed as a fairy tale by someone like Thomas Hobbes, who perceived humanity's initial state in nature as a "solitary, poor, nasty, brutish and short affair." Today however, anthropologists would be more inclined to agree with Hesiod's interpretation of humankind's early history. Studies of the few remaining hunter-gatherer societies bear out much of Hesiod's account. Detailed examinations of the African bushmen and other hunter-gatherer groups provide some real surprises for those of us who like to believe that human history has been a progressive journey from the backbreaking toil and labor of the early primitives to the comfortable, leisurely life of twentieth-century America.

We moderns take pride in the fact that we only have to work forty hours a week and that we can take off two or more weeks each year for vacation. Most hunter-gatherer societies would find such conditions intolerable. The fact is, contemporary hunter-gatherers work no more than twelve to twenty hours per week, and for weeks and months each year they do no work at all. Instead, their time is filled with leisure pursuits including games, sporting events, art, music, dance, ceremonies, and visiting with neighbors. Contrary to popular opinion, studies of the few remaining hunter-gatherer societies show that some are among the healthiest people in the world. Their diets are nutritious, and many—like the bushmen in Africa—live well into their sixties without the aid of modern medicine. Many hunter-gatherer societies place a premium on cooperation and sharing, and show little inclination for warring and aggression against each other or outside groups.

According to Hesiod, the Golden Age came to an abrupt end when Pandora lifted the lid on the box containing the evils of life. From then on each succeeding age has been more harsh and exacting than the one before it. The final age, according to Greek mythology, is the Iron Age. Speaking in the eighth century before Christ, Hesiod laments:

For now in these latter days is the Race of Iron. Never by day shall they rest from travail and sorrow, and never by night from the hand of the spoiler. The father shall not be of one mind

25

with the children, nor the children with the father, nor the guest with
the host that receives them, nor friends with friends. . . . Parents
shall swiftly age and swiftly be dishonored. . . . The righteous
man or the good man or he that keeps his oath shall not find
favor, but they shall honor rather the doer of wrong and the proud
man insolent. Right shall rest in might of hand and truth shall be
no more.[52]

The Greeks believed that while the world was created by the
Deity and was therefore perfect, it was not immortal. It had
within it the seeds of decay. History, then, is the process whereby
the original order of things maintains itself in perfection during
the Golden Age, only to begin an inevitable process of decay
during the subsequent ages of history. Finally, as the universe
approaches ultimate chaos, the Deity intervenes once again and
restores the original conditions of perfection. The whole process
then begins once again. History is seen not as a cumulative
progression toward perfection but as an ever repeating cycle
moving from order to chaos.

This idea of history as a decaying cyclical process heavily
influenced the Greek conception of how society should be ordered. Plato and Aristotle believed that the best social order was
the one that experienced the fewest changes; there was little room
in their world view for the concept of continuous change and
growth. Growth, after all, did not signal greater value and order
in the world, but the exact opposite. If history represented the
continued chipping away of the original perfect state, and the
using up of the original fixed bounty, then the ideal state was
the one that slowed down the process of decay as much as possible.
The Greeks associated greater change and growth with greater
decay and chaos. Their goal, then, was to hand down to the next
generation a world as much preserved from "change" as possible.

The Christian World View

Imagine a time warp that could put us face to face with a medieval Christian serf. The thirteenth century is not so very long ago. Only forty generations separate us from the feudal world. In fact, there's much about that world that we would immediately recognize. In England, students were already graduating from Cambridge, *Beowulf* had been written, and a form of English was being spoken—although we would find it difficult to understand. Still, even without a language barrier we and the serf would have very little of interest to say to each other after the usual chitchat about the weather. That's because we would probably be interested in finding out what his goals in life were. What contribution did he hope to make to the world? How was he bettering his lot in life? What kind of largesse did he expect to leave his children? What were his ideas about happiness and the good life? We might even want to probe a little deeper into his psyche, asking him about his personality traits and identity problems.

Of course, we shouldn't expect much in the way of a response. In fact, if all we see in his eyes is a blank expression, it's not because we're talking over his head, or because his mind isn't developed enough for the exchange of ideas. It's just that his ideas about life, history, and reality are so utterly different from our own.

The Christian view of history, which dominated western Europe throughout the Middle Ages, perceived life in this world as a mere stopover in preparation for the next. The Christian world view abandoned the Greek concept of cycles but retained the notion of history as a decaying process. In Christian theology, history has a distinct beginning, middle, and end in the form of the Creation, the Redemption, and the Last Judgment. While human history is linear, not cyclical, it is not believed to be progressing toward some perfected state. On the contrary, history is seen as an ongoing struggle in which the forces of evil continue to sow chaos and disintegration in the earthly world.

Equally important, the doctrine of original sin precluded the possibility of humanity ever improving its lot in life. In fact, the idea of people making or changing history would have been unthinkable. After all, to the medieval mind the world was a tightly ordered structure in which God controlled every single event. The Christian God was a personal God who intervened in every aspect of life. If things happened or didn't happen it was because God willed it. God made history, not people.

There were no personal goals, no desires to get ahead or to leave something behind. There were only God's decrees to be faithfully carried out. As historian John Randall points out, for the medieval Christian "everything must possess significance not in and for itself, but for man's pilgrimage." The purpose of every action, of every unfolding event, was tied to the "purpose it served in the divine scheme."[53]

The Christian world view provided a unified and all-encompassing picture of history. There was no room for the individual in this grand theological synthesis. It was duties and obligations, not freedoms and rights, that cemented and unified the historical frame of medieval life. Like the Greeks, the medieval concept of history was not one of growth and material gain. The human purpose was not to "achieve things" but to seek salvation. Toward this end, society was viewed as an organic whole, a kind of divinely directed moral organism in which each person had a part to play.

Toward the Modern World View

There is no way to know how many professors have delivered lectures and how many students have been forced to sit through them over the course of history. Only a tiny handful of those lectures have ever made history. Jacques Turgot, a history teacher at the Sorbonne, is among those who have earned a place in this elite club. In 1750, he walked into a classroom in Paris, took out his notes, and began a two-part lecture in Latin on a new concept of world history. Turgot took on Plato, Aristotle, Saint Paul, Saint Augustine, and all of the intellectual giants of the ancient and medieval worlds. By the time he had finished his last sentence, he had changed the entire construct of world history. The lectures, observed Frank Manuel, "framed a new conception of world history from remotest antiquity to the present and constituted the first important version in modern times of the ideology of progress."[54]

Turgot rejected both the cyclical nature of history and the concept of continued degradation. He argued, rather pugnaciously, that history proceeds in a straight line and that each succeeding stage of history represents an advance over the preceding one. History, said Turgot, is both cumulative and progressive. Unlike the steady-state philosophers of Greece and the theologians of the Roman Church, he heralded the virtue of constant change and movement. Turgot was willing to acknowledge that progress is uneven and that occasionally it becomes bogged down or even retreats a few steps. Yet he held steadfast to the conviction that history demonstrates an overall advance toward the perfection of life here on earth. Bold thoughts! But Turgot's world was ready for them, as evidenced by the fact that Turgot was neither relieved of his appointment by the university nor condemned by the ecclesiastical authorities. A very radical change had taken place in the European mind between the time the giant cathedral at Chartres was being erected in the thirteenth century and that rather remarkable lecture in the year A.D. 1750. That change was the development of the modern world view. The story of its growth and maturation is the story of the world you and I have inherited.

Though we are largely unaware of it, much of the way we think, act, and feel can be traced back to the tiny strands and fragments that were woven together into the historical paradigm that took shape and form during those centuries of transition. It is ironic indeed that only now as that tapestry begins to fray and unwind is it possible to really see the stuff we and our modern world are made of.

The Machine Age

The modern age is the Machine Age. Precision, speed, and accuracy are the premier values. We are forever asking, "How fast will it go?" or "How long did it take you to get there?" The highest compliment we can pay is to say that something is so well made or thought out or planned that it virtually runs itself. We love the feel of metallic finishes, of aluminum, steel, and chrome. We find nothing more aesthetically pleasing than to ignite an engine or turn a switch. Our world is a world of pulleys and levers and wheels. Playtime is caught up with tinkering with contraptions; worktime with adjusting monitors and fine-tuning instruments. We regulate our daily routine by a machine—the watch. We communicate by a machine—the telephone. We learn by machines—the calculator, the computer, the television set. We travel by machines—the automobile, the jet. We even see by a machine—the electric light. The machine is our way of life and our world view rolled up in one. We view the universe as a grand machine set in motion eons ago by the supreme technician, God. So perfectly engineered, it "runs itself," without ever missing a beat, and with a predictability of movement that can be calculated down to the nth degree.

We are mesmerized by the exactness we perceive in the universe, and we seek to duplicate its grandeur here on earth. History for us is a continuing exercise in engineering. The earth is like a giant hardware store, made up of all sorts of parts that need to be assembled into a functioning system. Our job is never done. There are always new designs to consider and new jobs to be performed, all requiring the constant rearrangement of parts and the enlargement of processes. Progress then is "geared" toward the perfection of the machine. There is the constant tying together of loose ends, the elimination of flaws, and the expansion of the machine process into every aspect of life. This is the historical paradigm of our age. We live by the dictates of the machine, and although we are quite willing to acknowledge its importance to our external way of life, we are much less willing to see how it has penetrated to the center of our being.

The machine is now so firmly entrenched inside of us that it is difficult to know where it stops and we start. Even the words that come out of our mouths are no longer our words, they are the machine's words. We "measure" relationships with other people by whether we are in "sync" with them. Our feelings are reduced to good or bad "vibrations." We no longer initiate activity; instead we are a "self-starter." We avoid "friction" at work and choose to "tune in" rather than pay attention. We think of people's lives as either "running smoothly" or "breaking down." If the latter, then we expect that in short order they will be put back together or "readjusted."

The Architects of the Mechanical World View

Every world view has its architects—those who sketch out the blueprint that the rest of us end up filling in. There were many preliminary drawings before the final plans for the Machine Age were agreed upon. By the middle of the eighteenth century all of the key elements of the mechanical paradigm had been carefully integrated into a unified schema. The world was ready to turn the switch on the Machine Age. The mechanical world view is a testimonial to three men: Francis Bacon, René Descartes, and Isaac Newton. After 300 years we are still living off their ideas.

Francis Bacon laid the groundwork for the machine paradigm with an attack on the world view of the ancient Greeks. His *Novum Organum*, published in 1620, was a masterful piece of propaganda. Bacon sneered at the collected works of Plato, Aristotle, and Homer as nothing but "contentious learning."[55] The Greeks, he snapped, "assuredly have that which is characteristic of boys; they are prompt to prattle but cannot generate; for their wisdom abounds in words but is barren of works."[56] Bacon took stock of the Greek world view and concluded that, for all of its pompous claims, it had not "adduced a single experiment which tends to relieve and benefit the condition of man."[57] Bacon saw the world with different eyes. He didn't want to sit around contemplating nature. He wanted to find a methodology for controlling it. For the Greeks, the science of learning was intended to ask the metaphysical *why* of things; Bacon on the other hand thought that a science of learning should be committed to the *how* of things. "Now the true and lawful goal of the sciences is none other than this: that human life be endowed with new discoveries and powers."[58]

Some parts of Bacon's *Novum Organum* read more like an interoffice memorandum than a classical philosophical tract. For example, how many times have we heard our boss tell us to start dealing with the world as it is, not with how we would like it to be? Well, the boss is most likely unaware of it, but he's quoting Francis Bacon, who argued that we should begin "building in the human understanding a true model of the world, such as it is in fact, not such as a man's own reason would have it to be."[59] Bacon goes on to make it clear that a new method for dealing with the world is in order, one that can "enlarge the bounds of human empire, to the effecting of all things possible."[60] The new method Bacon alludes to is the scientific method, an approach that would separate the observer from the observed and provide a neutral forum for the development of "objective knowledge." According to Bacon, objective knowledge would allow people to take "command over things natural—over bodies, medicine, mechanical powers and infinite others of this kind."[61]

Bacon is the original pragmatist of the modern age. The next time you hear someone say to you, "Try and be objective" or "Prove it to me" or "Just give me the facts," think of Francis Bacon. He started it all off in 1620 with what he believed was a better idea for organizing the world.

Bacon had barely opened up the door to the new world view when René Descartes, a mathematician by trade appeared on the scene. Descartes was not a modest man. One rather cold day, according to his biographers, he was confined to his room by the severe weather. And that's when the idea hit him. The key to understanding the world, to deciphering its hidden secrets, to controlling it for human purposes was to be found in one word: *mathematics*.

As I considered the matter carefully, it gradually came to light that all those matters only are referred to mathematics in which order and measurement are investigated, and that it makes no difference whether it be in numbers, figures, stars, sounds or any other object that the question of measurement arises. I saw, consequently, that there must be some general science to explain that element as a whole which gives rise to problems about order and measurement. This I perceived was called universal mathematics. Such a science should contain the primary rudiments of human reason, and its province ought to extend to the eliciting of true results in every subject.[62]

Descartes concluded with an observation that has since become the overriding axiom of the mechanics paradigm: "To speak freely, I am convinced that it [mathematics] is a more powerful instrument of knowledge than any other that has been bequeathed to us by human agency, as being the source of all things!"[63] Here then was a man convinced, the first "true believer" in the mechanical world view. Descartes wasted no time in popularizing his revelation. By the time he died in 1650, his mathematical view of nature had become accepted by the best minds all over Europe.

Descartes had succeeded in turning all of nature into simple matter in motion. He reduced all quality to quantity and then confidently proclaimed that only space and location mattered. "Give me extension and motion," he said, "and I will construct the Universe."[64] Descartes's mathematical world was tasteless, colorless, and odorless. Mathematics represented total order, and so in a single stroke of genius Descartes had successfully eliminated everything in the world which might in any way be thought of as messy, chaotic, and alive. In Descartes's world everything had its place and all relationships were harmonious. The world was one of precision, not confusion.

The Greek view of history as unfolding chaos and decay was deemed unmathematical and therefore false. The Christian world view fared little better. How could one ever know the workings of the natural order with precision if a personal God was constantly intervening in the affairs of life? In order to work as a world view, the mechanical paradigm had to be, above all, completely predictable. There was no room for a Divinity who could change the operating rules whenever He chose. God, then, was delicately retired from the scene. Of course, at first He was congratulated for being the supreme mathematician who had engineered the whole plan and set it in motion, before going on to some other activity in the cosmic theater. Eventually, God was forgotten altogether, as succeeding generations became more and more intoxicated with the power of this newfound paradigm.

While Descartes gave human beings the "faith" that they could unravel the truths of the world and become its masters, it was Isaac Newton, another great European thinker, who provided them with the tools they needed to do it. Newton discovered the mathematical method for describing mechanical motion. He argued that one law could explain why the planets move the way they do and why a single leaf falls from the tree in the manner it does. Subjecting all of nature to the laws of mathematics, Newton proclaimed that "all the phenomena of nature may depend upon certain forces by which the particles of bodies, by some causes hitherto unknown, are either mutually impelled toward each other, and cohere in regular figures, or are repelled and recede from each other." According to Newton's three laws:

1. A body at rest remains at rest and a body in motion remains in uniform motion in a straight line unless acted upon by an external force.
2. The acceleration of a body is directly proportional to the applied force and in the direction of the straight line in which the force acts.
3. For every force there is an equal and opposite force in reaction.[65]

Soon after Newton published his mathematical method it was being taught at all the major universities. His fame spread to every corner of Europe, and when he died in 1727 he was given a royal funeral.

The mechanical world view dealt exclusively with material in motion, because that was the only thing that could be mathematically measured. It was a world view made for machines, not people. By separating and then eliminating all of the qualities of life from the quantities of which they are a part, the architects of the machine paradigm were left with a cold, inert universe made up entirely of dead matter. It was a short journey from the world as pure matter to the world of pure materialism, as we shall see in the next section.

Alfred North Whitehead delivered perhaps the single most devastating piece of commentary on the limitations of the Newtonian world machine as a historical paradigm. Noting that mechanics deals only with the space-time relationships of matter in motion, Whitehead remarked to his students:

> As soon as you have settled . . . what you mean by a definite place in space-time, you can adequately state the relation of a particular material body to space-time by saying that it is just there, in that place: and, so far as simple location is concerned, there is nothing more to be said on the subject.[66]

The mechanical paradigm proved to be irresistible. It was simple, it was predictable, and above all it worked. Here, it appeared, was the long-sought-for explanation of how the universe functioned. There *was* an order to things, and that order could be ascertained by mathematical formulas and scientific observation. Still, as European scholars looked around them, they wondered why the normal activities of people in society often seemed so muddled and chaotic. The erratic behavior of people and the imperfect workings of government and the economy didn't seem to square with the well-ordered mechanical explanation of the world that Bacon, Descartes, and Newton had put forth. The dilemma was quickly resolved: if society was misbehaving, then it could only be due to the fact that it was not adhering to the natural laws that govern the universe.

The only thing that was needed, then, was to figure out exactly how the natural laws applied to human beings and social institutions and then apply them. Obviously, this would be a long and difficult process—but no longer an impossible one, because the universal laws were now known. Besides, it would be well worth the time and effort, since the final payoff would be a perfectly ordered society. Humanity now had a new purpose in life. Gone was the medieval goal of seeking salvation in the next world. In its place was the new idea of seeking perfection in this world. History was now seen as a progressive journey from the rather disordered and confused state that society found itself in to the well-ordered and wholly predictable state represented by the Newtonian world machine.

Two men immediately set about the task of discovering the relationship between these universal laws and the workings of society. John Locke brought the workings of government and society in line with the world machine paradigm, and Adam Smith did the same with the economy.

Like most intellectuals of his period, Locke was deeply impressed with how the mechanical model had made sense out of a seemingly incomprehensible natural world. But why, he asked himself, were the affairs of human beings so chaotic? The answer, he concluded, was that the natural laws of society were being violated because the social order was built upon irrational traditions and customs that originated from the theocentrism that had ruled the world for so long. With the aid of reason, Locke set out to determine the "natural" basis of society. He immediately concluded that religion could not form the social foundation simply because, by definition, God is unknowable. How can the unknowable be the proper basis for government? And so, in a monumental break with his philosophical predecessors, Locke argued that while religion could rightly be a private concern of each person, it could not serve as the basis of public activity.

Having removed God from the affairs of people—as Bacon had removed Him from nature—Locke was left with human beings, all alone in the universe. No longer was the human being to be considered as part of a divinely directed organism. Now, men and women became just what Bacon, Descartes, and Newton had made of nature: mere physical phenomena interacting with other bits of matter in the cold, mechanical universe. This being the case, on what basis could a social order be formed? Locke provided an argument that has continued to dominate the modern world view down to the present. Once we cut through useless custom and superstition, argued Locke, we see that society, being made up solely of individuals creating their own meaning, has one purpose and one purpose only: to protect and allow for the increase of the property of its members. Pure self-interest thus becomes, in Locke's formulation, the sole basis for the establishment of the state. Society properly becomes materialistic and individualistic because, Locke maintains, reason leads us to conclude that this is the natural order of things. By the laws of nature, each individual is called upon to act out his role of social atom, speeding through life, attempting to amass personal wealth. There is no value judgment to be made here; self-interest is simply the only basis for society.

For Locke, the purpose of government was to allow people the freedom to use their newfound power over nature to produce wealth. Thus, from Locke's time to our own, the social role of the state has been to promote the subjugation of nature so that people might acquire the material prosperity necessary for fulfillment. "The negation of nature," Locke declared, "is the way toward happiness." People must become "effectively emancipated from the bonds of nature."[67]

But won't this constant and unmoderated scramble for personal affluence result in a savage war of each person against the other, with some members of society being victimized in the process? Not at all, says Locke, for human beings are not naturally evil or fallen, but inherently good. It is only scarcity and lack of property that make them evil. As people are naturally acquisitive, it is therefore only necessary to continue to increase the wealth of society and social harmony will continue to improve. People need not fight among themselves because nature has "still enough and as good left; and more than the unprovided could use."[68] People can have liberty of action because their self-interest will not conflict with others. Locke, then, became the philosopher of unlimited expansion and material abundance.

Still, are there no limits at all to the amount of wealth individuals can amass? After all, philosophers from Aristotle to Aquinas had argued that, beyond a certain point, property becomes a barrier to happiness. Not so, argues Locke. In a state of nature, he admits, it is true that primitives can only accumulate a limited amount of property from the bounty of nature. If a primitive attempts to take more property than his crude knowledge will allow him to consume, then it will spoil and possibly rob other members of the community of their own chance for accumulation. But in a commonwealth founded upon reason, where money as a medium of exchange exists, an unlimited amassing of property is permissible, indeed natural, for that is the purpose of money. Since money cannot possibly spoil, it is impossible to possess too much of it. Obviously, some individuals will amass more property than others, but this too is natural, for the world was given to "the use of the industrious and rational." He who applies reason the best will benefit the most.[69]

Locke does not stop here. The ownership of property (value extracted from nature) is not only a right in society; there is also a duty to generate wealth. In an environmentalist's nightmare, Locke writes that "land that is left wholly to nature . . . is called, as indeed it is, waste."[70] Nature is only of value when we mix our labor with it so that it will be productive:

> He who appropriates land to himself by his labour, does not lessen but increase the common stock of mankind. For the provisions serving to the support of human life, produced by one acre of inclosed and cultivated land, are . . . ten times more than those which are yielded by an acre of land, of an equal richness lying waste in common. And therefore he that incloses land and has a greater plenty of the conveniences of life from ten acres than he could have from a hundred left to nature, may truly be said to give ninety acres to mankind.[71]

Using this early version of the "trickle-down theory" (the more one makes individually, the more society collectively benefits), Locke goes on to declare that a person should "heap up as much of these durable things (gold, silver, and so on) as he pleases; the exceeding of the bounds of his just property not lying in the largeness of his possession, but the perishing of anything uselessly in it."[72] Reading Locke from our present-day concern with ecology, one has the unnerving feeling that he would not be satisfied until every river on earth were dammed, every natural wonder covered with billboards, and every mountain turned into rubble to produce oil shale. So rigidly productivist and materialistic is Locke that he condemns American Indians as a handful of people living in one of the richest lands in the world, idly refusing to exploit their riches: "A king of a large and fruitful territory there feeds, lodges and is clad worse than a day-laborer in England."[73]

With Locke, the fate of modern man and woman is sealed. From the time of the Enlightenment on, the individual is reduced to the hedonistic activities of production and consumption to find meaning and purpose. People's needs and aspirations, their dreams and desires, all become confined to the pursuit of material self-interest.

Like Locke, Adam Smith was enamored of the mechanical world view and was determined to formulate a theory of economy that would reflect the universals of the Newtonian paradigm. In *The Wealth of Nations,* Smith argues that just as heavenly bodies in motion conform to certain laws of nature, so too does economics. If these laws are obeyed, economic growth will result. But government regulation and control of the economy violated these immutable laws by directing economic activity in unnatural ways. Thus markets did not expand as rapidly as they could and production was stifled. In other words, any attempt by society to guide "natural" economic forces was inefficient, and for Adam Smith, efficiency in all things was the watchword.

An inquiry into the laws of economics, Smith declared, will lead us to the inevitable conclusion that the most efficient method of economic organization is laissez-faire—the notion of leaving things alone and allowing people to act unhindered. Smith, like Locke, believed that the basis of all human activity is material self-interest. Since this is natural, we should not condemn selfishness by erecting social barriers to its pursuit. Rather, we should recognize people's desire to satisfy themselves for what it is—a virtuous activity that, in fact, benefits everyone. It is by each individual operating selfishly that scarcity may be overcome by surplus:

> Every individual is continually exerting himself to find out the most advantageous employment for whatever capital he can com-

mand. It is his own advantage, indeed, and not that of society which he has in view. But the study of his own advantage naturally, or rather necessarily, leads him to prefer that employment which is most advantageous to the society.[74]

Smith explicitly removes any notion of morality from economics, just as Locke had done with social relations. Any attempt to impose morality on economy simply leads to a violation of the "invisible hand," which Smith asserted was a natural law that governs the economic process, automatically allocating capital investment, jobs, resources, and the production of goods. People could use reason to understand this law, Smith allowed, but just as human beings cannot control gravity, they cannot improve on the invisible hand. Since nothing can be more efficient than this "natural" force controlling the rational market, wealth can best be produced only through free, unfettered trade and competition among rational, acquisitive individuals. Because the purpose of economics is a continually expanding market, anything that promotes growth is to be welcomed.

Believing that men and women are basically egoists in pursuit of economic gain, Smith's theories subordinate all human desires to the quest for material abundance to satisfy physical needs. There are no ethical choices to be made, only utilitarian judgments exercised by each individual pursuing self-interest.

Bacon, Descartes, Newton, Locke, and Smith were the great popularizers of the mechanical world view. Many others preceded and followed them. Still, their basic assumptions remain with us today. Those assumptions can be summarized in a few short sentences. First, there is a precise mathematical order to the universe that can be deduced from an examination of the motions of the heavenly bodies. Unfortunately, here on earth most things in the primal state are in a chaotic and confused condition. Therefore, things need to be rearranged to bring the same order to our world as appears to exist in the rest of the cosmos. The question then arises as to how best to arrange the stuff of nature so that it reflects the same kind of order that exists in the universe. The answer, it was assumed, was to use the scientific principles of mechanics to rearrange the stuff of nature in a way that best advanced the material self-interests of human beings. The logical conclusion to this grand new paradigm was simply this: *The more material well-being we amass, the more ordered the world must be getting.* Progress, then, is the amassing of greater and greater material abundance, which is assumed to result in an ever more ordered world. Science and technology are the tools for getting the job done. This, in a nutshell, is the chief operating assumption of the mechanical world paradigm.

The mechanical world paradigm has not been without its critics over the years. It has been ridiculed, attacked, and battered from many different quarters. Some of its assumptions have even been modified. Still, when one rereads Descartes, Locke, or Smith, one cannot help but be impressed with how contemporary they sound. Every time a businessman, politician, or scientist speaks out in public on some pressing issue it is as if his speech had been ghostwritten by these long-dead seminal thinkers. Therefore, if the pronouncements tendered by our civic and public leaders seem more and more divorced from reality and less capable of explaining the problems facing our society, the blame is not altogether theirs. If we are going to place the blame somewhere, then we should place at least part of it on Descartes, Locke, Smith, and their colleagues. After all, it is their methodology and ideas we are using.

The mechanical world paradigm experienced its greatest triumph in the aftermath of Charles Darwin's publication of *On the Origin of Species* in 1859. Darwin's theory of biological evolution was every bit as impressive as the scientific discoveries of Newton in physics. It could well have pushed the mechanical world view off center stage and claimed hegemony for itself as a completely new organizing principle for society. It never happened. Instead Darwin's theories became an appendage to the Newtonian world machine. The full implications of Darwin's discoveries were never really explored. Instead, some of the more superficial trappings of his theory were immediately taken hold of and exploited in a way that further legitimized the mechanical world view.

Social philosophers like Herbert Spencer seized on Darwin's theory of the evolution of species as a kind of proof positive of the existence of progress in the world. Spencer and the so-called social Darwinists turned the concept of natural selection into the concept of the survival of the fittest. In so doing, they provided further support for the mechanical world view that holds that self-interest leads to increased material well-being, which leads to increased order.

Survival of the fittest was interpreted to mean that in the state of nature, each organism is engaged in a relentless battle with all other creatures. Those who survive and pass on their traits to their offspring are simply those best able to protect their own material self-interest. Evolution was seen as a process of ever-increasing order brought about as a result of each succeeding species' being better equipped to maximize its own self-interest and provide for its material needs. And so, Darwin's theory became a complete regurgitation of the chief assumption of the mechanical world view.

The mechanical age has been characterized by this notion of progress. Reduced to its simplest abstraction, progress is seen as the process by which the "less ordered" natural world is harnessed by people to create a more ordered material environment. Or to put it another way, progress is creating greater value out of the natural world than what exists in its original state. Science, in this context, is the methodology by which people learn the ways of nature so that they can reduce them to consistent principles or rules. Technology, in turn, is the application of these rules in specific instances, the purpose being to transform parts of the natural process into workable forms of greater value, structure, and order than exist in the primal state.

The mechanical world view, the world view of mathematics, science, and technology, the world view of materialism and progress, the world view that claims to explain the world we experience, is beginning to lose its vitality because the energy environment upon which it was nourished is nearing its own death. (This argument will be examined later on in detail.) If there is a history to look back on, future generations will shake their heads in disbelief at the 300 years we call the modern age. The world as a machine will appear as naive to them as the Greeks' five ages of history have appeared to us. For they will be living under an entirely new world paradigm, one whose broad contours we will now explore.

PART TWO

THE ENTROPY LAW

The Entropy Law

An anthropologist, Max Gluckman, once remarked that "a science is any discipline in which the fool of this generation can go beyond the point reached by the genius of the last generation."[1] The first and second laws of thermodynamics are now taught in introductory physics courses. What they proclaim seems simple and commonsensical. Yet the path that led to their final articulation was an arduous one, littered with complex theories and the musings and speculations of many fine minds. Strangely enough, while scientists have anguished over the proper meaning of these two laws for longer than anyone cares to remember, they were already well established in the everyday folklore of just about every culture on earth. How many times have we heard the statement "You can't get something for nothing" or "It does no good to cry over spilt milk" or "You can't beat the system." If you are familiar with these sayings and have seen them verified over and over again in your own everyday experience, then you know about the first and second laws of thermodynamics.

Thermodynamics sounds like a very complicated concept. In actuality it is both the simplest and at the same time the most impressive scientific conception we know of. Both laws of thermodynamics can be stated in one sentence:

> The total energy content of the universe is constant and the total entropy is continually increasing.[2]

What this means is that it is impossible to either create or destroy energy. The amount of energy in the universe has been fixed since the beginning of time and will remain fixed till the end of time. The first law is the conservation law. It says that while energy can never be created or destroyed it can be transformed from one form to another.

Science writer Isaac Asimov provides a simple example:

> Suppose we take a quantity of heat and change it into work. In doing so, we haven't destroyed the heat, we have only transferred it to another place or perhaps changed it into another energy form.[3]

To be more specific, consider an automobile engine. The energy in the gasoline is equal to the work done by the gasoline motor, plus the heat generated, plus the energy in the exhaust products.

The most important thing to remember, again, is that we cannot create energy. No person has ever succeeded in doing it and no person ever will. The only thing we can do is transform energy from one state to another. This is a heady realization to come to when we stop to consider that everything is made out of energy. The shape, form, and movement of everything that exists is really only an embodiment of the various concentrations and transformations of energy. A human being, a skyscraper, an automobile, and a blade of grass all represent energy that has been transformed from one state to another. When a skyscraper or a blade of grass is formed, it is made of energy that has been gathered up from somewhere else. When the skyscraper is razed, and the blade of grass dies, the energy they embodied does not disappear. It is merely transferred back somewhere else into the environment. We have all heard it said that "there's nothing new under the sun." You can prove it to yourself with the next breath you take. You have just inhaled about 50 million molecules that were once inhaled by Plato.

If the first law of thermodynamics were all that we had to consider, then there would be no trick at all to using energy over and over again without ever running out of it. But we know that's not the way the world works. For example, if we burn a piece of coal, the energy remains but is transformed into sulfur dioxide and other gases that then spread out into space. While no energy has been lost in the process, we know that we can never reburn that piece of coal and get the same work out of it. The explanation for this is to be found in the second law of thermodynamics, which says that every time energy is transformed from one state to another a certain penalty is exacted. That penalty is a loss in the amount of available energy to perform work of some kind in the future. There is a term for this; it's called entropy.

Entropy is a measure of the amount of energy no longer capable of conversion into work. The term was first coined by a German physicist, Rudolf Clausius, in 1868. But the principle involved was first recognized forty-one years earlier by a young French army officer, Sadi Carnot, who was trying to better understand why a steam engine works. He discovered that the engine did work because part of the system was very cold and the other part very hot. In other words, in order for energy to be turned into work, there must be a difference in energy concentration (i.e., difference in temperature) in different parts of a system. Work occurs when energy moves from a higher level of concentration to a lower level (or higher temperature to lower temperature). More important still, every time energy goes from one level to another, it means that less energy is available to perform work the next time around. For example, water going over a dam falls into a lake. As it falls, it can be used to generate electricity or turn a water wheel or perform some other useful function. Once it reaches the bottom, however, the water is no longer in a state to perform work. Water on a flat plane cannot be used to turn even the smallest water wheel. These two states are referred to as *available or free energy states* versus *unavailable or bound energy states*.

An entropy increase, then, means a decrease in "available" energy. Every time something occurs in the natural world, some amount of energy ends up being unavailable for future work. Part of the unavailable energy is pollution, dissipated energy that accumulates in the environment and that poses a grave threat to the ecosystem and to public health.

Now let's get back to Clausius, the man who thought up the word *entropy*. Clausius realized that in a closed system the difference in energy levels always tended to even out. Everyone who has ever taken a hot poker out of a fire has observed the same thing that Clausius made into a law. When a red-hot poker is removed from the fire and placed in the air, we soon notice that the poker begins to cool while the surrounding air begins to heat up. This is because the heat always flows from the hotter to the colder body. Finally, after enough time has elapsed, we can touch the poker and then place our hand in the surrounding air and, lo and behold, we find that they have reached the same temperature. The experts call this the equilibrium state, the state where there is no longer any difference in energy levels. This is the same state the water is in when on a flat plane. In both cases, the cooled-off poker and the flat water are no longer able to perform useful work. Their energy is bound energy or unavailable energy. Now that does not mean that the water cannot be lugged up to the top of the dam again in buckets and dropped over or that the poker cannot be reheated. But in each case, it means that a new source of free or available energy has to be used up in the process.

The equilibrium state is the state where entropy has reached a maximum, where there is no longer free energy available to perform additional work. Clausius summed up the second law of thermodynamics by concluding that "in the world, entropy [the amount of unavailable energy] always tends toward a maximum."

Here on earth there are two sources of available energy: our terrestrial stock and the solar flow from the sun. Economist Herman Daly explains the difference between the two:

The terrestrial stock consists of two kinds of resources: those renewable on a human time scale and those renewable only over geologic time and which, for human purposes, must be treated as nonrenewable. Terrestrial low-entropy stocks may also be classified into energy and material. Both sources, the terrestrial and the solar, are limited. Terrestrial nonrenewables are limited in total amount available. Terrestrial renewables are also limited in total amount available and, if exploited to exhaustion, become just like nonrenewables . . . the solar source is practically unlimited in total amount but strictly limited in its rate and pattern of arrival to earth.[4]

While the sun's energy is degrading with every passing second, its entropy will not reach a maximum until long after the earth's available terrestrial stock has been completely used up.

Every time you light a cigarette, the available energy in the world decreases. Of course, as already pointed out, it is possible to reverse the entropy process in an isolated time and place, but only by using up additional energy in the process and thus increasing the overall entropy of the environment. This should be especially understood when it comes to recycling. Many people believe that almost everything that we use up can be totally recycled and reused if only we develop the appropriate technology. This just is not true. While more efficient recycling is going to be essential for the economic survival of the planet in the future, there is no way to achieve anywhere near 100 percent reprocessing. For example, recycling efficiency today averages around 30 percent for most used metals. Recycling requires the expenditure of additional energy in the collecting, transporting, and processing of used materials, which increases the overall entropy of the environment. Thus, things can only be recycled by the expenditure of new sources of available energy and at the expense of increasing the entropy of the overall environment.

A point that needs to be emphasized over and over again is that here on earth material entropy is continually increasing and must ultimately reach a maximum. That's because the earth is a closed system in relation to the universe; that is, it exchanges energy but not matter with its surroundings. With the exception of an occasional meteorite that falls to earth and some cosmic dust, our planet remains a closed subsystem of the universe. To those who mistakenly believe that the solar inflow of energy can be used to produce matter, economist Nicholas Georgescu-Roegen responds that "even in the fantastic engine of the universe matter is not created from energy 'alone' to any significant extent; instead, huge amounts of matter are continuously converted into energy."[5] The point is, the sun, by itself, does not generate life. You can let the sun flow into an empty glass jar from now until the final heat death of the solar system and still no life will come forth. For life to unfold, the sun must interact with the closed system of matter, minerals, and metals on the planet earth, converting these materials to life and the utilities of life. This interaction facilitates the dissipation of this fixed endowment of terrestrial matter that makes up the earth's crust. Mountains are wearing down and topsoil is being blown away with each passing second. That is why, in the final analysis, even renewable resources are really nonrenewable over the long haul. While they continue to reproduce, the life and death of new organisms increase the entropy of the earth, meaning that less available matter exists for the unfolding of life in the future.

Every farmer understands that even with recycling and constant sunshine, it is impossible to grow the same amount of grass on the same spot year after year in perpetuity. Every blade of grass today means one less blade of grass that can be grown sometime in the future on that same spot. That's because, like everything else, topsoil is part of the entropic flow. It contains the organic matter and inorganic minerals that allow the grass to grow. But the topsoil is only temporary. It begins as rock formations and organic refuse and much of it will end up as dust scattered into the wind or silt washed out to sea. In other words, topsoil is not a permanent fixture, but merely a particular concentration of matter along the entropic flow. In the short run (human time scale), it is possible to maintain the topsoil near a steady state as long as erosion does not occur faster than nature can degrade rock formations and organic wastes into new topsoil. Even in the short run, however, topsoil often erodes faster than nature can replenish it, as a result of natural forces at work (wind storms, droughts, floods, etc.) or as a result of human intervention. Overcultivating the land and the destruction of natural ecosystems often lead to demineralization of the soil and soil erosion, resulting in entropy patches for topsoil in isolated geographical pockets. It takes a thousand years to replace twelve inches of topsoil. Obviously, within the context of human time scales entropy of topsoil is a very real and continuous phenomenon. Matter is continually dissipating. The recognition of this fact was first advanced by Nicholas Georgescu-Roegen: "In a closed system, the material entropy must ultimately reach a maximum."[6]

This is a difficult truth for most of us to accept because every child, when first introduced to elementary principles of biology, is taught that all matter recycles itself. Of course, this is true and is merely a restatement of the first law of thermodynamics, that matter (and energy) can neither be created nor destroyed. Unfortunately, the second law of thermodynamics is generally ignored. It tells us that while matter is continually recycled, a price has to be paid each time in terms of degradation. For example, suppose we extract a chunk of metallic ore from beneath the earth's surface and fashion it into a utensil. During the lifetime of that utensil, metal molecules are constantly flying off of the product as a result of friction, and wear and tear. Those loose metal molecules are never destroyed. They eventually find their way back into the earth. But now they are randomly dispersed throughout the soil and are no longer in a concentrated form to perform useful work, like the original chunk of metallic ore. A way might be found to recycle all of these randomly dispersed metal molecules but only at the expense of an increase in entropy in the process. A mechanical device would have to be assembled to collect the metal molecules and an energy source introduced to run the machine. Since the machine itself is made out of metallic ore from the earth, it would be losing its own metal molecules to friction and wear and tear even as it was recycling the other random metal molecules. At the same time, the energy used to run the recycling machine would also end up increasing the entropy.

When energy becomes unavailable we use the term "heat death." When matter becomes unavailable we use the term "matter chaos." The result in both cases is entropy: a randomization of energy and matter making both less concentrated and thus less fit to perform useful work.

Some scientists have argued that in the very long run, the sun, acting upon the earth's crust, might somehow reconstitute all of the random metal molecules into a concentrated state once again. This may be statistically possible, but is of little help to the human species since the time frame being discussed is measured in geological units, namely billions of years. In the short run and in specific geographical pockets, entropy of energy and matter is a very real observable phenomenon.

The Entropy Law is something that needs to be felt as much as understood. The essence of this law is the essence of reality itself, and so getting hold of its meaning requires a kind of intuition. For this reason, it will be helpful to look at the Entropy Law from some other directions.

Another way of talking about energy levels and entropy has already been touched upon—namely concentrations. Why is it that when you open up a bottle of perfume, the odor begins to escape into the air, and after a short time it pervades the room? Or let's say we open the door of the room into an even larger room only to find, a few minutes later, that the perfume can now be smelled in both rooms although the smell is much less intense than when it was in only one room. Bertrand Russell explains the process:

> Whenever there is a great deal of energy in one region and very little in a neighboring region, energy tends to travel from the one region to the other, until equality is established. This whole process may be described as a tendency towards democracy.[7]

Again, this is just another way to understand the second law. Energy always moves from the more concentrated state (in this case the perfume bottle) to the less concentrated state (both large rooms). In the process, free or available energy is used up or dissipated (the odor loses its potency). If you were to look at the perfume on a molecular level, you would notice that while they are cooped up in the bottle, the molecules are bombarding each other at an incredibly fast rate. As soon as they are allowed to escape from the bottle, however, the molecules begin their random journey into the larger space. As they begin to spread out over the room they collide with each other less frequently until they are uniformly distributed throughout the whole room.

There have been many attempts to find a way around the Entropy Law. In fact, it has been one of the favorite pastimes of scientists and philosophers alike. Perhaps the most impressive challenges to the Entropy Law came from two highly respected scientists, J. C. Maxwell and Ludwig Boltzmann, in the late nineteenth century. Both challenges only ended up strengthening the position of the second law, and for that reason they deserve mentioning.

Maxwell suggested that an intelligent being tiny enough to handle individual molecules might be capable of violating the second law. No matter that we have yet to come across any such little fellow; the argument is still interesting for what it says about the lengths the scientific community was willing to go to try to overcome the second law.

Maxwell posed the following hypothesis. Take an enclosure, he said, that is divided into two compartments, separated by a small door. The enclosure, which is totally isolated, contains a gas at a uniform temperature. Now at uniform temperature the Entropy Law says that no work can be performed. Maxwell proposed to get around that problem by putting a little demon at the tiny door separating the two compartments. The demon, being sharp of eye, would then open and close the door, permitting molecules with greater than average velocities to pass from left to right and molecules with less than average velocities to pass from right to left. "Since high-speed molecules correspond to a high temperature and low-speed molecules to a low temperature, the gas in the righthand compartment would become hotter and the gas in the lefthand compartment colder." Need we say more? "Once the difference in temperature was established, it could be used to drive a heat engine that would deliver useful work."[8]

Starting from maximum entropy or a total equilibrium state of uniform energy, Maxwell proposed to reverse the entropy process without any outside energy being used; this would have violated the second law. First, it is obvious that in the real world we would never be able to produce such a demon. But just to humor Maxwell, let's assume an appropriate demon could be found and that it would be willing to take on the job. Could it perform its work without violating the second law? Stanley Angrist and Loren Hepler, writing in *Texas Quarterly,* put the demon to the test and discovered that even it could not get around the Entropy Law:

[Maxwell] supposed that his demon would be able to sense the velocity (speed and direction) of individual molecules and then act accordingly. . . . As the demon peers into either side of the isolated enclosure at uniform temperature, the uniformity of radiation throughout does not permit him to see anything. The sameness in the enclosure would allow him to perceive the thermal radiation and its fluctuations, but he would never see the molecules. . . . We conclude that the demon needs his own supply of light to disturb the radiation equilibrium within the enclosure, so we equip him with a light to enable him to see the molecules. The high quality energy that the light pours into the system provides the demon with the information he needs to operate the door to separate the high-speed molecules from the low-speed ones. Although the demon is able to increase the net order of the gas (and hence decrease its total entropy), a greater increase in disorder and entropy must occur in the light source. That is, for the entire system, light source, demon and gas, there will be a net increase in entropy as required by the second law, thus rendering the perpetual motion machine impossible.[9]

About the only thing this whole exercise proves is that "we cannot get anything for nothing, not even an observation."[10]

Maxwell's attempt to challenge the Entropy Law is worth remembering. It is, more than anything else, a reflection of the hardheaded refusal of the scientific community to acknowledge the full implications of what the Entropy Law means for science, philosophy, and life on this planet.

Adding embarrassment to fantasy, Ludwig Boltzmann jumped into the fray, determined to rescue classical physics from the steady encroachment of the Entropy Law. Boltzmann's "h-Theorem" is a remarkable sleight of hand designed to accommodate the second law while at the same time undermining its clout. Boltzmann acknowledged the validity of the second law up to a point. He was willing to admit that in a closed system, entropy increases, but was unwilling to claim that it was an absolute certainty. He preferred the word *probably* to *certainly* and in so doing attempted to turn the second law into a probability or statistical law. According to Boltzmann, while it was unlikely that energy would move from a colder to a hotter state, it was not impossible.

It is important to be clear on what Boltzmann was arguing because it is still taken seriously by many scientists. Sir Arthur Eddington gets right to the point about the likelihood of Boltzmann's probability theorem ever working, even once, in the real world. He proposes a vessel with two equal parts separated by a partition. The first compartment contains air, the second compartment a vacuum. The partition between the two compartments is opened, allowing the air to spread evenly through the vessel. Eddington allows that at some future time there is always the chance that all of those billions upon billions of molecules of air diffused through the entire vessel will in their individual random movements all end up in the righthand side of the compartment once again at exactly the same time. As to how probable such an occurrence is, Eddington concludes:

> If an army of monkeys were strumming on typewriters they "might" write all the books in the British Museum. The chance of their doing so is decidedly more favorable than the chance of the molecules returning to one half of the vessel.[11]

Even more to the point is Nicholas Georgescu-Roegen. He is worth quoting at length because his criticism of statistical thermodynamics zeroes in on the battle between the mechanical paradigm and the emerging entropy paradigm.

> It must be admitted, though, that the layman is misled into believing in entropy bootlegging by what physicists preach through the new science known as statistical mechanics but more adequately described as statistical thermodynamics. The very existence of this discipline is a reflection of the fact that, in spite of all evidence, man's mind still clings with the tenacity of blind despair to the idea of an actuality consisting of locomotion and nothing else. A symptom of this idiosyncrasy was Ludwig Boltzmann's tragic struggle to sell a thermodynamic science based on a hybrid foundation in which the rigidity of mechanical laws is interwoven with the uncertainty specific to the notion of probability. . . . According to this new discipline, a pile of ashes may very well become capable of heating the boiler. Also, a corpse may resuscitate

to lead a second life in exactly the reverse order of the first. Only, the probabilities of such events are fantastically small. If we have not yet witnessed such "miracles," the advocates of statistical mechanics contend, it is only because we have not been watching a sufficiently large number of piles of ashes or corpses.[12]

We have looked at the second law from the perspective of energy moving from available to unavailable states and from high concentrations to low. There is still another way to view the second law, the most profound way of all. The Entropy Law is also a statement that all energy in an isolated system moves from an ordered to a disordered state. The minimum entropy state, where concentration is highest and where available energy is at a maximum, is also the most ordered state. In contrast, the maximum entropy state, where available energy has been totally dissipated and diffused, is also the most disordered state.

This conforms to our everyday sense of the world around us. Left on their own, things do not tend to spontaneously move to more and more ordered states. Anyone who has ever had to take care of a house, or work in an office, knows that if things are left unattended they soon become more and more disorderly. Bringing things back into a state of order requires the expenditure of additional energy. For example, consider a deck of playing cards that is organized by number and suit. The deck is in a state of maximum order or minimum entropy. Fling the deck to the ground and the cards will scatter into a random, disordered state. Picking each card off the floor and then arranging them one by one back into their original ordered state will take the expenditure of more energy than was used to scatter them in the first place.

It must be emphasized that whenever the entropy increase is reversed in one place, it is only done by increasing the overall entropy of the surrounding environment. This is so because every time an event occurs, some amount of energy is dissipated in the process and thus made totally unavailable for future use. This dissipated energy is added to the sink of dissipated energy that has accumulated as a result of the occurrence of every other past event. The tremendous implications for society that flow from this are truly mind-boggling. To quote Angrist and Hepler: "Each localized, man-made or machine-made entropy decrease is accompanied by a greater increase in entropy of the surroundings, thereby maintaining the required increase in total entropy."[13]

Albert Einstein once mused over which of the laws of science deserved to be ranked as the supreme law. He concluded by making the following observation:

A theory is more impressive the greater is the simplicity of its premises, the more different are the kinds of things it relates and the more extended its range of applicability. Therefore, the deep impression which classical thermodynamics made on me. It is the only physical theory of universal content which I am convinced, that within the framework of applicability of its basic concepts will never be overthrown.[14]

Cosmology and the Second Law

Whenever scientists begin speculating about the second law, the question ultimately arises as to how broadly it can be applied. For example, does the Entropy Law apply to the macro-world of stars and galaxies that make up the universe? In fact, the Entropy Law is the basis of most cosmological theories. Scientist Benjamin Thompson became the first to draw the cosmological implications of the second law back in 1854. According to Thompson, the Entropy Law tells us that

> within a finite period of time past, the earth must have been, and within a finite period of time to come the earth must again be, unfit for the habitation of man as at present constituted, unless operations have been, or are to be performed, which are impossible under the laws to which the known operations going on at present in the material world are subject.[15]

Two years later Helmholtz formulated what has become the standard cosmological theory based on the Entropy Law. His theory of "heat death" stated that the universe is gradually running down and eventually will reach the point of maximum entropy or heat death where all available energy will have been expended and no more activity will occur. The heat death of the universe corresponds to a state of eternal rest.

Today the most widely accepted theory about the origin and development of the universe is the big bang theory. First conceptualized by Canon Georges Lemaître, the big bang theory postulates that the universe began with the explosion of a tremendously dense energy source. As this dense energy expanded outward, it began to slow down, forming galaxies, stars, and planets. As the energy continues to expand and become more diffused, it loses more and more of its order and will eventually reach a point of maximum entropy, or the final equilibrium state of heat death. The big bang theory coincides with the first and second laws. It states that the universe started with complete order and has been moving toward a more and more disordered state ever since. If this theory appears familiar, it should. Both the ancient Greek and the medieval Christian view of history share much in common with the cosmologists' notion of the history of the universe.

It is strange indeed that we in the modern world are willing to see the history of the universe as beginning with a perfect state and moving toward decay and chaos and yet continue to cling to the notion that earthly history follows the exact opposite course, i.e., that it is moving from a state of chaos to a "progressively" more ordered world. This contradiction is so blatant that it should not come as too big a surprise that there have been attempts to formulate other cosmological theories to get around the Entropy Law. For a few years the "theory of continual creation" was the vogue. Back in 1948 three young scientists, Fred Hoyle, Thomas Gold, and Herman Bondi, suggested that while the universe is definitely expanding, heat death or maximum entropy could be avoided by interjecting negative entropy into the universe from "without." If just the right amount of new negative entropy were introduced to compensate for entropy loss, then the universe would continue to go on forever with new galaxies forming at the same time as others are burning out, like a kind of cosmic perpetual motion machine. So, while there would be losses in parts of the universe, the gains in other parts of the cosmic theater would assure that the entire system never degraded. Unfortunately for Hoyle, Gold, and Bondi, subsequent scientific experiments have invalidated their theory. In the 1960s, astronomers began counting the number of radio sources back through time and out into space. In order for the continual creation theory to be proven correct they would at least need to show that there had been no substantial change in radio sources between the past and present. The results of the experiment proved devastating to the continual creation theory, because they showed that there were more radio sources in the distant past than there are now, thus reconfirming the big bang theory and the second law, that the entropy of the universe is moving toward a maximum and heat death.

Other evidence continued to come in invalidating the continual creation theory and offering additional support for the big bang theory. It was found that quasars, which are some of the the most distant objects known, were, like radio sources, much more numerous in the past. Finally two scientists, Penzlas and Wilson, delivered the crushing blow to the continual creation theory with their discovery of "universal background heat radiation." There was simply no way to account for this phenomenon in the continual creation theory of the operation of the universe.

There have been other theories as well. The cyclical theory, for example, holds that the universe is forever moving through endless series of expanding and contracting phases without beginning or end. According to this theory, the last big bang is just one of an infinite chain of big bangs that have occurred and will continue to occur forever. As the present expanding universe reaches maximum entropy, it will then begin to contract back to a more and more ordered state until the entire universe is condensed into a critical mass the size of an atomic nucleus, at which time it will explode into the cosmic reaches once again. At the present time, the cyclical theory remains highly speculative, since so little experimentation has been done to confirm or refute its central thesis. For the moment all we can say for sure is that, for our tiny solar system and the planet earth, the Entropy Law still holds "the supreme position among the laws of nature."

Time, Metaphysics, and Entropy

Nowhere is the Entropy Law more important than in the determination of time. Saint Augustine once wrote, "I know what time is, if no one asks me, but if I try to explain it to one who asks me, I no longer know."[16] The mechanical world view of time is very different from the entropy world view. In classical physics, time can go in either direction. Because Newtonian principles are based on mathematics, every change in matter in motion must be reversible in theory. For example, imagine a film showing billiard balls colliding with each other. Now reverse the film and run it backwards. It still seems to make perfect sense, even in the reverse order. As long as we are dealing with simple matter in motion, in the Newtonian sense, time can be represented equally well as both $+T$ and $-T$. But now suppose we run a second film showing water plunging over Niagara Falls. As soon as we reverse this second film, everything looks ridiculous. The water is now flowing from the bottom up to the top of the falls. While the Newtonian model based on mathematics tells us that, in theory, the water could reverse itself and run uphill, we know it can't happen. The reason is explained by the second law.

"Time waits for no one." "Time goes on." "You can't go back in time." Indeed! The point is, time as we experience it is irreversible. Time only goes in one direction, and that is forward. That forward direction, in turn, is a function of the change in entropy. Time reflects the change in energy from concentration to diffusion or from order to increasing disorder. If the entropy process could be reversed, then everything that has been done could be undone. In the words of Lord Kelvin: "Boulders would recover from the mud and would become reunited to the mountain peak from which they had formerly broken away."[17]

Time goes forward because energy itself is always moving from an available to an unavailable state. Our consciousness is continually recording the entropy change in the world around us. We watch our friends get old and die. We sit next to a fire and watch its red-hot embers turn slowly into cold white ashes. We experience the world always changing around us, and that experience is the unfolding of the second law. It is the irreversible process of dissipation of energy in the world. What does it mean to say, "The world is running out of time"? Simply this: we experience the passage of time by the succession of one event unfolding after another. And every time an event occurs anywhere in this world energy is expended and the overall entropy has been increased. To say the world is running out of time, then, is to say the world is running out of usable energy. In the words of Sir Arthur Eddington, "Entropy is time's arrow."

Both the ancient Greek and the medieval Christian world views, with their idea of history as a process of movement from order to decay, reflected an understanding of the true direction of time's arrow and the entropy process. By ignoring the truths of the Entropy Law, the existing world paradigm of Newtonian mechanics has provided the illusion that time is an autonomous process in the world, independent of the workings of nature. This sense of alienaton from nature began with Bacon's suggestion of total separation between people and the environment. The crux of the scientific method is the establishment of complete detachment and neutrality between the observer and the observed, so that nature could be manipulated from a distance and used to advance the material interest of humankind.

Having hit upon a method of organizing the world that effectively separated people from nature, the true relationship between life, time, and the entropy process was severed from people's consciousness. From there it is not hard to understand how

Locke and his friends could devise a world view that went completely counter to the real workings of the world. While the Entropy Law states that all things in nature can only be transformed from a usable to an unusable state, Locke argued the opposite. Claiming that everything in nature was waste until people took hold of it and transformed it into usable things of value, he and the other architects of the existing mechanical paradigm argued that the world was in fact "progressing" from chaos to order. As to the passage of time, they reasoned that the faster nature was transformed, the more progress would occur, the more ordered the world would become, and the more time would be saved.

This view of time and history is completely backwards. As already mentioned, time can only exist as long as there is available energy to perform work. The amount of real time expended is a direct reflection of the amount of energy used up. As the universe runs out of available energy, fewer and fewer occurrences can happen—which means less and less "real" time is still available. Eventually, as the final equilibrium state of heat death is reached, everything will stop occurring. Time, then, will no longer exist as we experience it, because nothing will any longer be occurring. Therefore, the faster the energy of the world is used up, the fewer are the possible occurrences left that can unfold, and, correspondingly, the less time that is left in the world. The fact is, we never save time by expending greater amounts of energy. On the contrary, the more energy we expend, the more time we use up. The next time someone asks you how much time you saved by expending more energy to do a particular thing faster, think about the Entropy Law and time's arrow, and then think about the peculiar way we have come to view history over the past 400 years.

There is one more aspect of entropy and time that deserves attention. While entropy tells us the direction of time, it does not tell us the speed. The fact is, the entropy process is constantly changing speed. With every occurrence in the world, entropy increases—but sometimes slower, sometimes faster. Its speed depends upon how many babies are being born, how many blades of grass are dying, how many cars are being built, how many raindrops are falling to the ground, how much wind is blowing, and how many pebbles are being ground into sand as the waves wash up on the beaches of the world.

Humans have always debated the question of whether history is predetermined, or whether we are able to exercise a measure of free will over the unfolding of events. The Entropy Law, more than any other concept we have discovered, goes a long way toward resolving that question. In establishing the direction of time, the second law sets the limits we are forced to work within. We cannot reverse time or the entropy process. It is determined for us. But we can exercise free will in determining the speed by which the entropy process moves. Every action we human beings take in this world either speeds up or slows down the entropy process. By the way we choose to live and behave, we decide how quickly or how slowly the available energy in the world is dissipated. Here is the point where science joins metaphysics and ethics. The full implications of this juncture between free will, determinism, and the entropy process will be explored in depth in later sections when we look at the nature of technology and economic theory.

Life and the Second Law

If the overall entropy of the world is always increasing, then how do we explain the process of life? Certainly, living things exhibit a great deal of order. Evolution itself appears to represent the continued accumulation of greater and greater order from disorder. No one would deny that as a little baby continues to grow it stores up greater amounts of energy. Every time we look at a plant or animal we marvel at how well organized are all of the billions of molecules that make it up. Life, then, must violate the second law, right? Wrong! For a long time, scientists were confused on this point. Now they acknowledge that, like everything else in the world, life cannot escape the iron hand of the Entropy Law. Says Harold Blum, in his pioneering book on the subject, *Time's Arrow and Evolution,* "The small local decrease in entropy represented in the building of the organism is coupled with a much larger increase in the entropy of the universe."[18]

Living things are able to move in a direction opposite to that of the entropy process by absorbing free energy from the surrounding environment. The ultimate source of that free energy is the sun. All plant and animal life is dependent on the sun for survival—either directly, in the case of plants performing photosynthesis, or indirectly, in the case of animals that eat plants or other animals. Every living thing survives, in the words of the Nobel Prize-winning physicist Erwin Schrodinger, "by continually drawing from its environment negative entropy. . . . What an organism feeds upon is negative entropy; it continues to suck orderliness from its environment."[19]

In other words, in all living things the natural tendency is to move toward equilibrium. We human beings, for example, are constantly dissipating our energy every time we think a thought or twitch a finger. In order to prevent ourselves from dissipating to an equilibrium state of death, we require a constant flow-through of free energy (negative entropy) from our larger environment. Anyone not convinced of this truth has probably never seen a dead body. Within hours of death, the body begins to completely unravel, dissipating into total random chaos.

At first, scientists had a difficult time figuring out how living systems fit into the second law because equilibrium thermodynamics is concerned with closed systems—systems in which energy but not matter can be exchanged with the outside surroundings. Living systems, however, are open systems. Both matter and energy are exchanged with the outside. Living systems can never obtain an equilibrium state, while they are alive, because an equilibrium state means death. So, living things maintain themselves far away from an equilibrium state by continuing to feed off the available energy around them. This state is called the "steady state." If matter and energy cease flowing through a living organism, the steady state is abandoned, and the organism drifts to equilibrium and death. In living systems then, free energy flow, not entropy, is the primary concern. This branch of science is called nonequilibrium thermodynamics. While nonequilibrium systems cannot be explained in the same way as equilibrium systems, they do conform with the broad imperative laid down by the second law, as we shall continue to see.

"Every living thing," said Bertrand Russell, "is a sort of imperialist, seeking to transform as much as possible of its environment into itself and its seed."[20] In this process of energy scavenging, every living thing on this planet dissipates energy as that energy flows through its system, making at least part of it unavailable for future use. It is also true that even the tiniest plant maintains its own order at the expense of creating greater disorder in the overall environment. In the case of the plant, it survives by photosynthesis—sucking negative entropy from the sun's rays. In the process, only a tiny fraction of the solar energy is actually picked up and used by the plant; the rest is simply dissipated. Compared with the tiny entropy decrease in the plant, the energy lost to the overall environment is monumental.

The entropy increase is even more graphically illustrated in the normal food chain. Chemist G. Tyler Miller sets up a very simple food chain to make the point. The chain consists of grass, grasshoppers, frogs, trout, and humans. Now, according to the first law, energy is never lost. But according to the second law, available energy should be turned into unavailable energy at each step of the food chain process, and therefore the overall environment should experience greater disorder. In fact, this is exactly what happens. At each stage of the process, when the grasshopper eats the grass, and the frog eats the grasshopper, and the trout eats the frog, and so on, there is a loss of energy. In the process of devouring the prey, says Miller, "about 80-90% of the energy is simply wasted and lost as heat to the environment."[21] Only between 10 and 20 percent of the energy that was devoured remains within the tissue of the predator for transfer to the next stage of the food chain. Consider for a moment the numbers of each species that are required to keep the next higher species from slipping toward maximum entropy. "Three hundred trout are required to support one man for a year. The trout in turn, must consume 90,000 frogs, that must consume 27 million grasshoppers that live off of 1000 tons of grass."[22]

Thus, in order for one human being to maintain a high level of "orderliness," the energy contained in 27 million grasshoppers or a thousand tons of grass must be used. Is there any doubt, then, that every living thing maintains its own order only at the expense of creating greater disorder (or dissipation of energy) in the overall environment?

Energy is continuously flowing through every living organism, entering the system at a high level and leaving the system in a more degraded state. Organisms survive by being able to accumulate negative entropy from their environment. The struggle for existence depends upon how well equipped each organism is to capture available energy. Biologist Alfred Lotka was one of the first to relate energy flow-through and biological evolution. Lotka said that every species can be looked at as a different type of "transformer" for capturing and using available energy. Each transformer or organism is equipped with an array of devices that it uses to suck in energy from its surroundings.

According to Lotka, "The close association of the principal sense organs: eyes, ears, nose, tastebuds, tactile papillas of the finger tips, with the anterior [head] end of the body, the mouth end, all point to the same lesson."[23] That lesson is that organisms are designed to be collectors and transformers of energy. If they weren't so designed, they wouldn't be able to survive. From the point of view of evolution, Lotka argues that natural selection favors those organisms that are able to "increase the total mass of the system, rate of circulation of mass through the system, and the total energy flux through the system . . . so long as there is presented an unutilized residue of matter and available energy."[24]

Lotka's assertion that natural selection favors those organisms that maximize the flow of energy through the system has since been modified (even by Lotka himself). It is now acknowledged that maximizing flow-through is a common response in the early stages of an ecological system's development, when there is still an excess of available energy present. However, as various species begin to fill up a given ecological habitat, they are forced to adapt to the ultimate carrying capacity of the environment by using less energy flow-through more efficiently. The early stage of maximum flow-through is generally referred to as the colonizing phase, and the later stage of minimum flow-through as the climactic phase.

On the whole, Homo sapiens has yet to move from a colonizing to a climactic phase. Human beings, especially in the highly industrial societies, continue to increase energy flow-through in both the human and the social systems. The worldwide human crisis today is a crisis of transition. In the next age, humanity will have settled into its climactic phase, ordering its activity in such a way as to minimize energy flow-through in the human and social processes. If it doesn't, it will likely go the way of other species who were unable to make the transition in the past. Life's epic is strewn with extinct species; it would have little trouble accommodating at least one more on the long list of names.

We are so used to thinking of biological evolution in terms of progress. Now we find that each higher species in the evolutionary chain transforms greater amounts of energy from a usable to an unusable state. In the process of evolution, each succeeding species is more complex and thus better equipped as a transformer of available energy. What is really difficult to accept, however, is the realization that the higher the species in the chain, the greater the energy flow-through and the greater the disorder created in the overall environment.

The Entropy Law says that evolution dissipates the overall available energy for life on this planet. Our concept of evolution is the exact opposite. We believe that evolution somehow magically creates greater overall value and order on earth. Now that the environment we live in is becoming so dissipated and disordered that it is apparent to the naked eye, we are for the first time beginning to have second thoughts about our views on evolution, progress, and the creation of things of material value. More about the implications of this in later sections.

Explanations and rationalizations aside, there is no way to get around it. Evolution means the creation of larger and larger islands of order at the expense of ever greater seas of disorder in the world. There is not a single biologist or physicist who can deny this central truth. Yet, who is willing to stand up in a classroom or before a public forum and admit it?

If this explanation of evolution appears too depressing to consider, it is only because we are so locked into the existing world paradigm that all other ways of organizing our thoughts seem totally unacceptable. Yet, not until we recognize and acknowledge that the second law is the basis of both life and evolution will we be able to make the transition from our present colonizing phase to a climactic phase of existence.

Exosomatic Instruments and Energy

While all living things are engaged in a continuous struggle to secure available energy from their surroundings, only Homo sapiens is equipped with external aids to help facilitate the process. Other creatures must rely on their own anatomy—their eyes, ears, nose, teeth, claws—to gather up energy. Human beings, however, because of our more highly developed nervous system and brain, have succeeded in augmenting and extending our natural biological apparatus with the creation of all sorts of tools. Scientists and anthropologists refer to these instruments as exosomatic in nature to distinguish them from the endosomatic organs we are born with.

When we talk about exosomatic instruments, we are really including the entire range of tools that people use to capture, transform, and process available energy (or negative entropy) through our systems. We develop tools and machinery to extract energy from the environment; we build homes to capture heat and maintain our body warmth; we build roads, construct bridges, and engineer new ways of traveling to facilitate the transport of energy from one location to another; we devise languages, customs, economic institutions, and governments to better organize the processing and distribution of energy.

All of these exosomatic activities together constitute a large part of human culture. Social development, after all, is basically the attempt to create pockets of order to advance human survival. Since we human beings, like all other living creatures, survive by our ability to maintain a constant flow-through of energy, our cultures serve as an instrument for the withdrawal of energy from the larger environment. The first and second laws of thermodynamics, then, serve as the supreme operating principles for every culture and civilization, just as they do for the rest of the universe. The belief that we can leave these laws outside the city gates is as dangerous as the notion that we can survive without a constant flow of energy through our systems.

If we were to abstract all of the complex activities that go on in a culture into a few categories, the terms *transforming, exchanging,* and *discarding* of energy would no doubt top the list. People are always busily engaged in one or more of these processes. Yet, it is often hard for us to see these processes for what they are, because they have become so associated with activities that seem to have no relationship whatsoever to nature itself. Still, if we take the time to strip away all of the layers upon layers of cultural paint that have accumulated over the centuries, we will notice that at the bottom, it is really available energy that is being constantly transformed, exchanged, and discarded. If this sounds hard to believe, test it out yourself. Take an entire day to observe everything you come in contact with: things that you see, hear, touch, smell, feel, or consume; things that you change; and things that you exchange. Then try to trace each experience or item in both directions, back to its original source and forward to its final destination. Chances are better than excellent (in fact, guaranteed) that they all started off as some form of raw material (available energy), and that they will all end up somewhere as unusable waste (unavailable energy).

Energy is the basis of human culture, just as it is the basis of life. Therefore, power in every society ultimately belongs to whoever controls the exosomatic instruments that are used to transform, exchange, and discard energy. Class division, exploitation, privilege, and poverty are all determined by how a society's energy flow line is set up. Those who control the exosomatic instruments control the energy flow line. They determine how the work in society will be divided up and how the economic rewards will be allocated among various groups and constituencies.

Of course, anthropologists have long recognized that the energy basis of a given environment is a primary determinant in the shaping of culture. Anthropologists divide the major periods in history by the changes in how people organized their environment. For this reason, it is important to take a look at the distinguishing features of some of these epochal periods and the common thread that runs through all of them. That thread is the Entropy Law.

PART THREE

ENTROPY: A NEW HISTORICAL FRAME

History and Entropy Watersheds

Les gens heureux n'ont pas d'histoire. This old French proverb means, "Happy people don't make history." There is an American proverb that says "Necessity is the mother of invention." Put these two sayings together and much of history becomes understandable. Historians will protest. They will argue that the world is much more complicated than that. There are subtleties, nuances, hidden meanings, and unconscious drives to take into consideration. Arnold Toynbee will insist that social history is really a series of cultural and environmental challenges and responses. Oswald Spengler will argue that the history of civilizations is a cyclical process of birth, maturation, and death—like life itself. Ortega y Gasset will contend that history is a leveling process in which the tremendous creativity of charismatic minorities becomes taken over and absorbed by the masses and thus made dull and lifeless. Marx will lecture that history is really dialectical and material, and that each unfolding reality contains the seeds of its own destruction and the embryo of a new reality that will replace it.

Each of these scholars has identified part of the historical jigsaw puzzle. As with any other puzzle, however, the job of fitting all the separate pieces together is always more difficult when there is no prior knowledge of what the puzzle represents. The key to understanding the puzzle of history is the Entropy

Law and these two proverbs. Bring history down to a personal level and things immediately become clear. When you and I are feeling really happy and content with the way our life is going, we rarely if ever entertain the idea of a radical change in the way we go about things. Why should we? As the saying goes, "Don't knock a good thing."

On a personal level, we usually begin to think about radical changes in the way we do things when our present approach to life fails us in some way. We have all experienced the feeling of personal crisis, the trauma of having to reexamine our lives, and the fear of trying out something new and unexplored. Yet, it is exactly at these times, when the old way no longer works for us, that we begin to think, sometimes furiously, about ways out. The mental and emotional juices begin to flow, and we start to experiment helter-skelter with various alternatives. Finally, we hit on one or more alternatives that seem to make sense and take hold of them—at least until the next crisis hits.

Personal history is not very different from social history. In both cases happiness marks the blank periods and crises mark the inventive periods. Unfortunately, the exact opposite argument has been advanced by most (not all) modern historians, and for that reason we have to take leave of what our common sense tells us, just for a moment, to examine their thinking on this score.

The leisure, or surplus, theory of history argues that major changes occur in the way people do things when they have built up enough abundance or surplus to allow them the leisure time to think, experiment, and tinker. For example, it is often pointed out that hunter-gatherer societies could never have made the transition to agriculture unless they had first succeeded in building up a surplus. The reasoning is that people always on the brink of famine would "find it hard to devote resources to a future event— the harvest."[1] In other words, hungry people are not going to forgo hunting and gathering for five or six months in order to tend the fields.

This line of argument sounds reasonable at first, but upon closer examination it just does not hold up. First of all, let's assume that a hunter-gatherer society did succeed in establishing a surplus. This would mean that their environment was well stocked with more than enough animals, nuts, fruits, and berries to supply all of their needs. Why, then, would they consider uprooting their entire way of life to take up an uncertain, risky, and unexplored new existence tilling the ground? People simply don't destroy their way of life when things are going well.

Yet, according to the modern world view, history is a steady line of progress in which the surplus of each period provides the margin of free time necessary to invent new tools and technologies which, in turn, result in even more material surplus which frees even more time for the discovery of even more advanced tools and technologies which result in even more surplus and leisure time. The Newtonian world machine is constantly being streamlined, improved, and enlarged, and our own lives continue to become more secure and comfortable in the process. This is our world view—the way we look at things. No wonder the world around us is becoming so blurred. History, has, in fact, often unfolded in just the opposite way from how we have been conditioned to think.

All of the evidence suggests that the hunter-gatherers took up farming out of necessity. The game and edible plant life became increasingly scarce, new territories became exhausted, and further geographic expansion became impossible. The crisis of survival dictated experimentation. New ideas were tried out. Gradually, step by step, farming took over as the old hunting-gathering way of life proved less and less economical. Studies of the few remaining hunter-gatherer societies bear out the "deprivation, crisis, experimentation" thesis. Still, it is not necessary to focus exclusively on this one epochal shift in history because we do have records of other major changes in human culture since then, and with few exceptions they show that the great changes occurred not as a result of the building up of abundance but as a result of the dissipation of the existing stock of resources. What this means is that history is a reflection of the second law. The overall entropy process is always moving toward a maximum. With every single occurrence, some amount of energy becomes forever dissipated. In the course of history, critical watersheds are reached when all of the accumulated increases in entropy result in a qualitative change in the energy source of the enviroment itself. It is at these critical transition points that the old way of doing things becomes inoperative. The entropy of the environment becomes so high that a shift to a new energy environment occurs, along with the creation of a new mode of technology and the shaping of new social, economic, and political institutions.

The Entropy Law also tells us that each of these qualitative shifts in the environment is more harsh and exacting in terms of available energy than the preceding one. This is because, with each successive stage, the stock of available energy in the world has dissipated to a lower and lower level. The overall disorder of the world is always increasing; the amount of available energy is always decreasing. Since human survival depends upon available energy, this must mean that human life is always becoming harder and harder to sustain and that more work, not less, is necessary in order to eke out an existence from a more and more stingy environment. Because there is not enough time in a day for human beings alone to perform the additional work required by the harsher energy environments, more complex technologies must be devised at each stage of history just to maintain a moderate level of human existence.

Upholders of the Newtonian paradigm cannot stomach such thoughts. They argue that new and more sophisticated technologies continue to create greater abundances by replacing less efficient human energy with more efficient nonhuman energy—all of which lessens people's burdens in life. That's what progress is all about. In fact, it is not uncommon to measure cultural progress in terms of the increased use of nonhuman energy. In hunter-gatherer societies, people have to depend largely on their own muscle power as their primary source of energy. An average adult is capable of generating about one-tenth of one horsepower. Compare that figure with the thousands of horsepower or machine power that the average American has at his disposal today as a result of modern technology and it becomes obvious, say the upholders, that history is progress and that people are better off now than in the remote past. Behind this kind of thinking rests an essential assumption: that the greater the energy flow-through, the more efficient a society is, the more progress civilization is making, and the more ordered the world is becoming.

It is now time to dispel such foolish notions once and for all. It is true that each new major development in technique generally speeds up the process of extraction and flow of energy through the system. Remember, though, that energy can never be created or destroyed, and it can only be transformed one way—from available to unavailable. Therefore, every so-called advance in efficiency, as measured by new techologies designed to speed up energy flow, has only hastened the overall process of dissipation of energy and disorder in the world. As the process of energy flow has been speeded up, the period between each new entropy watershed has shortened. It took hundreds of thousands of years to exhaust the environment that supported hunter-gatherer societies before they had to make the transition to an agricultural base. It took tens of thousands of years before people finally "had to" move from an agricultural to an industrial environment. Within just a matter of a few hundred years people have exhausted the resource base (nonrenewable energy sources) of the industrial environment and today face a new entropy watershed.

Moreover, contrary to the prevailing wisdom, applying more and more energy per individual in order for each person to survive is not more efficient—not, that is, if efficiency is properly defined as a reduction in work. It is instead quite the opposite. Work, in the final analysis, is nothing more than the using up of available energy. Today, in the modern industrial world, we have to "use up" a thousand times more energy per person to maintain ourselves than was true in ancient times. If we have deluded ourselves into believing that, just because the work is being done by machines rather than by muscle power, somehow "less" work is being done, then we are sadly mistaken.

Throughout history, there have been exceptional cultures that have been able to survive for long periods of time within the same energy environment. They were able to make the transition from a colonizing to a climactic stage of existence. For all of these cultures, adapting to the existing environment meant slowing down the flow-through of energy and thus slowing down the entropy increase in the overall environment. Of course, in the real world, it is impossible even under the most adaptive climactic system to forestall an eventual qualitative change from taking place in a particular energy environment. The question is always one of how quickly or how slowly these successive entropy watersheds will be reached. It is interesting to observe that those cultures that have moved into a "steady state" with their surroundings have tended to see the world as a very closed system, a system they had already filled and from which there was no escape. For them, "living within their limits" was a matter of second nature.

The modern world view, however, reflects a very different conception. The machine paradigm emphasizes matter in motion. It puts a premium on locomotion and distance. It is bound up with the image of constant growth. Limits are a sign of defeat. The spirit of our age is one of expansion and conquest. Above all, there are always new worlds to conquer. Except now the human population is doubling every forty years, and every nook and cranny of the entire globe appears to be filling up, with standing room only. We find it harder and harder to locate sources of available energy and more and more difficult to find places to discard our energy wastes. We are finally reaching the outer limits of the planet earth, and as we begin to jostle each other back and forth, a new voice can be heard from deep inside the crowd. The voice is getting louder and it is saying that we must learn to "live within our limits." The colonizing stage for Homo sapiens is truly over.

Yet, there are those who refuse to accept the obvious. Today, the frontier mentality remains alive and well among space enthusiasts who claim that we can always move on to colonize and exploit other planets. Their expectations cannot be met. Sending up just the population increase on earth of six days of births would cost the equivalent of our entire gross national product for one year. Then, too, astronomers tell us that the nearest solar system to ours with planets that might possibly be comparable in climatic conditions is ten light-years away, and with our present technology it would take over a hundred years to travel there. And then there is no assurance that life as we know it could possibly be maintained. Finally, the idea that valuable resources could be mined and sent back to earth from other planets in the quantities needed is completely ridiculous. The cost of mining additional resources on earth is already becoming prohibitive. Even assuming we could locate planets with resources that would be usable in some way here on earth, there is no way we could ever afford the costs of mining and transporting the materials from these distant places.

Only by consciously choosing to respect the physical confines of this closed system we call the planet earth can we make the radical adjustment that is essential for our continuation as a species. Our survival and the survival of all other forms of life now depend on our willingness to make peace with nature and begin to live cooperatively with the rest of our ecosytem. If we do so, and allow the natural recycling process the time it needs to heal the wounds we have inflicted on the earth, then we and all other forms of life can expect a long and healthy sojourn on this planet.

If we steadfastly refuse to make the change and continue on in our colonizing ways, destroying everything in our path, we may find ourselves without a choice in the future. We will eventually reach that critical point where the matter-energy of the planet will be so depleted and the earth and atmosphere so polluted with greenhouse gases that even with a complete turnaround to a climactic mode, there will be too little time left to allow the natural recycling process to restore a measure of ecological balance for the continuation of life.

The transition from a colonizing to a climactic mode of existence is the most profound change our species will ever have to make. That crossroads is now before us.

The Last Great Energy Watershed

History does indeed follow the Entropy Law, as a brief survey of two major periods will demonstrate. Let's take a brief look at western Europe between the fourth century and the nineteenth century A.D. Historians separate this stretch of fifteen centuries into two parts: the Dark Ages and medieval era, and the industrial era. (The Renaissance is generally recognized as a transition time between the two epochs.)

Popular textbooks generally attribute the transition from the medieval era to the modern era to a great reawakening of the human mind—as if for some strange reason all of humanity had decided to stop thinking and simply hybernate for several centuries. While scholars argue back and forth about the significance of the Protestant Reformation, the rise of the bourgeois class and capitalism, and the opening up of trade routes in the great metamorphosis that occurred, few spend much time at all discussing another underlying cause for the changeover. Between the thirteenth and sixteenth centuries, western Europe experienced an entropy watershed. Wood, the energy base of the medieval way of life, became increasingly scarce. Population pressure further exacerbated the shortages, and the subsequent search for alternatives finally led to the replacement of wood with coal. The move from an energy environment based on wood to one based on coal radically changed the entire way of organizing life in western Europe. The transition from wood to coal was a principal factor behind the demise of the medieval era and the emergence of the Industrial Revolution.

A visitor to Europe today is likely to be impressed with how well used every available space is. Everything appears to be partitioned into neatly arranged geometric sizes and shapes. Even the open spaces have a measured look to them suggesting that the whole continent was meticulously planned out and sculptured down to the very last detail way back at the beginning of time. It would be difficult to imagine that in the fourth century the continent was a blanket of dense forest stretching from the Alps to the Scandinavian peninsula. A bird could fly over the treetops for hundreds and hundreds of miles seeing only an occasional clearing. In some of these tiny open spaces a little smoke might be coming from an open fire. Nearby, there might be a few thatched huts and twenty or thirty people scurrying back and forth near the edge of the forest.

The land in western Europe was very different from the land in the semiarid Middle East. There the soil was extremely light in composition; in the wetter climate of western Europe the soil was often sticky and heavy, making it much harder to plow. This difference in the environment necessitated some basic changes in cultivation that profoundly affected the future development of the continent.

The old Roman scratch plow was not strong enough to turn over the richer and heavier soils of Europe. By the middle of the sixth century, Slavic peasants began to use a new heavier type of plow with wheels and two blades. The cross plow was equipped with "a vertical blade to cut the line of the furrow, a horizontal plowshare, and a mouldboard to turn over the sod."[2] This new type of plow attacked the soil so violently that traditional cross-plowing of fields was no longer necessary.

The new cross plow changed the entire organization of agricultural life. Because it was so heavy, the cross plow required a team of eight oxen to move it. Since no single peasant family owned that many oxen, teams had to be used cooperatively.

Equally important, with the new cross plow it was no longer practical to fence off land into private strips. The big heavy plow performed best in long open fields. For both these reasons, communal farming became the pattern on most feudal estates in northern Europe.

By the ninth century, the cross plow had been introduced throughout much of the continent. Its unique effectiveness in plowing rich river-bottom soils led to the deforestation of mile after mile of low-lying timberland, as the expanding population brought more and more acreage into cultivation.

Two other technological developments followed the introduction of the cross plow. In parts of northern Europe, where the soil was richer, increased population pressure began exerting demands for increased crop yields. In response, the traditional two-field system of farming gave way to a three-field rotation. Under the two-field system, half the land was always left fallow in order to renew fertility; with the three-field system, only one-third of the land remained fallow each year. There were several advantages to this approach. First, production was increased by one-third. Second, there was a one-ninth decrease in the amount of plowing that had to be done. Of course, the short-range advantage in increased yield only resulted in exhausting the soil faster than it would have under a two-field system. By increasing the use of the land, the three-field rotation system speeded up the dissipation of the soil's energy and hastened the entropy process.

The three-field rotation system also made it possible to replace oxen with horses. Horses worked twice as fast but required grain as well as hay to survive. The increased yield of the three-field system provided the surplus oats necessary to maintain a stock of workhorses. Before horses could be effectively used, however, three technological improvements had to be made. By the eleventh century the modern horse collar had been adopted, horseshoes had been invented, and a method of tandem harnessing had been perfected. These three technological advances allowed horse teams to pull the heavier cross plows, thus greatly speeding up the tilling process.

The cross plow, the three-field rotation system, and horse teams greatly increased production on existing land and spurred the opening up of larger tracts of new land for cultivation. The agricultural surpluses of the ninth through the twelfth centuries resulted in a steady increase in population, which in turn resulted in increased pressure to overexploit existing farmland and deforest still more marginal lands for additional acreage. A vicious cycle had set in, the kind that precedes every major entropy watershed. Further refinements in technology were increasing the flow-through of energy, the population, and the entropy process. By the mid-fourteenth century the watershed had been reached. The population had outstripped its energy base. Soil exhaustion and a growing timber shortage were threatening the populations of western and northern Europe. The introduction, in some parts of Europe, of windmills in the twelfth century (and a greater use of water mills) helped bring previously unworkable land into cultivation—but at the expense of further depleting the forests and increasing the population even more.

According to historian William McNeill:

> Many parts of Northwestern Europe had achieved a kind of saturation with humankind by the 14th century. The great frontier boom that began about 900 led to a replication of manors and fields across the face of the land until, at least in the most densely inhabited regions, scant forests remained. Since woodlands were vital for fuel and as a source of building materials, mounting shortages created severe problems for human occupancy.[3]

The economic problem was greatly magnified by the expanding population in cities that needed to be fed. Cities had begun to spring up in the eleventh century as trading centers to handle the agricultural surpluses. Now, with population increasing faster than agricultural output, there were no more surpluses to be traded and the cities began to collapse. The whole fabric of medieval economic, social, and political life began to disintegrate. It was at this juncture that a new energy base took hold, one still partially with us today.

In order to comprehend the magnitude of the medieval energy crisis, it is important to understand how crucial wood was to the life of the times. Like fossil fuels today, wood was used for just about everything. Lewis Mumford drew up a list of some of the particulars:

> The carpenters' tools were of wood but for the last cutting edge: the rake, the oxyoke, the cart, the wagon, were of wood; so was the wash tub in the bathhouse; so was the bucket and so was the broom; so in certain parts of Europe was the poor man's shoes. Wood served the farmer and the textile worker: the loom and the spinning wheel, the oil press and the wine presses, and even a hundred years after the printing press was invented, it was still made of wood. The very pipes that carried water in the cities were often treetrunks: so were the cylinders of pumps . . . the ships of course were made of wood and . . . the principal machines of industry were likewise made of wood.[4]

Mumford sums up the importance of wood to the life of that period by observing that "as raw material, as tool, as machine, as utensil and utility, as fuel, and as final product wood was the dominant industrial resource."[5]

While the clearing of forests for cultivation greatly reduced the available wood supply, it was the quickened pace of commercial activity that led to a timber famine. For example, the new glass works and soap industry required large amounts of wood ash. But it was the production of iron and the building of ships that made the greatest demands. By the sixteenth and early seventeenth centuries, the timber crisis was so acute in England that royal commissions were set up to regulate the cutting down of forests. The regulations proved ineffective. In the 1630s wood had become two and a half times more expensive than it had been in the late fifteenth century.

The answer to the wood crisis was coal. But it was not just a simple matter of replacing one energy base with another. The cultures of Europe had been thoroughly integrated into a wood-based existence. The changeover necessitated the radical uprooting of an entire way of life. The way people made a living, the way people got around, the way people dressed, the way people behaved, the way governments governed—all of this was turned inside out, then upside down.

It started in England in the thirteenth century under Henry II. The people of Newcastle were without firewood and literally freezing to death. The king consented to the mining of coal as an alternative energy source.

In the fifteenth century, Pope Pius II wrote that while in Scotland on a visit he was surprised at the sight of people in rags lining up at church doors to "receive for alms pieces of black stone with which they went away contented. This species of stone they burn in place of wood of which their country is destitute."[6] By 1700 coal had begun to replace wood as the energy base for England. Within 150 years the same held true for much of western Europe.

Today we think of the substitution of coal for wood as a great leap forward, a singular triumph for the forces of progress. It would have been difficult to convince the people back then. Coal was treated with contempt as an inferior energy source. It was dirty and created a great deal of pollution. In 1631 Edmund Howes lamented that "the inhabitants in general are constrained to make their fires of sea-coal or pit coal, even in the chambers of honourable personages."[7]

Coal was also more difficult to extract and process than wood. It required the expenditure of a great deal more energy to transform it into a usable state. The reason is to be found once again in the operation of the second law. The available energy in the world is constantly being dissipated. The more available sources of energy are always the first to be used. Each succeeding environment relies on a less available form of energy than the one preceding it. It is more difficult to mine coal and process it than it is to cut down trees. It is still more difficult to drill and process oil, and even harder to split atoms for nuclear energy. Richard Wilkinson, in his book *Poverty and Progress*, reviews the history of human economic development:

During the course of economic development man has been forced over and over again to change the resources he depended on and the methods he used to exploit them. Slowly he has had to involve himself in more and more complicated processing and production techniques as he has changed from the more easily exploitable resources to the less easily exploitable. . . . In its broadest ecological context, economic development is the development of more intensive ways of exploiting the natural environment.[8]

Wilkinson's thesis is quite correct, although difficult for most of us to accept. We are used to thinking of great leaps forward in history occurring because someone came up with a better way of doing things. Actually, these so-called better ways are in reality only different ways of doing things occasioned by the need to readjust to harsher, less easily exploitable energy environments. And, as Wilkinson suggests, each new way of doing things ultimately requires the expenditure of more work (or energy) than the previous ways—although the work is carried out by nonhuman energy sources. The development of the steam engine is a good case in point.

When we study the Industrial Revolution in school we are taught that one day a bright young man named James Watt was tinkering and came up with a promising invention which he called the steam engine. The announcement was made to the world and within the blink of an eyelash the Industrial Age was off and clanking. We are told that the ancient Greek, Hero, had devised a steam engine in the third century B.C. but that it was only used as a toy for the amusement of the royal court. There was no thought of using it for the purpose of doing work because they had plenty of slaves for that. The Greeks aside, the story behind the development of the modern steam engine should be understood because it vividly demonstrates that major technological changes (not just refinements in existing technologies) follow changes in the energy environment.

The modern steam engine was designed and first used to facilitate the mining of coal. As mines had to be sunk deeper into the ground to extract available supplies, it became more difficult to ventilate the mines and to lift the hewn coal up the shafts. During the seventeenth century, mines faced still another problem. At a certain depth the water table was reached and drainage became a priority. All of these problems required a technological solution. The steam engine was the answer. The first steam pump was patented in 1698 by Thomas Savery.

The steam pump used in mining was only the first in a long series of mechanical and structural innovations to come directly out of the new coal environment. For example, no sooner had the problem of mining the coal been resolved with the introduction of the steam pump than a second and equally important problem arose—how to transport the coal to markets throughout the country. Because of its heavy bulk, coal could not easily be transported over land by horse-drawn wagons. English roads were for the most part unsurfaced. The sheer weight of the coal wagons created giant ruts in the roads, making it virtually impossible to travel during rainy periods when roads turned into muddy ditches. At the same time, the cost of maintaining transport horses became increasingly expensive. With farmland in critically short supply, it was not possible to grow food for both horses and people. The answer to the transporation crisis was the invention of the steam locomotive and railroad tracks. Like the steam pump, the steam locomotive was a direct technological response to the needs created by the new coal environment. Together, the steam pump and the steam locomotive laid the technological base for the industrial era that followed.

The steam pump and steam locomotive were much more complex energy-consuming technologies than the ax, horse, and cart of the wood era. But then, the energy environment was more exacting. Throughout history, qualitative changes in technology have always been toward more complexity and greater energy expenditure, because each major change in the environment has been toward less available, harder-to-reach sources of energy.

Not only has more work been required with each new environment, but the new way of doing things is usually perceived as an inferior substitute for the old way. Sometimes this perception is immediate, and sometimes not until well after the substitute has taken hold. Take, for example, canned and packaged food. Very few people today, if left with the choice of having processed food or fresh natural food, would choose the former, although for a long time it was touted as a superior substitute. In the case of processed foods, the amount of energy (or work) needed to produce the product is much greater than the amount used up by the older way.

Wilkinson offers still another striking example: clothes. In prehistoric times, people used leather to clothe themselves. As animal hides became more and more scarce they were forced to replace them with wool from sheep. By the seventeenth and eighteenth centuries, the population pressure on available farmland in Europe made sheep grazing less economical. "Sheep devour people" became a favorite slogan of the time, and demands were made to turn more grazing land to crop cultivation. This required a substitute for wool. The answer was found in cotton, which could be grown cheaply in the overseas colonies and imported back to the mother countries for conversion into cloth. People were not exactly overjoyed with the new substitute, as Friedrich Engels pointed out in his book *The Condition of the Working Class in England:*

> The working classes very seldom wear woolen clothing of any kind. Their heavy cotton clothes, though thicker, stiffer and heavier than woolen cloth, do not keep out the cold and wet anything like the same extent as woolens. . . . Gentlemen, on the other hand, wear suits made from woolen cloth, and the term broadcloth is used to designate the middle classes.[9]

Similarly, today, we are forced to rely more and more on synthetic fibers, but if given the choice many people would prefer clothes made of 100 percent cotton, or wool.

Though less desired, each successive clothes substitute has still required the expenditure of greater work (energy) to produce it than its predecessor. It did not take a great deal of work to kill an animal, tan its hide, and fashion clothes for an entire family. The feeding and grazing of sheep, the shearing and weaving of yarn, and the sewing of woolen garments meant that a great deal more human and nonhuman energy had to be put into the process. With the growing and processing of cotton, even more energy is expended. By the time we consider synthetics, the whole chemical process—beginning with the drilling of oil and leading up to the giant factories stamping out the final designs—requires an expenditure of work (energy) per garment that is astronomical compared with the killing of animals and tanning of hides.

This is what we call "progress." In the next two chapters we will explore in much greater detail some of the specific ways that changes in technology increase the use of work inputs per unit of output, hastening the entropy process, including the buildup of greenhouse gases and other pollutants.

Technology

Remove all of the mystique that surrounds technology, and what is left, naked and exposed, is a transformer. Every technology ever conceived by the genius of humankind is nothing more than a transformer of energy from nature's storehouse. In the process of that transformation, the energy flows through the culture and the human system where it is used for a fleeting moment to sustain life (and the artifacts of life) in a nonequilibrium state. At the other end of the flow, the energy eventually ends up as dissipated waste, unavailable for future use.

It is ironic that as technology has become more complex and has enlarged its domain in the world, we have come to see it as something independent of nature, as if it were generating its own energy from scratch or, through some mysterious process, were adding to the existing energy source to get more out of it than was there in the first place. The fact is, technology never creates energy; it only uses up existing available energy. The larger and more complex the technology, the more available energy it uses up. As awesome and impressive as our technology might sometimes appear, it too operates under the supreme reign of the first and second laws, just like everything else in nature. Those laws again: first, all matter-energy in the world is constant; it can be neither created nor destroyed but only transformed from one state to another. Second, the transformation of energy is always from an available to a dissipated form, or from an ordered to a disordered state. Technology is the transformer—nothing more, nothing less.

Even though all of this is rather obvious, we still continue to live under the delusion that our technology is freeing us from dependence upon our environment, when nothing could be farther from the truth. Life is not a closed system. Human beings, like all other living things, can only survive by exchanging with the environment. Without a constant flow-through of energy from the environment we would all perish within days. Technology makes us more dependent upon nature, even as it physically moves us farther away from it; we have become more dependent as we have required increasing doses of nature's energy to sustain our cultural patterns and our personal life-styles.

We also entertain the belief that technology is creating greater order in the world when, again, that is only part of the story. The Entropy Law tells us that every time available energy is used up, it creates greater disorder somewhere in the surrounding environment. For example, when we burn fossil fuels, we create dissipated energy in the form of carbon dioxide which is then spewed into the atmosphere, causing the greenhouse effect. The massive flow-through of energy in modern industrial society is creating massive pollution and waste in the world we live in. The faster we streamline our technology, the faster we speed up the transforming process, the faster available energy is dissipated, the more pollution and waste mounts.

In short, we live in a kind of nightmarish Orwellian world. We have convinced ourselves that the way we go about things is creating a world quite different from the one we are really making. Just as in Orwell's *1984,* where society was convinced that war was peace and lies were truth, we have come to believe that disorder is order, that waste is value, and that work is nonwork.

Even as our world slips deeper into chaos, we become less willing to identify the source of the problem. Instead, we wrap ourselves tightly in our technological garb, defending it against all criticism, unable to acknowledge what it is doing to the environment we live in, and even less able to acknowledge what it is doing to us. We continue to cling to the fiction that we are securely clothed and protected, even as we become more exposed and endangered by the disordered fragments of a world of our own making.

External Costs

It has become fashionable of late to talk about the "external costs" of technology. The term is used to refer to the unanticipated costs that arise as a result of the so-called secondary effects produced by a particular product, process, program, or service. Everyone is becoming more and more familiar with external costs. When a nuclear power plant breaks down and spews low-level radiation into the environment, the question immediately arises as to who should pay for whatever damage is done—the public, the utility, the designer, or the government. This is referred to as an external cost. Whenever politicians or economists talk about external costs, they convey the feeling that what is involved are the nuisance-causing side effects that sometimes accompany technologies. These side effects are often costly, but they are tolerable and absorbable because the benefits derived are always considered greater than the external costs generated. This just isn't so.

"External costs" is just a convenient dodge to try to avoid the consequences of the Entropy Law. The disorder created by each new technology is not a side effect. Nor is it less costly in the long run than the benefits derived from the particular technology. For example, consider the short-lived benefits derived from burning fossil fuels over the past two centuries against the long-term environmental and economic costs to the planet and civilization that are likely to result from the global warming trend. The truth is, every technology creates a temporary island of order at the expense of greater disorder to the surroundings. Twenty years ago, no one in America would have been willing to believe this. Back then we all believed that the benefits of technology always outweighed the harm. If technology sometimes failed or produced unfortunate side effects, then the solution was to be found in the application of new technologies to cover up the mistakes of the old. Today, tell people that a new technology is going to be introduced that will be of great benefit to them and society and their immediate reaction is likely to be one of skepticism. Whether it be a new government program, a new way to harness energy, or a new superdrug, the response is often, "Let's wait and see." While on the surface the benefits might appear worthwhile, there is always the doubt gnawing away at each of us that whispers: "I don't know when, or where, or how, but sooner or later this, too, is going to screw up and create greater problems than what I'm going to get out of it." Nuclear power—low-level radiation and cancer. Bigger and faster automobiles—carbon dioxide and the worsening greenhouse crisis. The Entropy Law is not selective. It works everywhere, all of the time. According to Jacques Ellul, the author of *The Technological Society* and perhaps the most renowned critic of technology, "History shows that every technical application from its begining presents certain unforeseeable secondary effects which are more disastrous than the lack of the technique would have been."[10]

The next time a technician, politician, or businessman tells you he or she can eliminate the secondary problems associated with a particular program, product, or process, with better planning or better leadership or better design, think about the second law. It is true that the secondary disorders caused by a particular technology can be temporarily solved by the application of additional technology. But the solution will inevitably result in even greater disorders than the one it solved. Again, says Ellul, "Every successive technique has appeared because the ones which preceded it rendered necessary the ones which followed."[11] That's the second law and there's no way around it. Still we wonder why it is that the more we technologize the world around us, the more things seem to malfunction and fall apart.

The world is becoming more disordered because each time we apply a new and more complex technological solution to a problem, it's like dousing a fire with gasoline. The faster we multiply the "transformers," the faster the available energy is used up, the faster the dissipation and disorder that result. The problems proliferate faster than the solutions.

There are those who would argue that every culture throughout history has used technology and, to a greater or lesser extent, has been able to adjust to it without catastrophic consequences. So why shouldn't we be able to do the same? They fail to recognize the key difference between technique in the modern culture and technique in cultures that have preceded us. In all the other civilizations before the industrial era, technique was limited in the functions it performed. It was a tool but not a way of organizing life. In the world machine paradigm, technique has become the way of organizing all of life's activities. A conscious attempt is made to bring technique into every aspect of our daily existence. The goal is predictability and synchronization. As long as parts of our culture remain outside of the technical process, they remain unpredictable and uncontrollable. It is argued that the system as a whole can never really function smoothly until these pockets of unpredictability are eliminated.

In our efforts to bring technique and order to all of life's activities, we are merely speeding up the transforming process and thus hastening the entropy process. Scientist Eugene Schwartz, in his book *Overskill,* compared our efforts to create the technological society to a giant squirrel cage "wherein technicians must run faster and faster to remain in the same place. Unlike the squirrel cage, however, the faster they run, the further they fall behind. Each quasi-solution has a multiplier effect on the residue of problems."[12] Moreover, each new set of problems is more difficult to solve than the ones that came before, because with the passage of each occurrence, the entropy of the environment has increased and the available free energy has decreased. It becomes harder to maintain order and more costly to generate order. The more we try to spread technique over the culture, the more fragmented society becomes. The whole process of increased complexity, increased problems, increased entropy, and increased disorder proceeds exponentially, and that is what makes the modern world crisis so frightening.

Lest we slip over the word *exponential* without much thought, just consider what it really means relative to the problems of a technological society. Exponential growth, in this context, is a doubling process at every step. According to ecologist G. Tyler Miller, if you were to take a piece of paper (about 1/254 inch thick) and double its thickness just 35 times, it would extend the distance from Los Angeles to New York City. If you doubled it 42 times it would reach from where you're sitting to the moon. If you doubled it just a few more times, say to just over 50 times, the thickness of that paper would extend 93 million miles, from you to the sun. The exponentiality of the technological fix is a one-way ticket to disaster for life and for the planet earth.

Diminishing Returns
of Technology

American business magazines are full of articles bemoaning the decline in American technology. This is of great concern because advances in technology have been the mainstay of American economic superiority in the world. There are various reasons given for the decline. Some blame it on inferior academic preparation. Others blame it on falling profit margins and disincentives to invest. It is argued that government regulations and restrictions extend the time between the discovery of new products and processes and their introduction into the marketplace, making research both costly and risky. Still others blame the downturn on environmental standards that restrict the way research can be conducted and the way the final product can be used. With all of the bickering over who or what is to blame and what can be done, very few of the experts seem to have understood the underlying reason behind the diminishing returns in technology.

Back once again to basics. Technology is not an independent, autonomous force. It is merely a transformer of energy. Therefore, major breakthroughs in technology come on the heels of qualitative changes in the energy source. This is because specific modes of technology are designed to transform the energy of specific types of energy environments. (For example, remember that the steam engine, which was the basic technology for the Industrial Revolution, was invented to transform coal energy from beneath the earth's surface.) During the early stages of a new energy environment, the new mode of technology expands in every direction. This is the time period in which the technological base of the new energy environment is being laid. There is plenty of experimentation, and a wide range of technological derivatives are created one after the other. Often the unit cost of the derivatives actually becomes cheaper and cheaper with further refinements in the technology.

However, as the mode of technology proliferates and the energy flow increases through the system, the entropy of the environment steadily moves toward a maximum, and diminishing returns begin to set in all along the line of energy flow. Sucking more energy out becomes more expensive and complicated. The pollution created by the past flow-through accumulates, exerting increasing pressure, and putting further restraints on new technological possibilities. A critical point is reached when the existing "type" of technology can no longer sustain the level of energy transformation that the society has come to depend on during the earlier stages. From this point on, less effort is put into new technological ideas and more is devoted to readjustments in existing technologies in an attempt to both solve the problems caused by increasing disorders to the overall environment and at the same time meet energy demands in the face of a depleted energy base. This is exactly what is happening in the United States today.

According to Mobil Oil chairman Rawleigh Warner, Jr., "Industry has been compelled to spend more and more of its research dollars to comply with environmental, health and safety regulations—and to move away from longer term efforts aimed at major scientific advances."[13] Some industries, like iron and steel, are now using up over 20 percent of their total capital expenditures on pollution-control equipment.[14] A study done by the Brookings Institution concluded that such expenditures accounted for a 17 to 20 percent decline in the U.S. economic growth rate in one recent year. By 1983, business was spending more than $39 billion on pollution control and abatements.[15] At the same time, the National Petroleum Institute estimates that as a result of the depleting energy base, it will take an additional $172 billion in the years just ahead to explore and process less easily exploitable sources of fossil fuel energy.[16]

Eventually the technology bottoms out altogether as the energy environment it was made for nears it own entropic watershed. In a cover story in *Newsweek* entitled "Innovation," the editors candidly acknowledge this basic reality: "To some extent, of course, erosion in America's technological edge is inevitable. No longer can the U.S. count on the natural abundance of its frontiers . . . the resources have been explored and sometimes depleted."[17]

It should be emphasized that all along the line of a particular type of energy flow, the dominant techniques and technologies used conform to a common energy bond. The kind of economic institutions, the form of transportation and communication systems, the location, design, and operation of cities and towns are all derived from a common energy flow. When that energy flow reaches an entropy watershed and a new energy environment takes over, the various technological forms that served the old energy flow are either radically changed or, more often than not, allowed to simply atrophy as the old energy spigot runs dry. Even a casual examination of the technological and institutional changes that took place when society moved from a wood to a coal energy base and from a coal to an oil energy base bears out this simple observation.

Institutional Development

Historians have observed that at a certain stage in the development of a culture or civilization, a process of universalization sets in. That is, there is a concerted attempt to consolidate the various economic and political activities under more centralized control. Eventually a point is reached where it is impossible to further consolidate and the culture or civilization begins to break down and fragment. But before that point is reached, each succeeding crisis is met by an escalation in centralized control. Certainly, that has been the case with all of the industrializing nations. Each new social or economic crisis is inevitably dealt with by the establishment of some new form of control or regulation, and a greater measure of authority is placed in fewer and fewer hands. Rarely does a crisis get resolved by decentralizing power and placing responsibility and control with a greater number of people. The tendency of institutions and processes to become larger, more complex, and more centralized is the same tendency we see with various forms of technology. The reason for this can be found in the operation of the Entropy Law.

Economic and political institutions, like machinery, are transformers of energy. Their job is to facilitate the flow of energy through the culture. During the first stage of a new energy environment, the economic and political institutions are generally more flexible. This is because, in this early stage, the energy flow

104

is being used primarily to create the new transformers (technologies) for the new energy environment. While some energy is flowing through the larger systems, much of it is still lavished on the creation of the transforming machinery. At this stage, the economic and political institutions serve more as designers and coordinators. Their role is an innovative one and therefore requires a great deal of maneuverability.

Even in the case of societies that place a heavy emphasis on regimentation of the population during the takeoff stage of technology development, the economic and political institutions still have to remain relatively flexible and uncomplicated in order to take advantage of all of the technological possibilities that need to be explored and experimented with.

In the takeoff stage of a new energy environment, the population at large is always deprived of a great deal of energy flow because it is being diverted into the building of the new base of energy transformers. The harsh living conditions and the regimentation are generally tolerated because the population is desperate, having experienced the tremendous deprivation and disorder that accompanied the last stages of the old energy environment. Certainly this was true for many millions of European peasants forced off the land and into the urban slums in the seventeenth, eighteenth, and nineteenth centuries. As bad as conditions in the factories and industrial towns were they were no worse than the conditions in the countryside where timber shortages, exhausted soil, and overpopulation were producing starvation and panic.

In the second stage of a new energy environment, more and more energy begins flowing directly through the social system. At this stage, the initial technological base is in place, and from here on the technology begins to multiply. It is at this point that the weight of the entropy process begins to exert itself. The flow-through of energy creates greater secondary disorders all along the flow line.

The disorders are of three general kinds: those precipitated as a result of the transformation of energy into various products or services; those resulting from the exchange of energy between individuals and groups; and those resulting from the discarding of energy wastes. As mentioned earlier, people depend upon energy flow for their survival and are continually involved in the process of transforming, exchanging, and discarding energy. We work for a living, we buy things, and we throw things out or exchange them for other things. This is what the energy flow line and economic life are all about. Every time we add our own labor to a product or perform a service we expend energy and increase the overall entropy of the environment. Every time we exchange money for a product or a service, the legal tender we use represents payment for previous energy that we expended. Money, after all, is nothing more than stored energy credits. Salaries and wages represent payment for work done or energy expended. Every time we discard something, whether it be an old coat or yesterday's leftovers, energy is again being dissipated. At every stage in the flow line, energy is being transformed, exchanged, or discarded. In the process, energy is always being dissipated and the entropy of the environment is always increasing. The type, scope, and magnitude of the disorders, then, depend on how the flow line is set up. The way the work in a society is allocated (the transforming of energy), the way the energy is divided up between various people, groups, and constituencies (the exchange of energy), and the way the wastes are disposed of at each stage of the flow-through process (the discarding of energy) determine the social, economic, and political nature of the disorders that surface.

As disorders all along the flow line increase in number, the flow itself becomes impeded. To maintain maximum flow-through it becomes necessary to continue to reorder the total disorder that is proliferating faster and faster in every part of the system. Economic and political institutions enlarge their functions and expand their outreach. They begin to serve a maintenance and repair function. The bureaucracies grow with each succeeding crisis. When the disorder at any point along the flow line becomes so great that it threatens the continued functioning of part or all of the society, in moves the appropriate institution to remove the blockage. The institutions swell as they are forced to absorb and contain the mounting social and economic disorders and maintain the maximum flow-through. Periodically, the institutions burst as they can no longer manage to hold back the escalating disorder.

When that happens, new, even larger and more centralized institutions are designed to reorder the disorder, and so on.

At the same time, the state attempts, if at all possible, to extend its domain into new geographic territories in order to obtain new sources of available energy to compensate for the depletion of its existing stocks. Most imperial or colonial expansion is designed to secure new sources of energy. Of course, new conquests require the expenditure of even more energy to provide for armies, weapons, and bureaucracies to occupy and administer the new territorial possessions. The state's institutions become even more enlarged and centralized.

Finally the society reaches stage three, where its institutional complex (its economic and political organization) is so centralized and enlarged that it takes more energy to maintain it than the system can afford. Anyone who has looked at the escalating costs associated with the maintenance of giant multinational corporations and huge government bureaucracies cannot help but notice that more and more energy (or work) is expended operating them, while less and less work is gotten out of them. The institutional complex, which was supposed to facilitate the flow of energy through the culture, becomes a parasite, sucking up much of the remaining energy source. All along the energy line the flow slows up, and the society begins to atrophy. In the final stages, even the institutional complex cannot be maintained with the energy it needs from the environment. At this point the entire complex begins to disintegrate. The society becomes increasingly vulnerable to conquest by other nations or internal upheaval and revolution. An entropy watershed has been reached. The rise and fall of ancient Mesopotamia, Egypt, Rome, and the hydraulic civilizations of the Far East are all classic illustrations of how this whole process works. But every other major civilization that we know of has also followed the same course.

Humankind will remain trapped in this pattern of social development as long as society chooses to remain in a colonizing stage rather than move into a climactic stage of existence.

In a colonizing stage, the emphasis is always on increasing flow-through. As we have already seen, increasing flow-through always hastens the entropy process, speeding up the accumulation of disorder, which results in greater institutional control, complexity, centralization, and all of the other things just mentioned. It is no accident, by the way, that the term *colonization* is used. The colonizing of overseas territories by the great imperial powers in the eighteenth and nineteenth centuries is a graphic example of the truth of the historical development thesis just outlined. Colonial administrations were designed to increase the flow-through of energy from the colonies to the mother country. As the entropy process proceeded and disorders mounted, the colonial administrations had to enlarge their bureaucracies and their armies, diverting more energy away from the flow line and toward their own maintenance. Finally, the armies of occupation and the colonial administration could no longer be maintained by the mother countries and became so parasitic on the local energy supply that the native populations rebelled and overthrew them.

Only in a climactic framework can the process of increasing complexity and centralization be slowed down. By minimizing the energy flow-through, the entropy process slows down (it can never be stopped) and the disorders slow down as well. If the energy flow-through is maintained at a low constant level, the institutions responsible for transforming it through the social system can be maintained in a steady low-growth state. Only when a society attempts to get more and more energy out of its environment do the institutions (and other technologies) grow concomitantly in both complexity and control. A climactic existence, then, favors small, decentralized institutions; a colonizing existence favors large, centralized institutions.

Specialization

Specialization goes hand in hand with increased complexity and centralization. In a technological society everything becomes a component of the expanding social machine, including human beings. As the overall functions of a society become more complex and centralized, each individual function becomes more refined, more limited, and more dependent on every other function in the system for its survival.

Anyone who knows anything about machinery will tell you that the simpler the machine and the fewer the parts, the fewer the things that can go wrong. Simpler machinery is also more flexible and can be adjusted more easily to changing needs. In contrast, our technological society has become so specialized by function that whenever any part of the machinery malfunctions the entire system threatens to break down.

On November 9, 1965, some 30 million Americans experienced firsthand what can happen in an overly specialized society when just one tiny specialized function goes on the blink. On that day, late in the afternoon, a small electrical relay in a power station in Ontario, Canada, failed. Within minutes, almost the entire northeastern portion of the United States was without electricity. Thousands of people found themselves stranded in elevators and subway cars. The traffic lights all went off, creating massive traffic jams up and down the East Coast. As evening set in, that part of the nation was plunged into total darkness—without lights, without heat, and without many of the other accoutrements of the technological society that we have come to depend on for our very survival.

We find less dramatic but just as poignant demonstrations of the vulnerability of our overspecialized society in our everyday experience. For example, if a steel strike in Gary lasts too long, a person may be laid off from work even though he is a cashier at a department store in Denver. Without steel, the auto plants cannot produce cars. If the Big Three auto makers shut down or curtail production, then ancillary industries that provide autos with everything from plastic to glass must curtail their own operations. With one out of every six jobs directly or indirectly related to the auto industry, within weeks of a slowdown or a shutdown the economy would begin to slump. There would be a fall in consumer purchasing power, and the cashier at the department store in Denver might find himself in the unemployment line as a result of fewer purchases being made.

Technological specialization so limits the scope of operation of each function in society that it is virtually impossible to readapt a particular function to perform a different task. Every component is designed specifically to perform the task given it and no other. If the nature of the task changes, the component becomes worthless. This is equally true in the case of human specialization. Every day we encounter the limitations of expertise. For example, a podiatrist knows only about feet and cannot be expected to give sound medical advice about any other physical ailment. An antitrust lawyer only knows antitrust law and cannot be expected to know about divorce law. A geneticist knows only about genes and chromosomes and cannot be expected to understand the workings of a tropical ecosystem. The *Dictionary of Occupational Titles* now lists over 20,000 specialized jobs in America. We have come to the point where each of us knows more and more about less and less, until as a society we all know almost everything about nothing.

Overspecialization, say the biologists, is one of the most important contributing factors in a species becoming extinct. When a species becomes overspecialized in a particular type of ecosystem, it is usually unable to adapt to a change in environment. It does not contain the flexibility and diversification to enable it to make the transition. The same holds true with human society. Today we have become so overly specialized and adapted to the existing energy environment that we have lost much of the flexibility required to make a transition into a radically new energy mode.

World Views and
Energy Environments

Why did the Newtonian world view take hold when it did and why is it being challenged now by the new entropy paradigm?

As we have already seen, the basis of all of life is energy, ultimately derived from the sun. Technologies and institutions have served, throughout history, as transformers, facilitating the flow of energy from the environment through the human and social systems. The kinds of specific technologies and institutions that human cultures have developed have been a reflection of the kinds of energy environments they have lived in. This is so because different energy environments require different types of transformers. What should now be equally obvious is that the kind of world view a culture or civilization develops is also a reflection of the particular energy environment it finds itself in. A world view provides an explanation for why people organize life's activities in a certain way. When energy environments change, people are forced to change their ways of doing things— namely, the ways in which they transform energy from the environment. When people make these basic changes in the ways they relate to the world, their world view changes to reflect, rationalize, encourage, and explain the new circumstances.

That does not mean that only one kind of world view can emerge from one type of energy environment. In fact, similar energy environments have spawned different world views. However, whatever world view emerges must be at least compatible and consistent with the energy environment it interacts with. The various world views of different hunter-gatherer cultures would all be totally useless in any agricultural setting, just as all agricultural world views would be totally out of place in any advanced industrial environment. The energy environment, then, establishes the broad limits within which human beings make choices over the kind of belief systems they adopt.

Take, for example, the Newtonian paradigm. It emerged in the seventeenth and eighteenth centuries as European cultures were in the process of shifting from an environment based on renewable energy resources to one based, for the first time in history, on nonrenewable forms of energy. With the shift to nonrenewable energy forms humankind moved from a world of cycles and flows to a world of quantities and stocks. The world views shifted just as radically.

Cultures that were organized around the transformation of renewable energy sources perceived the world as a continual coming and going of seasons. The cycles of birth, life, death, and rebirth were qualitative processes. The energy sources were full of life and color. With renewable resources, the concept of order and decay was an ever-present reminder of the way the world unfolds. The world views of the ancient Greeks and the early Christians reflected the realities of an energy environment based on living, renewable energy sources.

Contrast the features of renewable energy sources with nonrenewable. Coal and oil are lifeless quantities. They can be divided and redivided and still the individual parts will contain the same attributes as the whole. A speck of coal is little different in composition from a chunk of coal, while the leaf of a plant is very different from the stem or roots. Nonrenewable resources represent a fixed stock. They can be easily quantified. They are subject to precise measurement. They can be ordered. Renewable resources, on the other hand, are forever changing and flowing. They are never still. They are always in the process of becoming.

They are hard to subject to precise measurement. With its mathematical formulas, its emphasis on measurement, and its concern with location and distance, the Newtonian world machine paradigm was tailormade for effectively harnessing an energy base of nonrenewable resources.

Scholars have often wondered exactly why the notion of unlimited progress took hold alongside the idea of the world as a machine. The answer is also to be found in the nonrenewable energy base. Here for the first time was a gigantic, seemingly endless stock of stored solar energy—3 billion years' worth. As society hungrily dipped into this storehouse of energy, the concept of cycles and seasons fell further and further into the background. With this bonanza of billions of years of stored solar energy, there was no longer any need to wait for the sun to come up each day and shine upon us, creating energy and life. We had all the energy we needed to replace the sun and would never again have to wait for nature to take its course. Time, then, lost its connection with the natural unfolding of things. Time became a function of how fast we could harness the stored solar energy that lay deep in the coal seams and oil reservoirs. Is it any wonder, then, that under the Newtonian paradigm time can be speeded up and slowed down and turned back and then forward?

With nonrenewable energy we could turn the sun off and on at will. We could make the sun stay out twice as long if we chose because we were dealing with the "stored sun"—sun that we could take out of the ground and manipulate at will. With nonrenewable energy sources people became increasingly convinced that they were no longer dependent upon nature, and that they could reorder the world to their own making. We no longer had to concern ourselves with the idea of dissipation, decay, and disorder. Time could be controlled, energy could be created, and material progress could be assured.

The Newtonian world view provided the rationale for this new way of looking at life and organizing its activities. It is being challenged now and will soon be abandoned, because we are about to make the transition away from a nonrenewable energy base toward renewable sources of energy once again.

PART FOUR

NONRENEWABLE ENERGY AND THE APPROACHING ENTROPY WATERSHED

The Energy Crisis

Addiction! There is simply no other way to accurately describe America's energy habit. The statistics are overwhelming. With only 6 percent of the world's population, the United States currently consumes over one-third of the world's energy.[1] Even the energy consumption in other highly industrialized nations pales in contrast to our own. In Sweden and West Germany, for example, per capita consumption of energy is only half that of the United States even though their standard of living is comparable to ours.[2] The United States consumes more energy per year than all the countries of Western Europe combined, even though their population exceeds ours by 75 percent.[3]

Although it is impossible to grasp the sheer magnitude of our energy flow-through, consider just the statistics on energy generation. In 1987, the United States consumed over 76 quadrillion BTUs of energy, more than the total consumption of Canada, France, Italy, Japan, the Netherlands, the United Kingdom, and West Germany combined.[4]

When U.S. energy consumption is contrasted to poor Third World nations, the figures become so great that comparisons become practically impossible to make. How does one even begin to calculate relative energy advantage or deprivation knowing that in a country like Haiti the energy consumption per capita is equivalent to 68 pounds of coal per year, while the per capita consumption in the United States is equivalent to 23,000 pounds per year?[5]

World energy needs are expected to increase in the late 1990s when population growth in developing countries and falling production in non-OPEC countries will cause demand to rise sharply.[6] The population statistics are already staggering. Every day 333,000 new babies are born on the planet. Even allowing for 134,000 deaths per day, the net increase in world population is now 200,000 every twenty-four hours. That's 73 million more people in the world next year—all of whom require inputs of available energy to survive.[7]

The population problem can only be grasped by placing it within a historical perspective. It took 2 million years for the human population to reach 1 billion. The second billion took only a hundred years. The third billion took only thirty years, between 1930 and 1960. The fourth billion took only fifteen years. Between 1960 and 1975 the world's population grew at a rate of 2 percent per year, going from 2½ billion to 4 billion people.[8] At current annual growth rates of 1.7 percent, the world's population will double once again to 8 billion by the year 2015 and to 16 billion by the year 2055. The regional population figures are even more ominous. In Africa, Nigeria which now hosts a population of 100 million is expected to grow to 532 million by the mid-twenty-first century. India's population is expected to double, reaching 1.7 billion people by the year 2010. In our own hemisphere, Mexico is projecting a population increase from 82 million to 199 million within the next twenty-five years.[9]

Exponential population growth is exerting a tremendous strain on the world's energy base. According to a United Nations study conducted by the Nobel Prize-winning economist Wassily Leontief, in order to meet a moderate rate of global growth over the years ahead, it will be necessary to increase the consumption of common minerals by fivefold and food consumption by fourfold.[10]

What is even more remarkable is the projection made by many international economists that in order to accommodate the minimum needs of the expanding world population, it will be necessary in the next thirty years to "build houses, hospitals, ports, factories, bridges, and every other kind of facility in numbers that almost equal all the construction work done by the human race up to now."[11] That work will require the expenditure of astronomical amounts of nonrenewable energy. When we stop to consider the worldwide energy problems we already face—the shortages, the mushrooming prices, the accumulating pollution and wastes—it should become more than obvious that the nation and the world cannot meet the projected future energy needs, regardless of how hard we try. The reality is that we are running out of the "available" stock of nonrenewable energy and moving dangerously close to an entropy watershed. While statistical studies vary, there is general agreement that the age of cheap nonrenewable energy is over.

A study, conducted under the auspices of MIT, and involving experts from industry, government, and academia from fifteen countries, concluded that the worldwide supply of oil "will fail to meet increasing demands before the year 2000."[12] According to this report, even if energy prices rise 50 percent above current levels, it is likely that the world will experience an oil crisis between 1985 and 1995.[13] Another study undertaken by the powerful Trilateral Commission—an international organization whose membership includes some of the most powerful business and political leaders of the Western nations—varies only slightly in its forecast. The commission concludes that global demands for oil will exceed supply by the mid-1990s.[14] Writing in the *Bulletin of Atomic Scientists*, economist Emile Benoit of Columbia says that if international consumption of oil continues to grow at its present rate, existing reserves would be exhausted within twenty-five years. Even if new oil finds equal to four times the present reserves could be discovered (which is a highly inflated estimate that most experts consider unlikely), it would only buy an additional twenty-five years before the total exhaustion of all oil reserves.[15]

In his book *The Twenty-Ninth Day*, ecologist Lester Brown computed in the late 1970s that there were enough recoverable oil reserves to provide every American with approximately 500 barrels. When refined, said Brown, a barrel of oil yields about forty-two gallons of gasoline. Consequently, if the average American drove 10,000 miles per year in a large car that gets around ten miles per gallon, he would use up his entire remaining share of the world's oil reserves in less than twelve years[16]

Ten years later, Brown reports that this catastrophe was averted largely through the increased efficiency of American automobiles, which improved from an average of 13.1 MPG in 1973 to an average of 17.9 in 1985. This improvement cut our gasoline consumption by twenty million gallons every year.[17]

The earlier forecasts on oil depletion have been confirmed by a major study conducted by the Complex Systems Research Center (CSRC) at the University of New Hampshire in the mid-1980s. According to the CSRC, between 1995 and 2005, the U.S. will be using more energy to explore for new oil and gas than the wells will produce.[18] By the year 2020, the U.S. will have exhausted its remaining oil and gas reserves.[19] In the interim, new energy efficiency programs and alternative energy technologies will not be able to fill the vacuum fast enough to prevent a long-term decline in the gross national product. That decline will be hastened as increased population demands exert greater pressure on a dwindling energy reserve.

The exhaustion of domestic energy reserves will force greater reliance once again on the OPEC cartel. Between 1995 and 2010, the OPEC nations are expected to cut back their production, forcing worldwide prices of oil up again, triggering a new world energy crisis similar to the one experienced in the 1970s.[20] This time, however, energy experts warn that the crisis will only deepen over time, plunging the world into a long-term depression. By 2025, nearly 88 percent of the world's original reserve of oil will be depleted, and by 2050, world oil and gas supplies will be effectively exhausted.[21]

As we approach an entropy watershed for oil and gas, industry is likely to push for greater reliance on coal. American politicians are now heralding the United States as "the Saudi Arabia of coal." In reality, the abundance is not nearly what is forecast. Government bureaucrats insist that the country contains enough coal for 500 years of use. What they do not say is that at current coal consumption growth rates of 4.1 percent annually, it is generally recognized that there are only enough coal reserves in the nation to provide for 135 years of energy.[22] While this still sounds rather impressive, as the country steps up coal production to offset declining availability of petroleum, the absolute time span will be greatly reduced to a few short generations. And as we push forward to extract the remaining coal from our land, we can expect that exorbitant government spending and higher inflation will be the result. Still more important, increased dependence on coal burning will result in a vast increase in the amount of CO_2 emissions being discharged into the atmosphere, exacerbating the greenhouse crisis and the global warming trend on the planet.

Nuclear Fission

Until recently, the hope for an energy alternative rested with nuclear power. Now, that hope is fading fast. Even before the near meltdown of the nuclear core at Three Mile Island in Pennsylvania, and the full meltdown at Chernobyl in the Soviet Union, serious problems inherent to the nuclear industry began to spell a dismal future for the "peaceful atom."

Extraordinarily high production costs have combined with severe health and safety concerns to greatly reduce the number of nuclear power plants being built. Projections of nuclear energy growth are now less than one-third of what they once were in many countries. In the United States there were thirty-six new nuclear power plants ordered in 1973 and twenty-seven in 1974. In 1975 the orders dropped to four, in 1976 to two, and in 1977 back up to only four.[23] No nuclear power plants have been ordered since 1978. As of 1987, 107 nuclear power plants were in commercial operation in the United States with another fourteen plants still under construction. Nuclear power now generates 17 percent of the electrical energy in the country.[24]

Aside from the fact that a nuclear power plant can cost up to $3 billion to construct,[25] hidden costs deflate the "cheap energy" myth of atomic energy. A congressional report made public in 1978 states:

Contrary to widespread belief, nuclear power is no longer a cheap energy source. In fact, when the still unknown costs of radioactive waste and spent nuclear fuel management, decommissioning and perpetual care are finally included on the rate base, *nuclear power may prove to be much more expensive* than conventional energy alternatives such as coal [emphasis in original].[26]

In addition to the cost factor, nuclear power generates many social and health problems for which there is simply no technical solution. Mining the uranium needed for the reaction can not only lead to cancer and other diseases among the miners, but can cause serious health side effects in communities located near uranium mines. This waste has a radioactive half-life of 80,000 years. In Colorado, where tailings have been used by construction firms as building materials in schools and homes, doctors have noted an increase in congenital birth defects among children whose parents live or work in buildings made of tailings.[27]

The reactors are also unsafe. The partial meltdown of the nuclear core at the Three Mile Island power plant in 1979 caused extensive damage to the facility but released relatively small amounts of radioactive materials into the atmosphere. In contrast, the explosion at the Chernobyl plant in the Ukraine in September 1986 released a thousand times more radioactive materials, affecting much of Europe.

The nuclear cloud traveled north to the Arctic Circle, south to Greece, and west to the British Isles.[28] Radioactive fallout from Chernobyl was recorded as far away as Washington, D.C., and Tokyo, and affected much of the northern hemisphere of the planet. Thirty-one people died in the immediate aftermath of the accident and 1,000 people were injured. Over 135,000 people were evacuated from their homes.[29] Radioactive fallout seriously affected produce, milk, and meat production throughout Europe, forcing 100 million people to radically alter their diets for months after the explosion.[30] Cattle grazing on contaminated grass were producing high levels of radioactive milk. Vegetables, berries, and freshwater fish were also contaminated with high levels of iodine and cesium from the fallout.[31] Ninety-seven percent of the reindeer in the Lapland region of Scandinavia were found to be radioactive and unacceptable for human consumption.[32]

In the area surrounding the Chernobyl plant, clean-up costs will be momentous. Contaminated forests extending over a wide region will have to be razed and topsoil will have to be removed for burial. Farmland will have to be quarantined and will remain uninhabitable for decades.[33]

Dr. Robert Gale, an American physician who assisted in the treating of victims of the Chernobyl disaster, estimates that upward of 50,000 people will die of cancer in the U.S.S.R. and Europe in coming decades as a result of radiation exposure from the Chernobyl plant.[34] Other studies project a death rate of 100,000 or more.[35] Nearly half of the population of Europe now favor shutting down all operating nuclear power plants.[36] The Swedish government has already announced a plan to decommission all nuclear power plants by the second decade of the twenty-first century. Antinuclear sentiment now runs deep in most countries of the world as a result of the catastrophic disaster at Chernobyl and the nearly disastrous accident at Three Mile Island.

The Three Mile Island and Chernobyl accidents were only the most serious of scores of breakdowns and radiation releases experienced by the nuclear industry. Every reactor in this country is constantly leaking small amounts of radioactive material into the environment. The industry, of course, is always quick to point out that the radiation discharge is now below officially acceptable limits. What is never said, however, is that the medical evidence suggests that all radiation, in however minute an amount, is potentially dangerous. Every dose of radiation is an overdose. It takes just one radioactive particle invading one cell to cause cancer or genetic mutations. The process, however, can be an insidiously slow one, taking perhaps two decades from the time of exposure to the onset of the disease. Because of that, we may be unleashing a future epidemic with today's nuclear power plants. The Union of Concerned Scientists has estimated that by the year 2000, close to 15,000 Americans will have died as a direct result of minor reactor accidents and leaks. Should there be a full "China syndrome," UCS predicts that 100,000 might die, and thousands of square miles of land would be contaminated for many years to come.[37]

An even more serious problem is that each nuclear reactor produces between 400 and 500 pounds of plutonium yearly. Plutonium is the basic raw material used in constructing nuclear bombs. At the current rate, every reactor in the country annually generates enough plutonium to manufacture up to forty atomic weapons. Within two decades, there will be enough fissionable material in international transit to make 20,000 nuclear bombs. Guaranteeing the safety of this material is an impossibility. Already, 700 pounds of plutonium is missing from reactors and storage sites around the country.[38] Given that all of the technical knowledge needed to build an A-bomb is already available on library shelves across the country, the continued production of plutonium is simply inviting someone to make and use their own nuclear device. In a study conducted by the Office of Technology Assessment, *The Effects of Nuclear War,* it was found that a relatively small terrorist device could completely destroy several blocks of a high-rise downtown area, sending out over a thousand times the amount of radiation considered allowable for human exposure, and causing deadly fallout in the suburbs. In fact, a bomb is not even necessary to cause incredible death and mayhem. If plutonium were dispersed in the open air over a city, an area of forty square miles would be contaminated for a period of 100,000 years.[39]

Then, too, there is the unresolvable problem of how to dispose of nuclear waste. As hard as it may be to believe, with all of the attention placed on nuclear research and development and after spending billions of dollars to erect existing plants, the scientific community, the energy companies, and the government have not yet figured out how to get rid of the radioactive waste. Says Harvey Brooks of Harvard University, who heads the National Academy of Sciences committee on the question of nuclear waste disposal: "I would predict that should nuclear energy ultimately prove to be socially unacceptable, it will be primarily because of the public's perception of the waste disposal problem."[40]

By the end of 1976, 3,000 metric tons of spent fuel rods lay in nuclear pools in the United States. By 1983, the amount had increased to 13,000 tons. As of 1987, nuclear storage pools at forty power plants were nearing the authorized capacity.[41] Solid wastes—contaminated clothes and equipment—are another huge problem.

In 1985, nuclear power plants generated a total of 1,348 metric tons of highly radioactive waste. It is projected that by the year 2000 there will be an estimated 41,000 metric tons of radioactive waste and spent fuel generation will have increased to 1900 metric tons per year.[42] While there are many plans centering on how to "safely" bury this massive amount of waste, none has proven effective simply because there is no way to guarantee that a lethal substance can be stored for thousands of years. After all, our nation has only existed for 200 years. Human civilization is but a few thousand years old. Imagine having the audacity to think that we can devise a program to store lethal radioactive materials for a period of time that is longer than all of human culture to date.

The long-term question aside, the industry has not even succeeded in finding adequate storage measures for the 1980s. Even with today's relatively small amount of nuclear waste, there are constant reports of leakage and accidents at dumping sites. Radiation leaks have been discovered at the U.S. government nuclear reservation in Richland, Washington. Over 500,000 gallons of liquid radioactive wastes have leaked from tanks stored at the facility. In June 1978, the state of Kentucky closed down its nuclear site at Maxey Flats in the wake of an EPA study showing that "radioactive particles were migrating offsite." Similar leakages have been reported at burial sites in Oak Ridge, Tennessee; Ocean City, Maryland; and near San Francisco, California.[43]

Even if U.S. nuclear power continues to level off, it will be necessary to find new burial sites every two to three years after the turn of the century to accommodate all of the waste. This in turn will necessitate strict monitoring and armed guards around the clock on each site for up to 250,000 years to insure against leakage into the biosphere: that is the average time needed for some of the radioactive wastes to become harmless.

Over $200 billion has been invested in nuclear power worldwide. [44] Yet, U.S. government studies indicate that a major accident at just one nuclear power plant near a large metropolitan area could result in losses of $150 billion and 140,000 lives.[45] It is no wonder that a majority of the public has come to believe that the short-term energy benefits of nuclear power pale in comparison with the potential long-term entropic costs involved in nuclear power. In 1985, *Forbes* business magazine aptly summed up the brief history of nuclear power in a single pithy sentence: "The failure of the U.S. nuclear power program ranks as the largest managerial disaster in business history, a disaster on a monumental scale."[46]

Nuclear Fusion

While nuclear energy generates problems that appear to be insurmountable, the nuclear genie dies hard. Twenty years ago, Americans were promised that fission power would usher in an age of "limitless, clean and too cheap to meter" energy. Today, even as this myth has been dealt a severe blow by accidents like the ones that occurred at Three Mile Island and Chernobyl, a new nuclear promise is being touted: the promise of fusion power. The claims of its proponents are eerily reminiscent of those made by fission advocates two decades ago.

Technically, fusion power is the reverse of fission. Instead of splitting apart one nucleus, as in fission, fusion slams together (fuses) two nuclei from different atoms. Fusion energy is nothing new; it is constantly taking place in the sun, releasing the life-nurturing energy that has bombarded our planet for billions of years. In the 1950s, humans learned how to unleash a fusion reaction through the hydrogen bomb. Scientists now hope to discover a method to harness the immense energy that can be generated in such an explosion by containing the reaction within a fusion power plant.

Proponents of fusion energy argue that the process is more efficient than fission, generates far less radioactive waste, and might one day rely for its fuel upon hydrogen, which could conceivably be taken in virtually unlimited quantities from the ocean. In a sense, fusion energy is the modern-day equivalent of the perpetual motion machine. But just as the Entropy Law precludes the workings of a perpetual motion machine, it sets severe restrictions upon the ability to develop fusion energy to meet human demands.

To begin with, no one can say for certain whether a contained fusion reaction can even be sustained. To be commercially useful, a reactor must fuse 100,000 billion hydrogen nuclei per second within each cubic centimeter of the reactor core. To date, a contained fusion reaction has been sustained for only a fraction of a second. Unless the reaction can be prolonged, the fusing process will require immeasurably more energy than it will produce. The most optimistic assessments speculate that it will be at least the year 2025 before fusion will be able to produce any commercial power, hardly soon enough to meet the energy crunch that now besets the world.[47]

Second, there are several kinds of fusion technologies. The type being explored now is called a deuterium-tritium reaction, because the process fuses together molecules of these two elements. Tritium is derived from lithium, a nonrenewable resource that is almost as scarce as uranium. Thus, fusion energy is not limitless; it can only be sustained as long as the lithium stock of the world remains. A fusion plant will also require huge amounts of other nonrenewable energy-intensive resources that are already becoming increasingly scarce, such as niobium and vanadium. Each 1,000-megawatt plant will require the mining of an additional 2.8 million pounds of copper, a metal that is also becoming relatively scarce.[48]

Third, the "clean" nature of a fusion reactor is a peculiar kind of cleanliness. Miners will still be affected by the extraction of lithium, just as uranium miners are now. Fusion reactors can hardly be said to be waste free, either. A large fusion plant might produce as much as 250 tons of radioactive garbage yearly.[49] The same containment problems that plague fission reactors would remain.

Further, there are tremendous technical and maintenance problems associated with any foreseeable fusion reactor design. One of the reasons scientists are experimenting with deuterium-tritium fusion is because it can operate at temperatures of 100 million degrees centigrade. (The hydrogen-buron reactor, which could be fueled with sea water, has a reaction temperature of 3 billion degrees.) These rather mind-numbing figures take on special meaning when it is realized that, at this point, we know of no materials that can withstand such sustained heat and tremendous radiation. Dr. Bowen R. Leonard, Jr., senior scientist at Battelle Pacific Northwest Laboratory, says that the heat and radiation generated by the reaction might make fusion power prohibitively expensive. "Radiation at that level destroys the strength of steel or other structural materials . . . making it dangerously brittle very fast. Parts would have to be replaced constantly and shutdowns would be frequent."[50] Some parts of the structure—such as walls nearest the reaction—might need to be changed every year, but because of the intensely radioactive nature of the reaction, no human could safely do the maintenance work. A new generation of industrial-maintenance robots will have to be designed at tremendous cost. No one even knows how long a plant will last, but estimates hover around the twenty-five year mark. Once the plant has been stressed beyond its operational capacity, it will have to be dismantled, transported, and buried.

In addition to all of these technical and resource questions, says Amory Lovins, a physicist and proponent of solar power, fusion energy represents "a way of doing something we don't want to do: that is build a complex, costly, slow-to-deploy, centralized, high-technology way to make electricity." All nuclear technologies, he believes, are the equivalent of using a chain saw to cut butter.[51]

Minerals

Energy—whether in the form of oil, coal, uranium, or solar radiation—cannot be viewed in isolation. If we want to extract energy from our environment, it must be done by using nonrenewable resources in the form of drilling rigs, tractors, and plants. And if we want the energy to perform work, it can only do so in conjunction with more nonrenewable resources such as those invested in machines and factories. Because of this, energy resource depletion is only part of the story of the physical limits we are now experiencing on our planet. The earth is fast running out of almost every major nonrenewable mineral necessary for the maintenance and growth of highly industrialized economies. Each year the U.S. economy alone uses nearly 40,000 pounds of new mineral supplies per person for our power plants, transportation, schools, machine tools, homes, bridges, medical uses, and heavy equipment.[52]

America is chiefly responsible for gobbling up the remaining stock of the earth's precious minerals. According to the U.S. Department of the Interior, the U.S. economy produces or imports 27 percent of the world's bauxite production, 18 percent of the world's iron ore production, and 28 percent of the world's nickel.[53] In order for the rest of the world to reach a par with the American standard of living, it would have to consume up to 200 times the present output of many of the earth's nonrenewable minerals (this assumes a doubling of world population between now and the early part of the twenty-first century). While catching up with the U.S. standard of living is the goal of most developing nations, it is obviously a pipe dream.[54]

Many experts predict that within seventy-five years or less (at current consumption rates) the planet's economies will have "exhausted presently known recoverable reserves of perhaps half the world's now useful metals."[55] Dr. Preston Cloud, a geologist at the U.S. Geological Survey, is one of those experts. Testifying before the Joint Economic Committee of the Congress in 1978, Cloud said that some of the minerals on the endangered resources list by early in the next century include copper, gold, antimony, bismuth, and molybdenum.[56] Domestically, by the year 2050 the United States will have run out of extractable quantities of tin, commercial asbestos, columbium, fluorite, sheet mica, high-grade phosphorus, strontium, mercury, chromium, and nickel.[57]

Increased reliance on foreign imports of most key minerals, combined with intense worldwide competition for the remaining scarce reserves, will raise prices and the bargaining leverage of the mineral exporting countries—just as was the case with oil for the OPEC nations.

The flow of nonrenewable resources through society also affects the consumption of renewable resources. While it is true that forests and fish are living organisms that create more of their own kind, the annual consumption of these resources appears to be increasing at a faster rate than they can be replenished. In effect, the high-entropy economic system "hot-wires" the renewable resources to the point where they become, for all practical purposes, nonrenewables themselves. Before the advent of the fossil fuel era, humanity relied almost exclusively on forests, fisheries, grasslands, and croplands for its energy flow. Now, however, evidence suggests that the productivity of each of these systems has peaked and is declining. Global forest productivity has steadily declined since 1967. Fisheries peaked in 1970, and now many traditional fishing areas of the ocean have essentially been "fished out." Cropland productivity, as measured by kilograms of cereals per capita year, peaked in 1976. As for grasslands per capita output of wool, mutton, and beef (all dependent on grazing) have all tailed off.[58]

Despite the overwhelming statistical evidence presented in United Nations, congressional, and academic studies, reports, and hearings, there are still a few souls who cling to the theory that at existing growth rates there are enough nonrenewable resources to provide for all the world's population forever—or at least for a good long time into the future. Their underlying assumptions, however, are without merit.

For example, it is often remarked that the entire planet is composed of minerals. What is overlooked is that only a tiny fraction of that amount is usable or potentially extractable. Assume, just for the sake of argument, that the entire weight of the earth was potentially convertible to productive energy—which would leave us all walking on thin air. At a current 3 percent growth rate in the use of ten leading minerals, we would literally mine the equivalent of the entire world's weight within several hundred years. That's not a very long time when one stops to realize that human beings have been on earth for over 3½ million years and that the earth itself has existed for 4 billion additional years.

Others argue that manganese nodules mined from the seabed could provide us with a source of nonferrous metals. According to some experts, this source could provide "copper equal to a quarter of current output, nickel equal to three times current output, and manganese equal to six times current output." These same experts believe it is possible to quadruple these figures sometime in the future. Again, these figures appear impressive on the surface until they are placed within the context of exponential growth. At current rates of consumption increase, demand for copper will be 90 times the current level in just a hundred years, nickel 28 times the current level, and manganese 17 times the present level, virtually wiping out whatever short-term advantage measured in years or decades that might accrue from these additional deposits.[59]

There are those who continue to believe that existing reserves of nonrenewable minerals can be maintained indefinitely by either replacing more-scarce minerals with less-scarce ones or by efficient recycling of existing mineral use. As to substitution, since most major metals are fast diminishing in supply, there is relatively little advantage in substituting one for another in the production process. As William Ophuls points out, "Substitutes (like aluminum for copper) are on the whole less efficient than the material they substitute for, and more energy is therefore required to perform a given function."[60] Then too, some minerals, because of their unique properties, are simply irreplaceable.

Recycling is often proposed as the answer to mineral resource depletion. Recycling already provides about half of the annual demand for antimony; one-third of the demand for iron, lead, and nickel; and one-fourth of our need for mercury, silver, gold, and platinum. However, it should not be forgotten that recycling also conforms to the second law of thermodynamics. Every time a mineral is recycled, some of it is inevitably, and irreversibly, lost. As already mentioned, recycling efficiency today averages around 30 percent for most used metals. Recycling also creates additional pollution and requires ever greater amounts of energy input to collect, transport, and transform the scattered material. While more efficient recycling is going to be essential data indicate that only a small percentage of our total mineral needs can be met in the foreseeable future through recycling.[61]

PART FIVE

ENTROPY AND THE
INDUSTRIAL AGE

Economics

The industrialized nations, and the United States in particular, are coming up against an entropy watershed. After 400 years, the world is now running out of the nonrenewable resource base that provided the industrial era with a massive flow-through of stored solar energy. At every stage of the energy flow line, disorder is mounting, and the technological and institutional transformers are becoming more complex, more concentrated, more specialized, and more vulnerable to breakdown.

One does not need to be an economist to understand the process. Since we all survive by transforming, exchanging, and discarding energy in all of its many forms, we experience first-hand the tremendous dislocations in the energy flow line as the society moves closer and closer to an entropy watershed. Nowhere is the process more apparent than in dealing with the ravages of inflation.

Inflation is tied directly to the depletion of our nonrenewable energy base. As it becomes more costly to extract less easily exploitable supplies of available energy from the environment, the costs associated with all of the transforming, exchanging, and discarding processes all along the energy flow line continue to rise. As a result, prices continue to rise for both the producer and the consumer. The accumulating disorder resulting from past flow-through adds additional economic, social, and political costs, further increasing prices for producers and consumers. The inflation spirals as the energy environment nears depletion. The reason again is simple: it takes more and more money to pay for more expensive, complex technology to extract and process the remaining energy and more money to pay for controlling or managing all of the disorder resulting from the dissipation of energy in the flow-through process.

While the energy induced inflationary spiral of the 1970s temporarily abated in the 1980s, many economists forecast a new round of inflation in the 1990s as energy shortages become more pronounced and environmental costs continue to rise.

According to Dr. Barry Commoner, all of the basic energy sources that we rely on suffer from the same flaw:

Because they are either non-renewable, or overburdened with unnecessarily complex technology—or both—they demand progressively larger investment of capital, become increasingly costly to produce, and—in the free market of the private enterprise system—higher in price.[1]

Commoner points to statistics that provide irrefutable evidence of how the Entropy Law affects the whole process. For every dollar invested in energy production in 1960, 2,250,000 BTUs of energy were produced. In 1970, says Commoner, every dollar invested was only producing 2,168,000 BTUs of energy. Just three years later, in 1973, the figure had dropped to 1,845,000 BTUs for each dollar invested. In just thirteen years there had been a *decrease* of 18 percent "in the productivity of capital in energy production."[2] (The data, by the way, were adjusted in terms of 1973 dollars to eliminate the effects of inflation.)

By the year 2020, the quality of domestic oil supplies will have become so low that other fuels will be used for most purposes.[3]

Because it costs more to extract less-available energy out of the environment, the amount of money that has to be diverted away from the rest of the flow line to pay for new capital for the energy industry continues to climb. The energy industry will need to raise over $900 billion to finance its operations over the next decade. Over half of that amount, however, will have to be raised externally, because these companies do not have sufficient retained earnings to finance their own needs internally.[4] This means that moneys normally invested in other areas of the economy will have to be diverted to maintain the energy industry.

By 1987, more than ten percent of the total fixed private capital in the United States was devoted to energy production.[5]

As more and more money is diverted into energy production, the energy transformers—both the machinery and the institutions—become more concentrated, complex, and powerful. Today America's energy institutions own $181 billion in assets or "29% of the assets (and sales) of the 500 largest corporations in the U.S." So large are energy companies such as Mobil, Exxon, and Texaco, that twenty of them now account for 18 percent of our total gross national product.[6] With the costs of a new petroleum refinery at $500 million, and the cost of a nuclear power plant at between $1 and $2 billion, only these corporate giants can afford to stay in the energy game.[7]

Energy, of course, is the basis for all economic activity. Therefore, as the costs go up at the source, they are passed along in terms of higher prices at each succeeding step in the energy flow line. Eventually the individual consumer pays the bill in terms of inflation.

Several years ago the Exploratory Project for Economic Alternatives, a Washington think tank, undertook a detailed study of the basic causes of inflation. It concluded, in its final report, that in the four basic consumer necessities—energy, food, housing, and health care—rising prices were tied to the increased costs associated with the transforming and exchanging of energy. While this seems obvious enough, most establishment economic thinking continues to center on secondary effects like wages or fiscal and monetary policy.

For 80 percent of American families, the four basic necessity areas comprise over 70 percent of their consumption budgets. The study isolated each of the necessity areas and then traced the cause of the inflation back to its source—the depletion of the nonrenewable energy sources, and the increased technological, structural, and institutional costs associated with the continued maintenance of the energy flow-through. For example, energy alone—gasoline, electricity, fuel oil, and coal—accounts for nearly 12 percent of the average household budget. The study found that energy inflation has "robbed ordinary Americans of 1% of household purchasing power per year."[8]

In the case of food, which accounts for approximately 28 percent of the average family budget, the report traced the inflation trend back to the higher energy costs associated with the farming, processing, transporting, packaging, and marketing of agricultural products, as well as the increased worldwide population demand for American foodstuffs.[9] In the areas of housing and health care, again, the higher cost of nonrenewable energy was at the source of the inflationary spiral. That is because all economic activity is traceable to the prevailing energy base.

Inflation, then, is ultimately a measure of the entropy state of the environment. The closer the entropy of the environment moves to a maximum, the more costly everything in the energy flow line becomes. As already shown, the costs associated with transforming energy rise as the sources of energy become more difficult to locate, extract, and process. The cost of exchanging energy between institutions, sectors, groups, and individuals also rises to reflect the increasing costs associated with the extraction and processing.

We have already seen how the consumer is ultimately affected by the higher costs in terms of being charged higher prices for basic necessities. The wage earner is also affected. That is, while wages rise, real purchasing power fails to keep up with the rise in the cost of living. Average weekly earnings in 1987 in constant dollars (consumer price index deflated) were lower than in 1962.[10] The growing gap between wages and real purchasing power is the money that is diverted away from the labor bill to pay for the increased costs of maintaining the nonrenewable energy flow. It works this way: as the costs go up at the beginning of the energy flow line, they are passed on to every other economic institution down the line as well. To compensate for the increased costs, all of the economic institutions along the entire flow line from extraction through retail sales attempt to reduce their wage component in order to maintain existing profit levels. The result is less "real" wages and less purchasing power. Less purchasing power really means that consumers are increasingly unable to meet their energy needs: food, clothing, health care, etc. In other words, as mentioned earlier, the energy flowing through the human system begins to slow down, as more and more energy (or money) is diverted to the maintenance of all the economic institutions and the machinery responsible for the energy flow itself.

While the consumer suffers from higher prices and the worker from lower real wages, the taxpayer suffers from the increased costs associated with the dissipated wastes and disorders that build up along the flow line. It is the taxpayer who has to pay the lion's share of cleaning up and disposing of the massive wastes generated by the flow of energy through the system. According to the annual report of the President's Council on Environmental Quality, the taxpayers shelled out more than $10 billion in 1983 to pay for pollution control and abatement.[11] The council estimates that the overall costs of pollution control over the next ten years will exceed $361 billion, much of it paid for by government tax dollars.[12]

The taxpayer also ends up paying for the economic and social disorders that arise as a result of the way the energy flow line is set up. For example, certain individuals, groups, and classes are located at the periphery of the transforming and exchange processes because of the way the system allocates jobs and distribution of income. As the entropy of the environment increases, and the costs all along the flow line escalate, this sector of the population is the first to feel the economic crunch. As more and more people in the poorer classes are thrown off the flow line altogether to compensate for the tightening economic condition, the government must step in and provide for their energy needs in terms of welfare and other benefits. Unemployment, after all, is the other side of the entropy process. The faster the energy is depleted, the more people become either unemployed or underemployed. Government institutions at all levels from local to federal have to enlarge their own involvement in order to provide relief for these frontline victims of the tightening energy crisis.

The government also has to enlarge its functions in other areas that are directly affected by the increase in unemployment and poverty, such as crime control and public health expenditures. As a result, still more money in the form of taxes has to be diverted away from the flow line in order to pay for the increased costs of maintaining these public bureaucracies. In 1988, 16 percent of the American work force was employed by a public institution or a governmental agency of some sort.[13] These government institutions continue to grow as they are forced to deal with and contain the mounting economic and social disorders arising along the flow line. Like the economic institutions, however, the government agencies end up using more and more money just for their own maintenance, thus increasing the tax burden and further decreasing the flow-through of energy for human consumption. This vicious process of energy diversion away from the people and toward the maintenance and enlargement of both the economic and governmental bureaucracies proceeds faster and faster until the entire social mechanism crashes headlong into an entropy watershed.

It should be clear by now that classical economic theory cannot solve the growing crisis facing the world's economies. There is no room in either socialist or capitalist economic analysis for the Entropy Law. Yet, the second law is the supreme governing principle of all economic activity. Failure to recognize this ultimate truth and to reorient economic policy accordingly is shortening the road to economic and ecological disaster for the planet.

Today, as 200 years ago when Adam Smith first laid out the principles of modern economic theory, both socialist and capitalist nations model their economic assumptions along the lines of classical mechanical doctrine.

Capitalist economists continue to view the economic system as a mechanical process in which supply and demand functions are continually readjusting to each other in forward and backward motion like the swings of a pendulum. Pick up any introductory economics textbook and it will tell you that economics is nothing more than the give and take of supply and demand curves. When consumer demand for a commodity or a service goes up, the sellers will raise their price accordingly to take advantage of the situation. When the price becomes too high, demand will slacken off or move to some other commodity or service, forcing the sellers to lower the price to the point where demand is rekindled.

Many qualifications and refinements have been added over the years, but the basic concept of the market mechanism of supply and demand still remains at the center of all classical economic thinking.

While socialist economists reject the market mechanism, they agree with the capitalist economists that the overall economic environment is never depleted. As to where the new supply is supposed to come from, both capitalist and socialist economists assume that new technology can always find a way to locate and exploit previously untapped resources. The resource base is considered inexhaustible.

According to capitalist and socialist theory, economic activity turns waste into value. Remember Locke's belief that everything in nature is to be considered waste until human labor is added to it, transforming it to something of value that can be exchanged and consumed in society. By turning the first and second laws upside down, modern economic theory has completely misinterpreted the entire basis of all economic activity. Again, the first law says that all energy is fixed, and it can neither be created nor destroyed but only transformed. The second law, in turn, says that it can only be transformed in one direction, from available to unavailable, or from usable to unusable. Whenever energy is extracted from the environment and processed through society, part of it becomes dissipated or wasted at every stage, until all of it, including that which is made into products, ends up in one form or another as waste at the end of the line.

Most economists simply cannot accept this simple truth. They are wedded to the idea that human labor added to nature's resources creates greater value, not less. Because machine capital is ultimately viewed as past human labor mixed with resources, it too is considered to be creating economic value. They cannot get it into their heads that machines and people cannot create anything. They can only transform the existing available energy supply from a usable to a wasted state, providing only "temporary utility" along the way.

Economists steadfastly cling to the idea that human labor and machinery create only value, because they believe in the paradigm of permanent and unlimited material progress. But we know from the second law that every time human energy or mechanical energy or any other form of energy is expended to make something of value, it is done at the expense of creating even greater disorder and waste in the overall environment. We also know that even the things of value that we make eventually end up as waste or dissipated energy. Thus, there is no such thing as "material" progress in the sense of accumulating a "permanent" store of usable goods, for everything we make in the world eventually ends up as dust in the wind.

The implications here are extraordinary. Consider for a moment the concept of productivity. Capitalist and socialist systems define productivity in terms of speed per unit of output. A premium is placed on performing a given task as fast as possible. A more appropriate thermodynamic measure of productivity would emphasize the entropy produced per unit of output as opposed to speed per unit of output. A study was done several years ago on how much energy was required to make an automobile. The study concluded that many times more energy was actually used than was necessary to make the automobile. Why was all the additional energy expended? To get the automobile off the assembly line faster. The greater the emphasis on speed of conversion, the more energy that is used up than is essential in making the product. Much of the energy wasted in modern industrial economies is the price we pay for speed.

Interestingly enough, anyone who has ever been caught with a nearly empty gas tank while driving along a lonely highway has understood the difference between defining productivity by speed per unit of output vs. entropy produced per unit of output. Faced with the prospect of running out of gasoline and not knowing how far up the road the next gas station might be, the driver has two choices available to him. He can accelerate in order to try to reach the gas station faster. Or he can drive more slowly. It is not surprising that many of us, when faced with this situation, generally react by accelerating, believing that the increased speed will somehow enhance our chances of getting to that gas station. In truth, the opposite is the case. By using the gas more judiciously, a further distance can be traveled. It takes longer, but the time lost is made up by the energy saved that can be used to travel a longer distance. In terms of thermodynamic efficiency, then, productivity is a measure of entropy produced per unit of output, not speed per unit of output.

The Entropy Law also tells us that every time we increase the rate of energy expended by either human or machine labor, the decrease in entropy or enhanced value of the product results in an even larger increase in disorder somewhere else in the overall environment. Therefore, as long as productivity is measured in terms of speed per unit of output, more energy will be used than necessary in converting resources into economic utilities and this increased energy flow-through will result in greater disorder or entropy buildup which ultimately has to be paid for by the society. "Haste makes waste" is an age-old adage that reflects an intuitive understanding of the Entropy Law at work.

As long as there was an abundant supply of fossil fuels and the particular metals used to fashion and maintain the industrial mode, it seemed logical to define productivity in terms of speed per unit of output. Now that the existing matter-energy base is becoming depleted, and the entropy from past economic activity is accumulating at a rate beyond the system's ability to absorb, a major reformulation of the notion of productivity will need to be made by economists in order to adjust to the requisites of thermodynamic efficiency in the economic process of production and consumption.

The economics profession has still not understood that "the entropy law is the basic physical coordinate of scarcity."[14] Nowhere is this more obvious than in discussions about "balancing budgets." While it is generally recognized that a society cannot continue to consume faster than it produces, the economists remain ignorant of the fact that the ultimate balancing of budgets is not within society, but between society and nature. Conventional economic theorists have been unable to address the problem of deficits because they have failed to take into consideration the larger environmental context within which economics actually takes place. Approximating a balanced budget requires that society not consume faster than nature can recycle the wastes and replenish the resources. The buildup of greenhouse gases in the atmosphere and the global warming trend is the tragic result of our civilization's refusal to balance its production and consumption schedules with nature's recycling schedules. We have been spewing CO_2, NO_2, CFC^s, and urethane into the atmosphere faster than the earth's ecosystems can absorb and recycle them, creating a global ecological and economic crisis of unprecedented proportions.

Ecosystems operate as near to a steady state as possible (the laws of thermodynamics tell us that a perfect steady state is impossible to attain). The entire conversion process from low entropy to high entropy is maintained at a speed commensurate with the system's ability to manage a relative balance between production, consumption, and recycling. Wastes are generated, absorbed, and recycled for reuse, maintaining a balanced ecological cycle. While 100% recycling is thermodynamically impossible, natural ecosystems come as close as possible to the ideal state of a balanced budget between production, consumption, and recycling.

Economic activity is merely human intervention in the ecological cycle, borrowing low-entropy inputs, converting them into temporary utilities, and eventually discarding them back into the ecological cycle in the form of high-entropy wastes. If society borrows low-entropy matter and energy, converting it into utilities, then waste, at a speed far exceeding the conversion process in nature itself, the deficit escalates. Wastes are dumped back into the system faster than they can be absorbed, creating mounting disorder in the environment and escalating external costs for society. At the same time, available matter and energy is being depleted faster than nature can recycle and reproduce, causing increased scarcity in nature and mounting supply costs for society. Of course, any use of nonrenewable resources like oil and natural gas automatically increases the deficit. For all practical purposes these nonrenewable resources represent a fixed store of ecological capital that can only be used once.

By minimizing the use of nonrenewable resources and by using up renewable resources only as fast as they can be replenished, it is possible to minimize the deficit between consumption in society and production in nature.

Closely related to the misunderstanding about the nature of balanced budgets and deficits is the problem of money and debt. Over the years a few scholars like Frederick Soddy and Herman Daly have attempted to point out the obvious contradiction that exists between the social conventions of money and debt on the one hand, and the entropic flow of nature on the other, but their critique has been ignored within the economics profession. Money, for example, is a form of national debt. It represents a lien against the total physical wealth of the community which an individual is free to exchange for actual physical wealth sometime in the future. The problem that economists completely ignore is that the generation of physical wealth by the community is not inexhaustible. The laws of thermodynamics set ultimate limits to the amount of physical wealth that can be generated. However, there is no limit to how much money can be produced and put into circulation. The problem becomes apparent with the introduction of debt and compound interest. As Nobel chemist Frederick Soddy pointed out over fifty years ago:

Debts are subject to the laws of mathematics rather than physics. Unlike wealth, which is subject to the laws of thermodynamics, debts do not rot with old age and are not consumed in the process of living. On the contrary, they grow at so much per cent per annum, by the well known mathematical laws of simple and compound interest.[15]

Economist Herman Daly explains the inevitable consequences that result when society pits the mathematical notion of compound interest against the physical reality of thermodynamics. He says that while debt can grow at compound interest forever, real physical wealth cannot continue to grow at the same speed "because its physical dimension is subject to the destructive force of entropy.[16] Echoing Frederick Soddy's earlier analysis, Daly concludes that:

Since wealth cannot continually grow as fast as debt, the one to one relation between the two will at some point be broken—i.e. there must be some repudiation or cancellation of debt. The positive feedback of compound interest must be offset by counter-acting forces of debt repudiation, such as inflation, bankruptcy, or confiscatory taxation, all of which breed violence.[17]

At every step in the entire production and exchange process, work is done; namely, energy is expended by both humans and machines.

Part of that energy is absorbed into the product and part is wasted. This means that the more stages in the economic process, the more energy is lost. The same principle is at work in the production process as in the simple food chain described in Part Two. In highly industrial societies the stages of the economic process continue to proliferate, meaning more and more energy is dissipated all along the line; and the resultant disorders create even greater long-range problems for society.

Take, for example, your morning English muffin. As we will show in the next chapter, the very process of modern petrochemical agriculture used to grow the wheat is extremely energy inefficient. But once grown and harvested, the folly is compounded manyfold thanks to our national mania for processed food. Here are just some of the energy steps that go into making your English muffin. (1) The wheat is taken by a fossil-fuel-driven truck made of nonrenewable resources to (2) a large, centralized bakery housing numerous machines that very inefficiently refine, enrich, bake, and package English muffins. At the bakery, the wheat is (3) refined and often (4) bleached. These processes make for nice white bread, but rob the wheat of vital nutrients, so (5) the flour is then enriched with niacin, iron, thiamine, and riboflavin. Next, to insure that the English muffins will be able to withstand long truck journeys to stores where they will be kept on shelves for many days, or even weeks, preservative (6) calcium propionate is added, along with (7) dough conditioners such as calcium sulfate, monocalcium phosphate, ammonium sulfate, fungal enzyme, potassium bromate, and potassium iodate. Then the bread is (8) baked and placed in (9) a cardboard box that has been (10) printed in several colors to catch your eye on the shelf.

The box and muffins are placed within (11) a plastic bag (made of petrochemicals), which is then sealed with (12) a plastic tie (made of more petrochemicals). The packages of English muffins are then loaded into (13) a truck which hauls them to the (14) air-conditioned, fluorescent-lit, Muzak-filled grocery store. Finally, you (15) drive two tons of metal to the store and back and then (16) pop the muffins in the toaster. Eventually, you will throw away the cardboard and plastic packaging, which will then have to be disposed of as (17) solid waste. All of this for just 130 calories per serving of muffin.

Tens of thousands of energy calories have gone into the entire process, and medical evidence suggests that both the additives and the lack of fiber in refined breads may pose a serious hazard to your health. In the end, the energy that was added to the muffins at each step of the process was insignificant compared with the energy that was dissipated at each step of the process.

Of the total amount of energy used in the food system, less than 20 percent actually goes into the growing of food. The other 80 percent is consumed by the processing, packaging, distribution, and preparation of the foodstuff. Almost twice as much energy is used to process your English muffin (33 percent) as was used to grow the grain it was made from (18 percent).[18]

The food-processing industry is now the fourth-largest industrial energy user in the nation—after metals, chemicals, and oil. Some sources estimate that food processing currently consumes nearly 6 percent of the country's energy budget. As far as the industry is concerned, apparently, the more the better.

Furthermore, between 1984 and 1988, the production of packaging containers alone increased by 19 percent, while the production of plastic containers increased by nearly 50 percent.[19]

The growth in packaging has been accompanied by a new industry: an entire army of "food technologists" now busy themselves making sure that our food supply is given just the right artificial color, scent, flavor, and texture. Nothing can be left to chance. As one food technologist puts it, "It's hard to compete with God, but we're making headway." Indeed they are. Some $500 million in synthetic chemicals is added to our food every year—2,500 additives. In 1979, each American consumed an average of nine pounds of additives, nearly double the amount in 1970. Four million pounds of dyes wind up in the food supply annually, a full sixteen times the amount used in 1940. Today, we eat more synthetic and artificial foods than the real thing.[20]

Convenience and processed foods, which are promoted as ways to liberate the individual from the "drudgery" of spending more time in the kitchen in food preparation, are in reality chaining humanity to the effects of ever greater entropy. The little time saved in the kitchen is more than outweighed by the amount of work time (human energy) given over to earning the money to pay for the increasing prices of the processed foods. Each step of the food processing takes energy, and as the energy flows through the food chain we witness a concentration of power in fewer and fewer food technology corporations, a decline in the healthfulness of the American diet, and an increased use of nonrenewable energy.

Food processing is representative of other major industries—such as petrochemicals, auto, truck, and air transportation, and synthetic fibers—that grew up in the era of high energy flow. All appear to be generating greater value (more products, more convenience) while all the time they are actually squandering the energy resources of the planet. Again, the economic system fosters the illusion of creating a more ordered, more materially valuable world, because consideration is given primarily to value added or entropy decreases, but rarely to energy dissipation and entropy increases.

If the Entropy Law were fully acknowledged, society would have to face up to the notion that every time we use part of the stock of available matter and energy it means two things: first, that one way or another, the individual, the institutions, the community, or the society ends up paying more for the disorder created in making the product than the value derived from the use of the product; second, less energy is available to be used in the future. This reality flies in the face of the way we have viewed the world for the past several hundred years. The entire modern world view is inspired by the principles of Baconian science, Cartesian mathematics, and Newtonian mechanics. Capitalist and socialist systems attempt to organize the physical world on the basis of these conceptualizations. Central to all three ideas is the notion of absolute repeatability of observation (the scientific method) and the absolute reversibility of all processes (universal mathematics and mechanical processes). In the real world, however, nothing is observable in the same manner twice and no occurrence is reversible. The Entropy Law tells us that all physical reality unfolds in only one direction and that while there must be a $-T$ for every $+T$ in math, there is no such reversibility in the physical world. It is indeed bewildering that we have been attempting to organize the world for these past few centuries on the basis of mechanics, mathematics, and the scientific method, when the real world simply does not conform to the central assumptions of reversibility and absolute repeatability. The reality is that when we leave this world, we leave it less well endowed as a result of our presence. When we glorify high energy production, what we are really promoting is an ever greater consumption of the store of resources of the planet. Seen in this way, the gross national product is more accurately the gross national cost, since every time resources are consumed a portion becomes unavailable for future use.

Actually, the term *consumption* is a misnomer, for nothing is ever consumed. A thing is used, usually for a very short period of time, and then discarded. The statistics are mind-boggling.

In 1987, we discarded more than 200 million tons of municipal solid waste. This included more than 18 million tons of metals, 16 million tons of glass, 80 million tons of paper and 4 million tons of rubber.[21] The figures are no less disturbing on the personal level. In 1974 the average American used 10 tons of mineral resources, including 1,340 pounds of metal and 18,900 pounds of nonmetallic minerals. In a lifetime, each American uses on an average approximately 700 tons of mineral resources, including nearly 50 tons of metals. If we add fossil fuels and wood, the per capita use more than doubles, to 1,400 tons. And this amount excludes water and food needs.[22]

It has been said before that the world could not possibly support another America. Looking at these figures, it becomes apparent that even one America is more than the world can afford. Imagine if the entire world tried to produce and consume as Americans do. It has been estimated that a middle-class American lives a style of life that is equivalent to the work produced by 200 human slaves.[23] Buckminster Fuller refers to us as possessing 200 "energy slaves" that run on nonrenewable resources. Another way of looking at it is in terms of the number of calories needed to sustain life. An average human diet consists of 2,000 calories daily. Yet the amount of energy calories we individually consume every day—in our cars, our electricity, our processed foods, and so on—amounts to about 200,000 calories, or more than a hundred times the quantity we absolutely need.[24] In terms of energy consumption, although Americans number only 225 million people, our energy needs are equivalent to those of over 22 *billion* individuals!

It should also be understood that there is no way to allow for the needs of future generations in classical economic theory. When we meet as buyers and sellers in the marketplace we make decisions based on the relative abundance or scarcity of things as they affect us. No one speaks for future generations at the marketplace, and for this reason, everyone who comes after us starts off much poorer than we did in terms of nature's remaining endowment. Imagine what it would be like if all future generations for the next 100,000 years could somehow bid for the oil our generation is using up. Obviously, the price of that energy would be so expensive that it would be prohibitive if future generations were allowed to participate in today's resource allocation decisions.

The illusion of material progress is exemplified over and over again in every major economic and social activity simply because the second law is swept under the rug. Take, for example, the areas of agriculture, transportation, urbanization, militarization, education, environment, and health. In all seven areas, we have convinced ourselves that we have made tremendous progress and that while there may be an occasional roadblock or retreat here and there, the progress is of a "permanent" nature. On closer examination such claims turn out to be illusory in the light of the second law.

In the following pages we will look at these seven areas as typical case studies of the effect of the Entropy Law on economic and social activity. The pattern that each follows is duplicated over and over again in every area in contemporary society.

Agriculture

American agriculture is the envy of the world. The bright yellow wheat fields stretching across mile after mile of Kansas flatland, the mechanized dairy farms scattered across the Wisconsin countryside, the lush fruit orchards planted along the entire rim of Southern California are all praised, studied, and copied by nations all over the world. Jonathan Swift once remarked that the man who can grow two ears of corn where only one grew before will deserve the better of mankind.[25] Can it be denied that American agriculture has succeeded beyond anyone's fondest expectations? Since 1940, crop output in the United States has grown at 2 percent per year. In 1985, U.S. grain production reached a record level of 347 million metric tons.[26] Where else, asked former Secretary of Agriculture Clifford Hardin, can one person raise 75,000 chickens in a modern, mechanized broiler-feeding system, or feed 5,000 cattle in an automated feedlot?[27]

Today, over 100 million people are starving to death all over the globe. Another 1½ billion people, nearly one-third of the human race, goes to bed malnourished each night.[28] With worldwide population expected to double in the next several decades, demand for increased food production will be greater than ever before in history. American agriculture is already producing 20 percent of the world's wheat and feed grains and exporting over half of it to countries around the planet.[29] Certainly, looking at the statistics, one would be hard pressed to deny what everyone accepts as gospel: that American agricultural technology is extraordinarily efficient. Yet, the truth is that it is the most inefficient form of farming ever devised by humankind. One farmer with an ox and plow produces a more efficient yield per energy expended than the giant mechanized agrifarms of modern America.

A simple peasant farmer can usually produce about 10 calories of energy for each calorie expended. Now it is a fact that an Iowa farmer can produce up to 6,000 calories for every calorie of human labor expended, but his apparent efficiency turns out to be a grand illusion when all of the other energy expended in the process is calculated in. To produce "just one can of corn containing 270 calories," the farmer uses up 2,790 calories, much of which is made up of energy used to run the farm machinery and the energy contained in the synthetic fertilizers and pesticides applied to the crop. So for every calorie of energy produced, the American farmer is using up 10 calories of energy in the process.[30]

Today agriculture accounts for 12 percent of all the energy used in the U.S. economy.[31] Where farming traditionally relied on human and animal labor for cultivation, natural manures and crop rotation for fertilizing and maintaining the soil, and natural pest enemies for controlling crop damage, nowadays sophisticated machinery and petrochemicals have been substituted. Heavy reliance on high-tech mechanized farm equipment and petrochemical fertilizer has resulted in a massive emission of carbon dioxide and nitrous oxide into the atmosphere over the past several decades. Modern agriculture is now a primary contributor to the global warming trend on the planet.

The more the energy flow-through has increased with the substitution of complex machinery and petrochemicals, the more centralized the agricultural industry has become. As the costs of maintaining the energy needs of U.S. agriculture have escalated, the small family farmer has been literally driven off the farm and replaced by huge agribusiness corporations. Today, twenty-nine corporations own over 21 percent of all of the cropland in America.[32] The next time you sit down to dinner, just think about this: your turkey probably came from Greyhound, your ham from ITT, your vegetables from Tenneco, your potatoes from Boeing, and your mixed nuts from Getty.[33] Agribusiness corporations now control 51 percent of our fresh vegetables, 85 percent of our citrus crop, 97 percent of our broiling chickens, and 40 percent of our eggs.[34] Only the large corporations can afford the mounting capital costs associated with a mechanized, energy-based agriculture. For example, it is estimated that the cost of farm machinery alone tripled between 1950 and 1971, from $12.1 billion to $33.8 billion in value.[35] And between 1972 and 1983, the amount of money necessary for the replacement of capital equipment more than doubled.[36]

Since World War II, the use of inorganic nitrogen fertilizer increased sevenfold—from 1 million tons in 1950 to 7 million tons by 1970.[37] The use of pesticides increased by even more.[38] These fertilizers and pesticides are all derived from fossil fuel energy sources. It would not be inaccurate to say that the food we eat today is grown from oil rather than soil. It is also true that it takes more and more oil to produce the same output of food each year. According to one authoritative study, it took five times more nitrogen fertilizer to sustain the same yield of crop in 1968 as it did in 1949. In other words, five times more energy or work had to be expended to produce the same results.[39] Between 1960 and 1987 the use of nitrogen-based fertilizer more than tripled.[40] Yet the annual wheat harvest was lower in 1986 than in 1974.[41]

This is because, in agriculture as in everything else, every time energy is expended, some is absorbed into the product and some is dissipated. In order to increase yield, American farmers have continued to increase the amount of energy used. While some of that energy has helped increase output, more and more of it has been wasted altogether. The marginal entropy decrease, represented by slightly expanding yields, is dwarfed by the greater increase in dissipated energy in the overall environment. Much of the dissipated energy runs off and contributes to polluting our land, rivers, and lakes. Nitrate pollution from fertilizer runoff accounts for over half of our water pollution and two-thirds of our solid waste pollution.

Chemical pesticides are the other major energy input in modern agriculture. The use of pesticides increased from 200,000 pounds in 1950 to over 6.4 billion pounds in 1986.[42] A good part of the reason for this gigantic increase rests with the kind of farming technology we rely on. The United States has replaced diversified farming with monoculture farming in order to increase output. Monoculture crops are not well suited environmentally to attract the natural enemies of insect pests. In their absence, massive doses of chemical pesticides have to be used against the insects. The results, however, have been anything but successful. Studies have shown that even with the intervention of massive amounts of chemical pesticides, crop losses due to pest damage have remained at about one-third of total production for the past thirty years.[43] There is a good explanation for this. The pests have developed genetic strains that are resistant to the chemicals employed. According to the annual report of the government's Council on Environmental Quality, there are now "305 species of insects, mites and ticks . . . known to possess genetic strains resistant to one or more chemical pesticides."[44] As the pest populations continue to develop more resistant genetic strains, more chemicals of a more virulent nature have to be applied, which results in the development of even more virulent pests, the cycle becoming more costly and brutal at each stage.

The long-range effect of pesticide escalation on the ecology of the soil is "frightening," says agricultural expert Deryel Ferguson. Like others who have begun to study the problem, he warns that damage to soil by pesticides poses a threat of incalculable proportions. "Every ounce of fertile soil contains millions of bacteria, fungi, algae, protozoa and small invertebrates such as worms and anthropods."[45] Ferguson points out that all of these organisms play an essential role in maintaining "soil fertility and soil structure." Pesticides are destroying these organisms and their minute but complex ecological habitats, thus greatly hastening the entropy process of the soil. The end result is massive soil depletion and erosion. The use of chemicals, both pesticides and fertilizers, is partially to blame for the destruction of 4 billion tons of topsoil, which is washed into tributary streams each year.[46]

According to the Council for Agricultural Science, "A third of all cropland is suffering soil losses too great to be restrained without a gradual, but ultimately disastrous, decline in productivity."[47] The National Academy of Science now estimates that one-third of all valuable U.S. farmland topsoil is already gone forever.[48] As the topsoil erodes, more chemical fertilizers have to be added just to make up for the deficit. In 1974, it would have taken $1.2 billion worth of chemical fertilizers to replace the natural nutrients lost through soil erosion.[49] Our farming technology, then, is caught in a vicious spiral of greater energy infusions in the form of fertilizers and pesticides and greater losses in the form of soil erosion and pest resistance.

As more and more energy is expended in American agriculture, the entropy of the overall environment increases. The accumulating disorder in the form of pollution and soil erosion increases the overall cost for both society and the agricultural sector. The increased cost leads to the further enlargement and centralization of the economic institutions controlling agriculture. As these giant agribusinesses grow they require more and more energy just to maintain their operations, which means more energy has to be diverted away from the flow line. The increased costs of maintenance are of course passed on along the entire flow line. The final victim of the process is the consumer at the checkout line at the neighborhood supermarket, who is forced to pay higher prices every week for the food—energy—needed to sustain life.

Every step of this high-energy agricultural process will continue to escalate as we move closer to the entropy watershed for nonrenewable fossil fuels.

Transportation

Our transportation system is the most advanced in the world. We spend more time on "saving" travel time than on any other single economic activity. Transportation now accounts for 21 percent of our gross national product.[50] Over 80 percent of our transportation dollars are spent on autos and trucks.[51] In 1987, all of our major forms of transportation used up over 28 percent of all of the energy consumed by the economy.[52] Even this figure grossly underestimates the amount of total energy consumed in transportation, because it does not include the cost of manufacturing and maintaining all of the transportation machinery. According to Dr. William E. Mooz of the Rand Corporation, when these figures are added in, the American transportation industry eats up over 41 percent of all of the energy used each year.[53]

Contrary to popular opinion, America's transportation system, like the agricultural system, has become less and less efficient over the years. That is, more and more energy inputs have been required to move the same amount of freight and passengers from one place to another.

Over the course of this century America's transportation system switched from primary reliance on the railroads to greater dependence on autos, trucks, and airplanes. Today, autos and trucks account for the most passenger and freight traffic respectively. Both are less efficient than other modes of transportation that have been either cut back or put into mothballs. It takes 8,100 BTUs of energy to transport one passenger one mile by automobile. In contrast, it takes only 3,800 BTUs of energy to transport the same person by mass transit.[54] Yet, over the past twenty-five years mass transit in this country has been greatly reduced. The figures for freight transport are even more telling. It takes only 670 BTUs of energy to ship one ton of freight one mile by train and over 2,800 BTUs to ship the same ton of freight by truck.[55] Even so, train transport of freight was cut from 50 to 33 percent between 1950 and 1970.[56]

All of our major modes of transportation run on nonrenewable fossil fuels. As the energy needs of America's transportation system have increased, the transportation industry has become more centralized in the hands of fewer companies. Where there used to be many domestic auto makers, today the industry is dominated by the Big Three auto firms—Ford, GM, and Chrysler. The same pattern occurred earlier with railroads, buses, and airplane traffic. Only these giant transportation firms can absorb the increased costs associated with the use of greater amounts of energy. Even they, however, are now feeling the crunch as the economy reels toward an entropy watershed. The auto industry, the undisputed leader of the American economy, is being forced to cut production and build smaller cars as the fuel crisis deepens. And as Henry Ford remarked, "Mini cars make mini profits."[57]

Smaller and fewer cars mean the entire economy suffers. Autos consume "20% of all the steel, 12% of the aluminum, 10% of the copper, 51% of the lead, 95% of the nickel, 35% of the zinc, and 60% of the rubber used in the U.S."[58] Way back in 1932, one auto zealot summed up the great possibilities for the entire economy in expanding auto production:

> Think of the results to the industrial world of putting on the market a product that doubles the malleable iron consumption, triples the plate glass consumption, and quadruples the use of rubber! . . . As a consumer of raw material, the automobile has no equal in the history of the modern world.[59]

In 1987, it required more than 23 weeks of income for the average American to buy a new car.[60] Every twenty-four hours

10,000 new drivers and 28,000 new cars are added to the road.[61] In addition to purchasing the automobile, the consumer pays for the insurance, the gasoline, the maintenance, the parking charges, the highway tolls, the traffic tickets, the state and federal taxes, and by the time he's done he has spent more money than he spends on food.

Today, one out of every six jobs is directly or indirectly related to the automobile.[62] The automobile is a central feature of our fossil fuel culture. The increased expense, then, in buying, running, and maintaining an automobile is a good measuring stick of the increased costs incurred all along the energy flow line as we run up against the end of the age of fossil fuels. The massive disorders caused by the automobile are also a good example of what happens when an economic system fails to take into account the effects of the Entropy Law until it is too late. Whatever we have received in benefits from the automobile over the past fifty years must now be judged in light of the even greater penalties we are now being forced to pay as the second law relentlessly drives its point home. The total bill is more than any of us can afford, as a brief survey of some of the costs suggests.

The first cost to consider is time itself. The automobile was supposed to reduce the amount of time it takes to get from one location to another. In truth it has done the opposite. With the widespread use of autos, Americans began to move farther away from their place of work. Forty years ago, most people lived within walking distance of their place of employment. Today people are spread out in suburbs, sometimes twenty or thirty miles from their job. While the automobile is a faster mode of transportation than walking, its speed becomes relatively meaningless when peak rush-hour traffic crawls at a pace of five to six miles an hour, as it now does entering and leaving many of America's major cities. It now takes most commuters anywhere from thirty minutes to an hour and a half each way to get to and from work—about the same time it took people forty years ago when homes were located nearer to the jobs and people could walk or take a trolley car.

Former Secretary of Transportation Alan Boyd once remarked:

If someone were to tell you he had seen strings of noxious gasses drifting among the buildings of a city, black smoke blotting out the sun, great holes in the major streets, filled with men in hard hats, planes circling overhead, unable to land, and thousands of people choking the streets, pushing and shoving in a desperate effort to get out of the city . . . you would be hard pressed to know whether he was talking about a city at war or a city at rush hour.[63]

In fact, the death and destruction wrought by the automobile is more gruesome than anything our country has ever faced in wartime. Automobile accidents kill 48,000 Americans every year.[64] The National Safety Council estimates that more Americans have been killed by automobiles than were killed in *all* of the wars this country has fought in the past 200 years. Imagine, over 1 million people have been killed by automobiles in just the past thirty years![65]

In dollar terms, the loss of health and property incurred by traffic accidents is ten times the total from all other crimes of violence combined. In 1969 the total losses from traffic accidents rang up at about $13 billion. By 1986 the societal costs of losses involving auto accidents reached $74.2 billion.[66]

Even these losses are only part of the picture. With the auto age came highways, and thousands and thousands of miles of concrete, asphalt, and cement. The environmental damage resulting from the lethal combination of highways and motor cars is phenomenal. The first Portland cement concrete was used to pave a small stretch of public road from Detroit to the Wayne County State Fairgrounds in 1909.[67] From these humble beginnings America set out on a public works project which has become the most costly ever undertaken in the history of the world. Between 1956 and 1970 alone, this country spent $196 billion in local, state, and federal moneys on highway construction. By 1986, annual highway costs for the federal government had exceeded $46 billion per year.[68]

The interstate highway system takes up 42,500 miles.[69] "The highway system," says transportation expert George W. Brown, "devours land resources and atmosphere at a rate that is impossible to sustain.''[70] According to the National Highway Users Conference, for every million dollars spent on the interstate highway system, 16,800 barrels of cement are consumed, along with 694 tons of bituminous materials; 485 tons of concrete and clay pipe; 76,000 tons of sand, gravel, crushed stone, and slag; 24,000 pounds of explosives; 121,000 gallons of petroleum; 99,000 board feet of lumber; and 600 tons of steel.[71]

There are 3,600,000 square miles of land in the United States and over 3,600,000 miles of road: that is one mile of road for every square mile of land.[72] Roads are proliferating so fast that they now take up 30 percent of the land use in fifty-three central cities.[73] Approximately two-thirds of the downtown land area of Los Angeles is now devoted exclusively to either the parking or movement of automobiles. In Chicago, Detroit, and Minneapolis nearly half the city land is "devoted to the movement and storage of automobiles."[74] While there is no way to calculate the total damage done to buildings and other city structures by the constant friction, weight, movement, and general wear and tear produced by inner-city auto traffic, city planners have begun to introduce the phrase "auto erosion" into their vocabulary when studying the cost factors of city traffic.

The entropy bill is now coming due for the nation's aging highway system. Many American roads and highways are twenty-five to fifty years old and incapable of withstanding current loads. It is estimated that one out of every ten miles of the 43,000 mile interstate highway system is in disrepair.[75] By the year 2000 more than one million miles of U.S. roads will need resurfacing.[76]

America's bridges are also aging and pose an increasing risk to public safety. Of the 575,607 bridges currently in use in the U.S., 131,562 are "structurally deficient" and another 112,084 are "functionally obsolete." It will cost over $50 billion to repair the nation's bridges in the coming decade.[77]

The small entropy decrease represented by every mile of highway and every shiny new car that travels along it is bought at the expense of a tremendous increase in entropy in the overall environment. Anyone who has been unfortunate enough to live right in the path of a highway construction route has felt the effects of the second law personally. According to D. R. Neuzil of the

Institute of Transportation and Traffic Engineering of the University of California, close to 100,000 persons per year are uprooted and displaced by new highway construction.[78] The destruction of neighborhoods has taken its toll in countless unforeseen ways, as sociological studies now confirm. The breaking up of long-established human living habitats has had an effect every bit as destructive as the breaking up of biological habitats. The resulting disorders have often been reflected in an increase in crime, unemployment, and mental illness, as familiar patterns of life have been suddenly and traumatically altered. Think of what it must do to the human psyche to see one's entire neighborhood of several square blocks suddenly razed to the ground. The sense of utter loss and confusion, say the psychologists, is often similar to that experienced after the ravages of bombing raids during wartime.

Finally, there is pollution to consider. Every time one of America's 150 million automobiles (or trucks or buses) travels along the highway, it is expending energy, much of which is dissipated as carbon monoxide, nitrogen oxides, and hydrocarbons. Today, 60 percent of the total air pollution in most U.S. cities is caused by auto exhaust.[79] In 1981, the National Academy of Sciences estimated air pollution damage to buildings and property at $2 billion per year.[80] It is now acknowledged that the dramatic rise in deaths caused by heart disease and cancer are also partially traceable to air pollution caused by the exhaust fumes of cars, trucks, and buses (more about this in the section on health).

Every day "250,000 tons of carbon monoxide, 25,000 tons of hydrocarbon, and 8,000 tons of oxides of nitrogen" are spewed out from auto exhausts. In 1970 the auto pollution totaled 111 million tons of sulfur oxides, 19.5 million tons of hydrocarbons, and 11.7 million tons of nitrogen oxide.[81]

Moreover, the entropy process often affects activities so far removed from the original energy expenditure that no relationship is even suspected. For example, a man driving an automobile down the highway would, no doubt, be shocked to learn that every time he puts his foot down on the accelerator he is potentially contributing to the brain damage of a five- or six-year-old schoolchild miles away. Studies over the past several years have demonstrated that children with learning disabilities, who show signs of "drowsiness, irritability, abdominal pains and vomiting . . . and in severe cases—paralysis, convulsions and coma," also have higher concentrations of lead in their blood.[82] Most of the lead poisoning comes from auto exhausts. According to the findings of one detailed study undertaken by Children's Hospital at Harvard Medical School:

> Teachers rated the classroom behavior of 2,146 of the children without knowing the lead levels of any of them. When these behavior ratings were later correlated with the findings from studies of the shed teeth (baby teeth), the scientists found a direct and regular relationship. The higher the level of lead contamination, the more likely were behavioral problems such as lack of persistence and organization, failure to follow simple directions, and tendencies toward lack of attention, impulsiveness, and excessive activity.[83]

Today's high-energy transportation system is largely responsible for depleting our remaining oil reserves. It is also one of the key contributing factors to the greenhouse crisis. According to the World Resource Institute, 30 percent of all U.S. carbon dioxide emissions in 1987 came from the transportation sector. (Electric utilities account for 35 percent of the CO_2 emissions, industry accounts for 24 percent and the operation of residential buildings accounts for 11 percent.)[84] If we are to effectively address both the energy crisis and the greenhouse crisis we must begin by focusing public attention and public policy on the task of radically reorienting the transportation system of the country.

Urbanization

"It's no news that America's major cities, on which much of the nation's growth depended for the last 200 years, are in decline. The challenge is whether this decline can be halted, or whether *all* big cities are to falter and eventually become ghosts of their once-thriving selves."[85] Foreboding words, to be sure; the kind you might expect from a radical sociologist or a "small is beautiful" advocate. But the message here is enhanced by its source, *U.S. News and World Report,* the most business oriented of the nation's newsweeklies.

Since World War II, and the advent of fossil fuel-based agriculture, America has been an urbanized country. Today, 80 percent of the population lives in urban areas. More than half of our people inhabit just 1 percent of the land.[86] Between 30 and 40 million of us live on just 10,000 square miles sandwiched in between southern New Hampshire and northern Virginia.[87] For a long time the city symbolized greater opportunity, more jobs, higher culture. No more.

Today, great numbers of Americans are becoming increasingly disenchanted with large cities. Polls have shown that most people actually want to live in smaller communities: 32 percent would prefer to live in small towns or cities; 25 percent in suburban communities; 26 percent in rural areas; and only 17 percent in big cities.[88] These sentiments are being translated into action. Between

1970 and 1976 the top seventeen metropolitan areas in the country actually suffered a net loss of nearly 2 million people.[89] From 1980 to 1986, five of the top seventeen cities continued to lose population.[90] When asked why they are leaving our great metropolises, the out-migrants are likely to respond in a variety of ways, citing crime, taxes, food and housing costs, crippling strikes of municipal workers, loss of jobs, pollution. All of these people are reacting to different facets of the same phenomenon: because of the massive energy inputs required to sustain contemporary city life, the entropy of the urban environment is rising dramatically, to the point where the continued existence of urbanization is being called into question.

The city as we understand it—millions of people packed together into giant megalopolises sprawling over hundreds of square miles—is a relatively new social institution, dating back to the birth of the era of fossil fuels. Before the rise of the modern urban center, people had lived in "cities" for thousands of years. But these were hardly cities by modern standards. Ancient Athens, for instance, had just 50,000 citizens; Babylon, a little more than 100,000. Centuries later, during the Renaissance, the size of urban areas had changed very little. Leonardo da Vinci's Florence claimed 50,000 residents, and when Michelangelo painted the ceiling of the Sistine Chapel, Rome's entire population hovered around 55,000. As late as the sixteenth century, the majority of European cities housed fewer than 20,000 inhabitants. At the time of the American Revolution, the two largest cities in the colonies— Boston and Philadelphia—had not yet reached 50,000, and New York City ranked a distant third in size.[91]

With the spread of the Industrial Revolution in the early nineteenth century, all of this began to change overnight. London became the first city with a population of 1 million, in 1820. By 1900 there were 11 cities with populations exceeding 1 million; by 1950, 75 cities; by 1976, 191 urban areas composed of 1 million or more people. At present there are 273 cities with populations over a million, the majority of these in Third World countries.[92]

As a percentage of the world's population, urban dwellers are moving toward a majority. Of the estimated 1 billion people alive in 1800, perhaps 25 million of them—or just 2.5 percent—lived in cities. By 1900, 15 percent of the world's population was located in urban areas. By 1960, one-third of the population. By 1987, nearly 43 percent of the world's population was living in urban areas. At the current growth rate, by the year 2000 more people will live in cities of 100,000 or more than lived in the entire world in 1960.[93]

This incredible explosion of urban life has come as a direct result of the global shift in the energy environment during the past two centuries. A city survives by virtue of its ability to gather available energy from the surrounding environment and store and use it for urban existence. Cities first originated thousands of years ago with the discovery of hard-grain cereal cultivation. Hard grains, unlike fruits and vegetables, lend themselves to long-term storage. Surveying the cities of the prefossil-fuel era, we can designate urban areas on the basis of their energy base as "rye cities, rice cities, wheat cities, and maize cities."[94]

While hard grains provided the energy foundation for urban life prior to 1800, they also set severe restrictions on both the size of the city's population and the physical size of the city itself. Traditional agriculture could not yield a large enough surplus to support a massive urban population of nonfood producers. Because the city was directly reliant on the surrounding countryside to provide it with energy (food), urban areas could not sprawl over the landscape as they do today for fear of destroying their local food base. The military walls surrounding ancient and medieval cities provided more than protection from invasion; they also ensured that the city would not grow beyond the limits of the carrying capacity of the energy environment. The great city of Babylon, for instance, encompassed an area of just 3.2 square miles; the medieval walls of London enclosed an area less than one percent of the city's present size. Nor could the traditional city rely upon food supplies brought in from great distances. Until the fossil fuel era, most transport was conducted through either animal or human labor, and thus the society's energy base set an absolute limit on the speed and distance over which food could be hauled.

The well-known exception to these historical limitations was the ancient city of Rome. At its peak, it grew to a population of nearly one million people. The Roman city could only be sustained, however, by attempting to colonize everything in its path. Without its vast pool of slaves, intensive farming techniques, massive aqueduct-building projects, and, most importantly, the empire's armies, Rome could not possibly have supported its population. In a sense, the entire known world had to be pillaged to overcome the natural limitation imposed by a solar-agricultural energy base. Murray Bookchin puts it well when he writes, "The Fall of Rome can be explained by the rise of Rome. The Latin city was carried to imperial heights not by the resources of its rural environs, but by spoils acquired from the systematic looting of the Near East, Egypt and North Africa. The very process involved in maintaining the Roman cosmopolis destroyed the cosmopolis."[95]

Once embarked on the course of urban expansion, Rome was in a losing race. The larger the city became, the more energy inputs that were required. The more energy flowing into the city, the greater the resulting disorder. The greater the disorder, the larger became the institutional infrastructure to deal with the various types of chaos. The process simply could not be sustained indefinitely. The energy supply lines maintained by the army became stretched so thin that the military absorbed more energy than it returned to the city. The agricultural system began to experience diminishing returns because of the intensive abuse of the soil. Slaves became too expensive to feed and house. The city's bureaucracy grew so big and costly that it could not be supported. Eventually, the overbloated city collapsed from within and without, returning after its military conquest to ecological equilibrium with its energy environment. After its fall, Rome claimed just 30,000 inhabitants.

Rome serves as a case study of what can happen when an urban area vainly seeks to ignore the growth limitations imposed on it by its surrounding resource base. Seeking out far-flung energy resources can serve to delay the collapse, but eventually the day of reckoning must come. Such is the case in our own time. Modern urban areas are supported through a kind of colonization of the world that is quite similar to that which sustained Rome. And like Rome, modern cities, because they have far outstripped the productive capacity of their local energy environments, are extremely vulnerable to collapse once the limits of their national and international resource base are reached.

Nowhere is this more evident than in the modern city's needs for food. A typical urban area of 1 million people requires a daily input of 4 million pounds of food.[96] To get these 2,000 tons of nourishment, the city is completely reliant upon our fossil-fuel-based agricultural system. Without the high yields of petroleum-chemical farming, and a national transportation system that moves wheat and oranges and beef thousands of miles to scattered urban areas, major cities would quickly become scenes of mass starvation. But as we have just seen, the declining availability and escalating cost of fossil fuels—the backbone of American farming and transportation—threaten the survival of the very agricultural system upon which the city is dependent.

Where will the food for New York, Chicago, and Los Angeles come from? Not from the surrounding countryside. Due to urban and suburban sprawl, tens of millions of acres of potential food-yielding land have been converted to concrete, plastic, and steel.[97] And not from within the city itself. In the historical city, a fair amount of land within the city walls would be set aside for small-scale agriculture. But as cities have grown bigger, more and more potential food-growing land has been converted to other uses.

Major urban areas are precariously reliant on other types of far-flung resources as well. A city of a million requires a daily input of 9,500 tons of fuel and 625,000 tons of fresh water.[98] Construction and maintenance of America's buildings (most of which are in large urban areas) require 57 percent of all the electricity produced in the country. Lighting them alone takes about one quarter of the nation's electricity.[99] Mammoth buildings like the World Trade Center draw 80,000 kilowatts of electricity, enough to service the entire city of Schenectady, New York. The Sears Building in Chicago uses more electricity than the people of Rockford, Illinois, a city of 147,000 inhabitants. Massive inputs of natural resources are also required. The Sears

Building, for instance, contains eighty miles of elevator cables and enough concrete to cover an area equivalent to seventy-eight football fields.[100] Resources are also necessary for upkeep. In cities around the country, steel is deteriorating so rapidly that the current annual replacement cost is estimated at $20 billion.[101]

Without the massive inputs of energy in its various forms, the city decays, jobs are lost, and urban life becomes intolerable. This process is already far advanced in some of the nation's oldest cities. According to a study done by the Urban Institute on the condition of America's urban infrastructure, basic facilities like sewers, streets, bridges, transit systems, and waterworks in the nation's major cities are finally wearing out and will require massive expenditures of funds to replace or repair in the coming decade. The figures are truly staggering. To avoid the collapse of its physical plant, New York City will require the expenditure of $12 billion for replacement, repair, and maintenance operations over the next ten years. Even a smaller city like Cleveland will have to spend over $700 million if it is to maintain its physical infrastructure in the years just ahead.[102]

Big cities require big inputs of energy to remain viable. As the energy flows into the urban area, however, it undermines the vitality of the city by generating various disorders. For example, a high energy flow into a city causes significant ecological changes. A large city's annual temperature averages three or four degrees hotter than surrounding areas. This is due to the emissions from power plants, automobiles, air conditioners, and the changes in solar reflection caused by highways and buildings. There are ten times more air pollutants in the city than in rural areas. Other meteorological phenomena created by an urban area's energy requirements include: 100 percent more winter fog and 30 percent more summer fog than in surrounding rural areas; 5 to 10 percent more rain and snow in the city; 5 to 15 percent less sunshine; and 20 to 30 percent less wind.[103]

The high levels of energy consumption and the resulting waste in cities seriously affect the health of urban residents. City dwellers have inordinately high cancer rates, along with more bronchitis, ulcers, and heart disease. The residents of large cities also exhibit far more antisocial behavior, hostility, and selfishness than those who live in lower-concentration energy environments. The suicide rate is higher in big cities; the percentage of admissions to mental hospitals is greater; schizophrenia, neurosis, and personality disorders are all considerably higher in urban environments. The crime figures alone are astonishing: there are 5.7 murders per 100,000 people in cities of 25,000–50,000 residents, but 29.2 murders per 100,000 in cities of over a million. A city of 100,000 averages 300 violent crimes annually; a city of over a million, 11,880.[104]

The density of high-energy urban life can affect human relationships and interaction in a more subtle way. For example, it has been estimated that a person can "meet" 220,000 people within a ten-minute radius of any place in midtown Manhattan. Obviously, it is impossible to pay attention to each person, so urban dwellers establish a kind of screening process, giving less time and consideration to each input. Urbanites typically disregard "low-priority" inputs such as panhandlers and drunks. Dozens may witness a crime and not report it or aid the victim. A simple walk down a street becomes a process of assuming an unfriendly face to ward off people who are undesirable "inputs." To preserve psychic energy, people in large cities become friendly with far fewer people than do those who live in sparsely populated rural areas. Neighbors are often totally anonymous. We become like sailors in a lifeboat: everywhere we are surrounded by water, but not a drop to drink.

Highly urbanized life tends to destroy effective political participation. In a small town, anyone might drop in to see the mayor to discuss a local issue. But in a major city, the individual's opinion and participation become nearly meaningless. A member of the New York City Council represents an average of 239,000 people. If he spent eight hours a day, every day of the year, doing nothing but talking for fifteen minutes with each of his constituents, a council member could only talk to 10,000 of them over the course of a year.

Kirkpatrick Sale, in a study analyzing the quality of life in large cities (of over a million) versus the small city (under 100,000), argues that in any area we care to look, major urban centers are inferior to small, decentralized communities. Not only are big cities vulnerable to massive unemployment during times of economic crises, but, on a daily basis, "there are higher transportation costs because of congestion, higher employee sickness and death rates because of air and water pollution, higher maintenance and cleaning costs because of air pollution, higher energy costs because of the 'heat island' effect over cities in the summer (and the inaccessibility of dense buildings to sunlight in the winter), higher security costs and higher loss rates because of crime, higher costs in training new workers because of bad schools."[105]

Urban expansion means higher energy flows and mounting disorders. As the various disorders build up, the city bureaucracy grows in an attempt to impose some order on the developing chaos. Still, every major city has discovered that there is just no way to adequately provide the necessary services—power, sewerage, schools, highways, police, public housing, and so on—that are required. One study indicates that the service demands upon a large city double every year. In New York City the number of municipal workers increased by 300 percent in the last decade, while the city's population actually declined.[106]

Obviously, the energy put into the city must also come out in the form of waste. The garbage problem in any major urban area is truly monumental. In metropolitan Washington, D.C., 4,000 tons of garbage are collected and compacted every twenty-four hours. If this daily accumulation of waste were dumped on the Mall in downtown D.C., it would stack up nearly half as high as the top of the Washington Monument. Where does all of this garbage go? In D.C., the urban area has five major landfills where waste is discarded. All five of these fills are beginning to spill over. Of course, more dumping sites could be built, but because the metropolitan area is so densely populated, any new landfill site would inevitably have to be placed near where thousands of people live. While everyone wants his garbage picked up and hauled away, no one wants a garbage dump built near his home. Faced with this problem, city authorities have two choices. Either the garbage will have to be burned, which will mean dirtier air and more pollution, or it will have to be packed into railroad boxcars and shipped to less populous areas of the country, a process that will use a considerable amount of energy and cause higher city income taxes.[107]

Maintaining a high energy flow-through and absorbing the increasing disorders that build up along the city's flow line require money. The Urban Institute has shown that a resident of a city of 1 million people will typically pay three times more in taxes than a resident of a small city of 50,000 inhabitants.[108] The bulk of this money will go into education, police, and health services. Yet by all statistical measurements, urban residents suffer more crime and have more inferior schools and worse health than those who live in small cities or rural areas. The entropy of the urban environment continues to build as a result of increased energy inputs, and the city's problems become unsolvable in conventional terms. Notes economist Leopold Kohr, "Social problems have the unfortunate tendency to grow at a geometric ratio with the growth of the organism of which they are a part, while the ability of man to cope with them, if it can be extended at all, grows only at an arithmetic ratio."[109]

Eventually, the city begins to run out of available resources and reaches the point where it is spending itself into bankruptcy. According to the Center on Environmental Quality, "expenditures in most distressed cities are growing much faster than increases in the value of real property, the chief tax base in most municipalities." In a city of 1 million or over, the average revenue per capita equals $426.90 in taxes, but the average local debt incurred by the city to pay for services equals $1,052 per resident.[110]

Even as the city attempts to preserve itself, it actually fosters its own economic decline. Rising taxes induce wealthy and middle-class residents, along with corporations, to leave the city. As the wealthy and middle class leave the city, less tax revenue is available to the bureaucracy and fewer jobs remain. Unemployment rises, crime goes up, and the city is forced to spend even more to keep down the disorder. The vicious cycle continues on and on.

The near fiscal collapse of New York and Cleveland in the 1970's is a sign of what lies ahead for our overgrown and outworn cities in the next two decades. The sober truth is that we can no longer afford to maintain these incredibly entropic urban environments.

The Military

The world has never seen a military machine the equal of our own. Of every dollar spent by the federal government in 1987, 53 cents goes to pay for wars—past, present, and future.[111] A recent military budget (fiscal 1989) allocated $300 billion for the nation's defense for just one year. In 1988, America's armed forces included at least 25,000 nuclear weapons, 2 million soldiers, 500 massive naval ships, 8,000 aircraft, and 871 domestic military installations.[112] Twenty thousand military contractors work to produce tens of thousands of different weapons systems. Counting workers employed directly under contract to the Defense Department, more than 5 million of our citizens owe their livelihood to the Pentagon.[113]

As far as many Americans are concerned, this is just as it should be. From the day the Japanese bombs fell on Pearl Harbor, most of us have felt that increased military spending is essential to maintain our national security. Many people also recall how Franklin Roosevelt brought us out of the Depression through massive military investment. Thus, defense spending has appeared for decades to be good for the economy. Yet, by any measure we care to use, it is becoming increasingly clear that the more resources and energy are devoted to the military, the less real wealth and security exist. As noted defense analyst Seymour Melman has written, "Far from being dependent on arms production for our prosperity . . . we paralyze the country as a whole by diverting the lion's share of our resources into the military sphere."[114]

Today, the U.S. military is the largest single institutional consumer of energy in the nation. Over 80 percent of the federal energy budget goes to the Defense Department.[115] When industrial defense contractors are included, the military uses 6 percent of the nation's total energy requirement, making it a primary contributor to carbon dioxide emissions and the global greenhouse crisis.[116] Moreover, since World War II, the defense establishment has been the largest single institutional user of capital and technology in the country. To sustain this infrastructure, fully one-half of the scientists and engineers of the past generation have worked either directly, or under military contract, for the Department of Defense.

The energy drained from society by the military causes tremendous social dislocation. Nowhere is this more readily visible than in the monthly unemployment figures. The common myth is that defense spending creates jobs. In fact, a study conducted by the Michigan Public Interest Research Group concludes that for every $1 billion added to the military budget, the nation as a whole loses 11,600 jobs. The study also found that in each of twenty-six states, which comprise 60 percent of the nation's population, as military spending in the state rose, unemployment rose as well.[117] The International Association of Machinists, in its own survey, showed that "a Pentagon budget of $124 billion costs the Machinists over 118,000 civilian jobs. When the 88,000 jobs generated by this level of military spending are subtracted, the net job loss to the union is 30,000 jobs a year." Another report, authored by Marion Anderson, indicates that the military buildup of 1981 to 1985 cost the jobs of 1,146,000 Americans.[118]

While it may appear paradoxical that investing money in military production actually produces unemployment, the issue is quickly resolved when we look at the nature of the jobs created. The types of jobs generated through military spending are necessarily highly capital and energy intensive. Human labor represents a very small ingredient in the overall mix of factors involved in weapons production. For example, the federal government awarded Lockheed Corporation a twenty-year contract that provided

$1 billion a year for the company to work on the most lethal and expensive weapon ever devised, the Trident submarine. The company employed at least 16,000 people on the project. This same $1 billion, however, could have been used to create 20,000 jobs in more labor-intensive, and less energy-consumptive, employment, such as the construction of solar collectors.[119]

Military spending is also a leading contributor to inflation. As *The New York Times* notes: "Virtually all economists agree . . . that military spending tends to be inflationary. This is because it puts money into the hands of workers without expanding the supply of goods they can buy—the consumer market for missiles and the like being somewhat limited—thereby driving up the prices of goods like autos and refrigerators and machine tools."[120] Military production also causes inflation in a more important sense. The first law of thermodynamics tells us that the quantity of energy and matter is fixed. Because the military sector consumes 6 percent of the nation's total energy use, along with massive quantities of nonrenewable mineral resources, the entropy increase represented by military hardware (the amount of energy no longer available to do work) causes tighter resource supplies, which in turn fuels inflation.

The rejoinder to all of this, of course, is that while energy-intensive military spending may indeed cause social disorder in the form of unemployment, inflation, and resource depletion, it at least provides us with a system of national security unparalleled in history. If security is to be measured in numbers only, then we would surely be the most secure nation on earth. If the lethal capacity of the nuclear arsenals of the world were broken down into tons of TNT, each man, woman, and child alive at this moment—nearly 5 billion of us—would be represented by four tons of explosive power. Some of our individual hydrogen bombs represent so much megatonnage that they each total more tons of dynamite power than all the bombs dropped by all sides during all of World War II. Using our atomic storehouse, we could blow up every major Soviet city fifty times over. And we daily produce two more nuclear bombs to add to our stockpile.[121]

Every dollar spent on national defense only generates greater global tension. Each time the United States develops a new weapon system, the Soviets feel threatened and therefore generate another as counterbalance. This, in turn, causes us to respond, and so on. Today we spend three times as much in real dollars as we did on defense in 1948,[122] but who could claim that we are three times more secure when, within twenty minutes of the commencement of an all-out nuclear war, 160,000,000 Americans would be dead?

Ever more sophisticated weapons systems mean greater energy concentration and flow-through. If the history of warfare teaches us one simple truth, it is this: the more concentrated the energy flow-through, the more deadly and depersonalized warfare becomes. At this moment, the Soviet Union and the United States are annually spending a combined total of $20 billion on the development of new weapons of war. The United States alone is experimenting with some 20,000 future weapons concepts.[123]

As American weapons systems become more energy intensive, more complex, and more expensive they suffer increasingly serious operational problems. Cost overruns become enormous and commonplace: the Trident submarine is currently $400 million over estimated costs. Some systems just do not work. The Department of Energy has admitted that 75 percent of all Polaris A1 missiles (a popular military item in the mid-1960s) would not have functioned had they been fired. Unexplained crashes of the most technologically advanced planes have become a regular occurrence.[124]

Finally, as the military seeks ways to embody more and more energy in destructive devices, weapons systems grow to such complexity that they approach the ludicrous. A current military proposal, much favored on Capitol Hill, is the MX missile system. The idea here is that 200 missiles will be hidden from "enemy" view by shuttling each warhead underground between twenty-five shelters. The theory is that the Soviet Union will never know where each individual missile is located, and so will have to launch 5,000 warheads to be certain to destroy them all. To construct the underground railroads and storage shelters necessary for this scheme, the Air Force will have to acquire an estimated 3½ million acres of land west of the Mississippi. This is an area roughly four times the size of Connecticut—just to house 200 missiles![125]

According to the governor of Kansas, a state in which the Pentagon hopes to build an MX tunnel, construction will disrupt 186,000 acres of prime western Kansas farm and range land; exclude the area's 40,000 inhabitants from 6,500 square miles of the state; suspend the existing uses of land in the area from farming, recreation, grazing, and human habitation for twenty to thirty years. On top of it all, construction crews and their families will bring in an additional 81,000 people to western Kansas, causing public service costs to rise by $37.5 million. And, asks the governor, how will the missiles be transported to their underground havens? Each weighs approximately 1 million pounds and is 150 feet by 22 feet in size. The entire cost of this Rube Goldberg scheme: $30–40 billion.[126]

The MX is just a small part of the various military systems being developed. Like something out of science fiction, the next generation of wars will be fought with missiles that read maps and guide themselves, and with killer satellites and particle-beam death rays hurled from outer space. By the 1990s the United States hopes to have a fully operational high-energy laser that can melt tanks or focus its beam to disable a satellite orbiting a thousand miles above the earth.

Yet, for all of our destructive capability, perhaps never has a nation's military supremacy been so precariously perched. While soldiers of the past moved on their stomachs (food being their primary energy source), today's military runs on oil. And oil is a diminishing resource. The total Department of Defense energy costs in 1978 exceeded $4 billion, more than twice the costs in 1973. Rising energy costs have "already caused the Defense Department to incur a lower margin of readiness than we might otherwise prefer," according to the Pentagon's Ruth Davis in testimony before Congress. Although DOD has managed to realize a 30 percent reduction in energy usage since 1973, the savings were accomplished by reducing men and operations. Says Davis: "Any further energy savings through reductions of this nature will have a serious impact upon our ability to maintain acceptable levels of force readiness." The oil embargo of 1973 and the revolution in Iran in 1979, "provide renewed awareness of our increasing susceptibility to the potential for political, economic or military pressure—pressure applied by those who either have the ability to control directly or who can indirectly influence the flow of oil to the U.S. and to its allies."

Even though the energy supply needed for our military operations is dependent on foreign sources, our war machine has become so specialized that there is very little that can be done to provide alternative sources of energy. Ninety percent of the DOD's daily use of petroleum is for "mobility fuels," used in aircraft, missile systems, and ships. "The DOD continues to design and build weapons systems under the implicit assumption that they can be fueled with petroleum-like products," says Davis. Until "well into the 21st century," she adds, the military will have to rely on liquid hydrocarbon fuels.

To cope with its declining fuel supply, the military must furiously scramble to develop new sources. In the old days, the troops might simply be sent into the Middle East oil fields; in fact, the Pentagon recently surfaced just such a proposal to test public reaction. But any such incursion might well lead to nuclear war, so the military has been forced to look closer to home. Already, the President has guaranteed that the armed forces will continue to receive 100 percent of their fuel requirements. This will clearly result in the further draining of energy away from other social and economic needs. To keep its energy flowing, the Pentagon has even recommended the establishment of a Defense Mobility Fuels Action Plan that would give the military unprecedented control over the nation's energy policies. Given the declining availability of petroleum, any attempt by the Pentagon to maintain its own high energy flow is certain to cause greater disruptions in other sectors of society.[127]

As our weapons systems become more complex, and our military presence in the world expands, more and more energy must be used up just to maintain the growing military bureaucracy. According to Earl Ravenal, former DOD analyst, "Less than 30% of our entire defense budget goes toward the direct defense of our country and its essential interests."[128] The rest is consumed by our national attempt to maintain a worldwide military presence. In one recent military budget, $35 billion was spent on the building of new weapons; the other $100 billion plus was used essentially for personnel and maintenance costs.[129]

Increased military spending represents a tragedy of monumental proportions. As the military fights to maintain itself and its own energy flow, it continues to take energy away from society's flow line, thus exacerbating other energy-based problems such as hunger and poverty. All of the nations of the world combined are currently expending $400 billion annually on weapons; nearly $1 million a minute.[130] Wars and preparation for wars consume roughly 10 percent of the world's total production of all goods and services.[131] This is the equivalent of the entire GNP of over half the world's population. With 800 million people barely surviving on $200 or less annually, and with 20 million dying of hunger each year, high-energy military spending becomes an obscenity. If just 2 percent of the world military budget for just one year were diverted, it could provide every rural Third World family with a stove.[132] Here in the United States, the cost of a single aircraft carrier—$1.6 billion—is almost twice the entire budget for occupational health and safety programs; the unit cost of an A-7E Corsair attack plane equaled two times the 1977 EPA budget for safe-drinking water programs.[133]

In the end, warfare, and its preparation, are the most highly entropic form of human activity. After all, there are only two things you can do with a missile—use it for destruction, or store it until it becomes obsolete and has to be scrapped. Either way, because the resources of the planet that went into making the weapon are fixed, "We are now beating the plowshares of future generations into present swords or warheads."[134]

Education

Most of us have gone through the painful experience of cramming for an exam. The "magic-marker syndrome" is a well-established academic phenomenon. That's when, the night before a test, the student takes out a yellow magic marker and proceeds to underline large sections of the textbook in the hope of memorizing and retaining giant chunks of data just long enough to regurgitate them back onto the test page in the classroom the following morning. Within twenty-four hours of the test, chances are good that little or none of the data has been retained. What has been retained, however, is a massive hangover which often lingers on for several days. Students get "up" for the exam and afterwards they "crash." This is the typical pattern set in the American education system.

The way the student prepares for his exam is not unlike the way an ear of corn is prepared on an Iowa farm. In both instances, a massive expenditure of energy results in a slight entropy decrease in the product (in the student's case, the amount of knowledge retained) at the expense of a greater increase in the entropy of the environment. With the corn, the entropy increase in the overall environment is called environmental pollution. Psychologists now refer to the dissipated energy that accumulates in the student's environment as information pollution. It can manifest itself in a hundred and one different ways, from the buildup of neurosis to nervous breakdowns.

Everything we do requires the expenditure of energy, even the learning process. The Entropy Law is always at work in the collection of information, as in every other endeavor. Of course, whenever we learn something, we generally believe that we are adding to the value and order of the world we live in. For a long time educators were convinced that at least the learning process was one activity that defied the second law by creating only greater order or the building up of megaentropy. No longer. With the introduction of cybernetics and modern information theory after World War II, scientists realized that information gathering and the storage of knowledge required the expenditure of energy, and therefore an entropy price had to be paid.

Back some seventy years ago, Henry Adams wrote an essay in which he suggested that even the human mind, in its gathering and storing of information, was subject to the entropy process. The essay, entitled "A Letter to American Teachers of History," was addressed to the American History Association.[135] In it, Adams dared to suggest that the development in human thought over the ages had proceeded in the same direction as every other activity in the world; that is, toward a more and more complex, highly dissipating state. That essay caused quite a stir in academic circles at the time, for Adams committed the ultimate heresy. Like a thief in the night, he had stolen his way into civilization's inner temple, boldly flinging the second law across the most sacred altar of all: the one erected in honor of the spirit of the human mind. In the seven decades that have elapsed since he first put his thoughts to paper, Adams's essay has been rediscovered over and over again by academic scholars and made a subject of intense debate and discussion.

If Adams is to be accused of heresy then so should the ancient Greeks with their belief in the tale of Pandora's Box and the Jews and Christians with their belief in the account of Adam and Eve in the Garden of Eden. Both stories hold that the original perfection of the world was undermined with the introduction of knowledge. When Pandora lifted the lid to the box, opening up the secrets of life, and when Eve ate the apple from the tree of knowledge, it marked the beginning of a long and torturous journey in which the accumulation and use of greater knowledge has led to greater disorder and fragmentation in the world.

Adams looked at the progression of the human mind—from instinct to intuition to reason to abstract mathematical thought—and concluded that each succeeding mental construct exhibited greater ordering, a higher energy flow-through, and, consequently, a greater dissipation of energy in the process. For example, comparing the instinctual responses of early man to his environment with the abstract rational responses of modern man to his environment, it is obvious, noted Adams, that in the former instance far fewer steps are involved in the mental process, and much less energy is dissipated.

In our own lives we sense that Adams's observation holds true. For example, we often hear people say that a gut reaction to a situation is more reliable than a reasoned decision. Or, that it is sometimes better to trust your own instincts in a given matter than your intellect. When asked why, the usual explanation given is that one's intuition or instinct is generally more closely attuned to the reality of what is occurring. That's true, and it has everything to do with the second law. As mentioned, the more stages in the mental process, the greater complexity, abstraction, and centralization, and the greater the dissipation of energy and disorder. The history of human mental development has been a history of removing the human mind farther and farther from the reality of the world we live in.

The evidence also suggests that our mental activities have become more complex and abstract as our energy environments have become more harsh and exacting. After all, a hunter-gatherer environment required little more than raw instinct to survive in. Agricultural environments, on the other hand, require a great deal more abstract thought to manage. Industrial environments require even more.

A primary purpose of mental activity is to help the human being to survive. People survive by being able to locate and process available energy. As our energy environments have become more difficult to exploit, we have had to rely on a greater array of mental tools to order (and facilitate) our search and transformation activities.

It is also true that as humankind has developed its mental activity from instinctual response all the way to abstract mathematical reasoning, it has generated greater disorder in the world around it. The hunter-gatherers afflicted the world with far less damage than modern man and woman with our greater power of abstract reasoning.

The "colonizing" period of human history has been characterized by the frantic depletion of one energy environment after another and the wreaking of greater and greater disorder on the earth. Still, the human mind continues to find new ways to collect, sort, store, and exploit greater amounts of information, in order to transform increased amounts of available energy through the system.

Today we are bombarded with information. Advertising, the mass media, our educational system are pounding on us with thousands and thousands of messages every day. From the time we get up in the morning until the moment we fall asleep at night, we are literally assaulted with bits of information. The advertising industry alone spent over $47 billion one recent year "educating" the consumer.[136] The average American is subject to the one-way flow of information from the television set for over five hours every day.[137] Economic historians like Daniel Bell assert that our economy is now making the transition from an industrial to a postindustrial mode, where communication and information systems will dominate the economic activity of the nation.

This massive increase in information translates into a massive expenditure of energy, mounting disorders, increased centralization and specialization, and all of the other features that accompany a speedup of the entropy process. Already, the information and communication institutions—in both the private and public sectors—are turning into giant bureaucratic fiefdoms exerting enormous power over the lives of every American. The collection, exchange, and discarding of information is proliferating at an unparalleled speed. The increasing energy flow of the so-called information revolution is already creating massive disorders all along society's energy flow line, requiring more energy to be diverted into the ever-increasing costs of maintaining the information and communication institutions and machinery.

The current computer and microchip "revolution" is a case in point. Its advocates are fond of pointing out that during the past thirty years, the prices for individual computers have plummeted dramatically, the size of the computer has decreased sharply, the amount of material resources as well as the energy necessary to run them has significantly dropped. At the same time, as computers have become smaller, cheaper, and less energy consumptive, the amount of information they can store, and the rate at which they can sift through facts, has increased astronomically.

Given all of this, it is easy to see why computer advocates argue that the computer is at least one example of how more and more can be done with less and less. The point should be self-evident, they say. After all, the day is near when the entire *Encyclopaedia Britannica*—all thirty-two volumes—can be stored on a single chip that costs just a few pennies. One day, it is forecast, we will have virtually all of the knowledge known to humanity at our fingertips and will never have to leave home to retrieve it. So, the computer actually uses less energy than traditional methods of accumulating information, makes it available faster, and opens it up for access to anyone who can afford the rather nominal computer purchase price. On the surface, this argument is rather convincing. However, notwithstanding these admittedly impressive points, the effect of the computer revolution, *in totality,* has been to dramatically increase the overall entropy of the world. Any energy and resource savings evidenced by individual computers has been more than compensated for by the total entropy impact of computerization.

First, it is important to understand that while the average individual computer today consumes fewer resources and energy than the prototypes of thirty years ago, this very fact has led to an astounding proliferation of computers, whose numbers have necessitated a massive consumption of the world's resources. In 1950, just a few years after the birth of the first modern computers, only sixty computers had been built. By 1959, 6,000 computers were on line; by 1966, more than 15,000; by 1970, over 80,000, performing tasks in more than 3,000 different categories. It is estimated that by 1990, nearly 50 percent of all American workers will be using electronic terminal equipment. In addition, some 38 million terminal-based work stations will be on-line in offices, factories, and schools. Nearly 34 million households are expected to have home computers by the next decade, while another 7 million portable terminals will be in use. Computers are fast becoming staples, finding their way into every conceivable nook and cranny of modern life.[138] All of these computers use nonrenewable resources.

Second, it should be remembered that the computer is designed to collect, store, and disseminate information. The computer deals with facts, but those facts only take on real importance, in terms of entropic flow, when they are used by society's technological transformers to collect, exchange, and discard energy. The computer is analogous to endosomatic sense organs. The mind uses the eyes, ears, and nose to see, hear, and smell; they are collectors of information. Yet, no animal could survive unless the sensory data that is collected is used by its other endosomatic transformers—its legs, claws, teeth, and jaws—to collect and consume available energy from the surrounding environment. The more sophisticated the sensory apparatus, the better equipped an animal is to collect the information necessary to locate and convert available energy.

Similarly, the faster information is generated by the computerized society, the faster the data is used by the society's transformers to collect and convert available energy. The increased energy flow-through, in turn, creates greater disorder, a faster depletion of the existing energy base, and a greater concentration and centralization of the society's economic and political institutions. The very purpose, then, of the computer is to provide more data, more rapidly, in order to facilitate the faster conversion of available energy through the system.

It is also worth noting that as computers proliferate into every conceivable social function, society necessarily becomes dependent upon their workings for its survival. The computerized society becomes increasingly complex, and with complexity comes the real potential for breakdown. A single computer malfunction, for instance, can trip a series of switches in a major electric plant, shutting the facility down for days. Anyone who has ever gone to an airline counter at a major airport when the computer is "down" quickly experiences the frustration, and even helplessness, that comes from a computer malfunction. When the whole system becomes dependent upon a computer for its effective functioning, the human being becomes hostage to the technology.

Strangely enough, it seems that the more information that is made available to us, the less well informed we become. Decisions become harder to make, and our world appears more confusing than ever. Psychologists refer to this state of affairs as "information overload," a neat clinical phrase behind which sits the Entropy Law. As more and more information is beamed at us, less and less of it can be absorbed, retained, and exploited. The rest accumulates as dissipated energy or waste. The build-up of this dissipated energy is really just social pollution, and it takes its toll in the increase in mental disorders of all kinds, just as environmental pollution threatens our physical well-being.

The sharp rise in mental illness in this country has paralleled the information revolution. That is not to suggest that the increase in mental illness is due solely to information overload. Other contributing factors include hereditary diseases, urban crowding, increased dislocation and migration of populations, and job-related stress. In less than twenty years, the concept of mental health in the United States has emerged from the academic halls to become a $15 billion industry. Today, upward of 40 million Americans, or one out of five, are being treated for various mental illnesses.[139] As mental illness reaches what some health authorities consider epidemic proportions, a frenzied campaign is under way to set up appropriate treatment facilities. There are more mental health workers in the country now than there are policemen. They are part of a growing complex which includes

some 1,100 free-standing psychiatric outpatient clinics; 300 general hospitals with psychiatric outpatient services; 80 veterans hospitals with psychiatric outpatient clinics; 500 federally funded community mental health centers; tens of thousands of nursing homes, board and care facilities, halfway houses, behavior clinics, child guidance clinics, child abuse, alcohol, and suicide prevention clinics.[140]

In the mid 1970s, Leopold Bellah, professor of psychiatry at New York University, compared mental health to public health, arguing that more needed to be done "to protect the community against emotional contamination."[141] While one might take exception to Dr. Bellah's harsh language, there is no doubt that the term *emotional contamination* accurately describes what is taking place as we move more and more into an information and communication society.

Each of us experiences the effects of information overload every day—at work, in school, in the home, and out in the community. We find ourselves increasingly in the position of not wanting to know any more about a particular thing or about the world in general because we just can't handle it. Our nervous system and brain are only equipped to take in and use a certain amount of information at a time. When too much comes our way we attempt to filter out part or all of it by simply turning off. When incoming information zooms in on us from every direction, along with all kinds of fragmented background noise of every type and description, we experience extreme anxiety.

Different people, of course, have different tolerances and thresholds. Everyone, however, has a limit beyond which the increasing flow of information and accumulated dissipation leads to breakdown and serious mental illness.

True to form, our society has devised a set of techniques to handle every imaginable human disorder, not realizing that the additional information infusion only alleviates one type of condition by bringing on other even worse ones. The image immediately comes to mind of the stereotyped therapy junky, a person who leapfrogs from one mental therapy program to another in a desperate attempt to gain peace of mind, tranquility, and an ordered life. By the time he has exhausted the entire smorgasbord of techniques and his own pocketbook, he is so overloaded with fragmented pieces of information, each with its own often conflicting prescription on how to "cope" with the world, that he is worse off than when he began.

Nowhere has the effect of the information revolution proven more deleterious than in our educational system. In the past fifteen years the cost of public education has quadrupled in the United States. In 1988, federal and state governments spent more than \$270 billion on education for some 40 million school children.[142] Yet in the same period students have shown a steady decline in actual learning. As of 1979, over 15 percent of all seventeen-year-olds in this country were functionally illiterate.[143] Many educators and parents are asking why kids are learning less when schools are equipped with more sophisticated teaching aids of all kinds, and a professional staff of teachers with specialized training in a host of academic fields. One woman who was interviewed in a CBS TV special on education summed up the apparent paradox. She pointed out that she had been educated in a tiny one-room schoolhouse in the South that contained some "scratched-up desks, a raggedy book and a few crayons, and a few scratched-up blackboards."[144] Still, she was perplexed as to why she was able to read and write but her children and their friends could not, even though their school had "all the latest equipment." Again, part of the answer is to be found in the speedup of the entropy process and the accumulation of disorders that follows.

Since World War II, the public school system has gone the way of many other institutions in American society. Smaller schools were absorbed into large centralized learning complexes. The uprooting of children from local neighborhoods and the increased bureaucratization and specialization that went along with centralized educational institutions began to exact a toll in terms of student alienation, loss of discipline, and other disorders. Then, too, centralized educational complexes were able to make available all sorts of fancy new information technologies and specialized programs to facilitate learning. All of these things combined have greatly increased the energy flow-through and resulted in problems ranging from increased learning disabilities to acts of vandalism and violence. Said one teacher on the CBS report:

> We have this vast proliferation of distractors, diversions. . . . We just keep pouring things into the school and on top of the kids' heads. And then suddenly someone realizes, "Hey, this kid can't read."[145]

The "techniquing" of education has become so oppressive, remarked one parent in the same school system, that it's a wonder the children learn at all. The parent told of visiting the school's "reading center" and becoming depressed at how many instructions on "exactly" how to read were plastered all over the room's walls. With that kind of overload, the parent remarked, "I just don't see how they would ever really get into the mood of reading. If I were a child it would turn me off just totally."[146]

The classrooms and corridors of America's giant school centers are overflowing with dissipated energy, much of it generated by the educational system. It is no wonder that children have a difficult time maintaining an attention span and that they exhibit a level of anxiety that often leads to outright violence. School vandalism now costs over $600 million a year.[147] Part of the blame, of course, rests with factors outside the school, many of which (but not all) are related to information overload. TV is perhaps the number-one culprit. Five or more hours a day of nonstop one-way information flow is bound to seriously weaken the child's ability to concentrate and absorb information. Says one educator:

> I think we've developed a generation that thinks of communication in terms of receiving messages, being talked to, rather than sending messages. And also, because of this great stimulation, when the child goes into the classroom they look at the teacher and, I think, make unhappy comparisons. . . . It's not the excitement of a fleeting picture. Learning is hard work, and it cannot come with images on the screen.[148]

As we become less and less able to deal with information overload, new techniques are devised by the media, the educational industry, and the information sciences to speed up, compress, and shove even more bits of information down us in the hope that enough will stay down long enough to be of some marginal economic or social value. Never once do they consider that the source of the increasing disorder rests with the very transformers that are directing the massive energy flow and increasing the entropy of the environment in the process. It reminds one of the story of the prison guards who were advised that increased punishment of the prisoners only increased their antisocial behavior and the incidences of violence. After careful consideration, the guards concluded that the answer to the problem was to "punish the increased violence."

The Environment

The Industrial Age has been characterized by an exponential flow of energy and matter through the economic system. We have been extracting, processing, and discarding energy and matter faster than the earth's ecosystems can recycle the waste and replenish the resources. The buildup of polluted waste in the form of dissipated energy and organic and inorganic garbage now threatens the survivability of the earth. The statistics are grim.

Domestic landfills are nearly filled to capacity. By the early 1990s more than half of the cities in the U.S. will exhaust their existing landfills, forcing a massive garbage crisis.[149] Already, cities are shipping garbage in barges around the world in desperate search of countries who will agree to store the waste. As the garbage heaps up and the available burial sites diminish, the cost of disposal continues to rise. In Minneapolis, the cost of burying a ton of garbage has risen from $5 to $30 in six years. In Philadelphia, the cost has risen from $20 to $90 per ton as the city has been forced to ship some of its garbage to Ohio and Virginia for disposal. California cities and towns are expected to spend over $1 billion a year to dispose of trash by 1990.[150]

With landfills brimming over, municipalities are increasingly turning to incineration, which further exacerbates the air pollution crises in urban areas around the country.

In 1987, the nation first became aware of a new more insidious form of garbage—infectious waste. This garbage is composed of disease-causing micro-organisms and can also include human and animal parts, blood-stained bandages, surgical equipment, tissue specimens, used needles, and surgical gloves. Over 1.5 million pounds of infectious waste are disposed of by the nation's 7,000 hospitals every day. Research labs, medical clinics, and nursing homes dispose of additional amounts of infectious waste.[151]

Infectious waste is being dumped illegally across the country and poses a serious public health hazard for millions. The horror stories are numerous. A few years ago, investigators uncovered a warehouse in the New York suburbs filled with five tons of medical wastes, including amputated limbs and hypodermic needles. The abandoned warehouse was less than 100 feet from a children's dance studio.[152] In June 1987, children in Indianapolis were found playing in a dumpster with vials of blood infected with the AIDS virus. In July 1988, homeowners in Manchester, New Hampshire, found their backyards littered with operating room wastes that had been washed onto their properties from a local hospital landfill after a heavy downpour.[153]

The National Solid Wastes Management Association estimates that 500,000 tons of infectious wastes are generated each year.[154] That figure is likely to rise dramatically in coming years, forcing local health authorities and the federal government to adopt more stringent regulatory requirements to prevent the spread of infectious disease-causing agents.

Pesticide contamination poses still another serious threat to the environment and public health and like infectious waste, the entropy accumulation is apt to affect the planet for generations and centuries to come.

In 1985, 1,350 people were poisoned after eating California-grown watermelons that had been sprayed with the pesticide Albicaib. More than a million watermelons were ordered destroyed to protect the public from mass poisoning.[155] In 1988 Cesar Chavez, the founder of the United Farm Workers, went on a prolonged fast to protest the use of pesticides on grapes, arguing that the chemicals threatened the health of farm workers. A recent epidemiological study estimates that 313,000 farm workers in the U.S. may suffer ill effects from pesticide exposure.[156]

Today, more than 50,000 pesticides containing 700 ingredients are registered for use in the U.S. Only 10 percent of the pesticides used ever actually comes into contact with the plant. The remaining 90 percent is scattered in the soil, water, and carried away by the wind.[157]

Pesticide contamination from agricultural runoff now threatens the nation's water supply. In Kansas, water in 72 to 78 percent of the wells tested in 1984 was contaminated with pesticides. In Iowa, 55 percent of the wells are now contaminated, and in Nebraska 70 percent have been tainted by pesticides.[158]

According to the U.S. Geological Survey's Pesticide Monitoring Network, one-quarter of all the water sampling stations contain the residue from atrazine, one of the most frequently used pesticides. DDT, chlordane, and dieldrin were found in one-third of the sediment in a nationwide study.[159]

More disquieting is the fact that some 496 ingredients in the pesticides used in the U.S. are commonly found on tomatoes, apples, grapes, lettuce, beans, and other produce in the grocery stores. In 1987, the National Academy of Sciences issued a warning that ''90% of all fungicides, 60% of all herbicides, and 30% of all insecticides may cause cancer.''[160] Despite these alarming statistics, little action has been taken by federal agencies to restrict the widespread use of pesticides on millions of acres of U.S. cropland.

Much of the dissipated energy and material waste that flows through the world economic system ends up back in the ecosystem, posing a serious threat to the environment and to public health. In the pre-Industrial Age the entropy accumulation was small enough to be absorbed and recycled by the planet's ecosystems. Today, the entropic flow is overwhelming the natural environment, forcing waste to back up and heap up in amounts that now threaten our very survival. The problem is compounded by the fact that nations are often unwilling to take any action to limit or curtail the use of a specific chemical or metal until the damage has become catastrophic and irreversible. For example, consider the use of lead and asbestos.

Lead is the fifth most used metal in the U.S. despite the fact that it is toxic and accumulates in the body. According to the EPA, 20 percent of Americans now drink water contaminated with unsafe levels of lead.[161] As mentioned in an earlier chapter, studies show that children are in a particularly high-risk category. Exposure to high concentrations of lead from water contamination, household paint, and automobile exhaust can damage both the brains and the nervous systems of young children.[162] Yet, even with these facts in hand, society is not willing to significantly retool its economic activity away from reliance on lead.

Asbestos is another poignant example of the tremendous social costs that accrue in waiting too long to address a crisis. Asbestos has been used for decades in insulation for office buildings, schools, and homes. If inhaled or ingested, the asbestos fibers can cause cancer. While asbestos has finally been banned for most uses, the material is so widespread that it will take decades, even centuries to remove it or tear down and rebuild structures containing it. At the present time, 15 million students and 1.4 million workers are exposed to asbestos just in the nation's schoolrooms.[163] Millions more are exposed daily to the material in offices and homes. The short-term economic benefits of using asbestos as a form of insulation pale in contrast to the long-term health bill that is likely to result from persistent exposure to this carcinogenic material.

As with other forms of modern economic activity, the problem is one of time frame. The benefits of increased energy and material flow-through seem impressive until measured against the long-term ill effects, which often cancel out the short-term gains. Nowhere is this more graphically illustrated than in the increasing deterioration of the very air we breathe.

We have long been aware of the fact that industrial activity increases air pollutants, threatening public health. Yet, until the last two decades, few regulatory protocols were established to curtail emissions. Even today, eighteen years after the passage of the Clean Air Act (1970), many American cities have failed to meet the minimum requirements mandated by the legislation.[164] Failure to act has resulted in an increased public health threat. In cities across the country, health authorities issue alerts for days and weeks each year, warning citizens that the air quality has reached dangerous levels and urging older citizens and those with respiratory ailments not to venture outdoors.

Now, new data suggest that the ozone level in major metropolitan areas is so high at peak times during the year that it may be posing a much more serious health threat than heretofore suspected by medical authorities. While the ozone layer in the upper atmosphere provides a critical shield against incoming ultraviolet radiation from the sun, high levels of ozone near the surface of the earth pose a serious health risk. Much of the ozone at ground level is formed by industrial pollutants, including hydrocarbons and nitrogen oxides spewed from automobile exhaust and factories. Recent animal studies suggest that chronic exposure to ozone can cause ''permanent damage to the lungs, including premature aging of that vital organ.''[165] The global warming trend of the past several years creates an ideal environment for increased ozone concentrations near the ground, according to researchers. The result: ozone levels in New York City in 1988 were 11 percent above the previous all-time high, recorded in 1983. Similarly in Washington, D.C., ozone levels were 22 percent above the record 1983 levels. In Chicago, health officials reported a 36 percent increase over the record set in 1983. Similar findings were recorded around the country.[166]

While the entropy penalty on land has reached crisis proportions, the oceans may well turn out to the ultimate victim of the Industrial Age. In the U.S. alone the number of people living within fifty miles of the ocean has increased from 42 million to 89 million in the period from 1940 to 1980.[167] Garbage from human settlements is seeping into the sea at an alarming rate, threatening the mass extinction of aquatic life. Warm-water seals in the Gulf of Mexico now have the highest pesticide level of any mammal. Fishermen along the entire U.S. east coast, from Chesapeake Bay to northern Maine, report catches of lobsters and crabs with holes in their shells and fish with rotted tail fins and ulcerous lesions.[168] In Louisiana, 35 percent of the state's oyster beds were closed as a result of sewage contamination in 1988.[169] San Francisco Bay is polluted with large amounts of copper, calcium, mercury, nickel, and other heavy metals discharged in industrial wastes.[170]

Plastic waste is now so numerous in the ocean that nearly 2 million sea birds and 100,000 marine mammals die annually after consuming the debris or becoming entangled in it. Sea turtles have been found choked to death inside plastic bags. Sea lions have been found strangled inside plastic mesh.[171]

Scuba divers report "swimming through clouds of toilet paper and half-dissolved feces, of bay bottoms covered by a foul and toxic combination of sediment, sewage, and petrochemical waste appropriately known as 'black mayonnaise.' "[172] The pollution of the great oceans of the planet has seriously compromised the commercial fishing industry and the food supply for millions of people around the world. Commercial fishing in the U.S. is a $3.1 billion industry. Fishermen, however, are reporting a dramatic decline in their catch. In some regions, clam and oyster catches have plummeted 50 percent in the past seven years.[173]

The fish are now so contaminated that state health officials are issuing warnings to consumers. Illnesses ranging from hepatitis A to cholera are being passed on to humans who eat contaminated fish. In New York state, authorities have warned women of childbearing age and children under age fifteen against eating most fish found in New York coastal waters. The regional EPA administrator in New England has remarked that "anyone who eats the liver from a lobster taken from an urban area is living dangerously."[174]

The cost of cleaning up the entropic waste of the Industrial Age is already staggering. The EPA estimates that it will cost $110 billion in the next twelve years to clean up national waterways. It will cost another $100 billion to clean up the 10,000 hazardous waste sites that dot the national landscape. Reducing acid rain pollution will cost an additional $30 billion in just the next half-decade. To dispose of radioactive waste will cost the tax-payer and industry another $37 billion. Reclaiming strip-mined land will cost $7 billion. The trail of figures seems endless. The entropy cleanup bill now exceeds $300 billion and we have barely scratched the surface.[175]

When the final entropy bill comes due for the Industrial Age, the costs are likely to exceed in magnitude the economic gains registered over the past several hundred years. The Age of Progress may well be recategorized by future generations of historians as the Age of Illusion as the laws of thermodynamics exact their toll on a civilization in which expediency has ruled over sustainability.

Health

Modern medicine, like almost every other activity in contemporary society, reflects the Newtonian world view. The mechanical approach to medicine has dominated the health care profession for the past 200 years. British health expert Thomas McKeown sums up the prevalent attitude:

> The approach to biology and medicine established during the seventeenth century was an engineering one based on a physical model. Nature was conceived in mechanistic terms, which led biology to the idea that a living organism could be regarded as a machine which might be taken apart and reassembled if its structure and function were fully understood. In medicine, the same concept led further to the belief that an understanding of disease processes and of the body's response to them would make it possible to intervene therapeutically, mainly by physical (surgery), chemical or electrical methods.[176]

Today, health care is the third-largest industry in the United States and accounts for nearly 9 percent of the gross national product.[177] Much of the $150 billion plowed into the medical field is for new, more complex, and more sophisticated technological gadgetry.[178] The modern clinic and hospital contain a plethora of diagnostic and therapeutic machinery. One of the

major reasons for the escalating costs of health care is the introduction of all of this medical hardware. The cost to the patient for
this machinery is skyrocketing. Between 1950 and 1988, health
costs per capita rose from $76 to more than $1600 dollars.[179]
Much of the increase went to pay for the enormous cost of
maintaining the ever-expanding medical institutions. Today, the
family doctor with a small individual practice has been eclipsed
by the giant medical complex—centralized institutions housing
hundreds of medical specialists and their machinery.

Centralization, increased specialization, and more elaborate equipment all translate into a greater expenditure of energy. As more
energy has been expended in the medical field, the corresponding
disorders have escalated. Although doctors do not like to talk
about it, the sad truth is that the medical industry is no more
immune from the Entropy Law than any other activity in society.

The chances are good that you have never heard of the term
iatrogenic, but every doctor has. Mention this ten-letter word in
front of a doctor and the response is likely to be one of instant
defensiveness mixed with a slight tinge of terror. Iatrogenic diseases are those that are actually caused by the physicians, hospital, drugs, or machinery used to treat the patient.

The fact is, a temporary alleviation in condition following a
medical procedure is often accompanied by an even greater long-
range health problem for the patient. Part of the explanation for
this lies in the fact that "75 to 80% of all patients seeking
medical help have conditions that will clear up anyway or that
cannot be improved even by the most potent of modern pharma-
ceuticals."[180] Still, the doctors perform operations and prescribe
various drugs, which create greater problems for the patients than
the ones that sent them for medical help in the first place. For
example, most of us are now aware that what little value (entropy
decrease) we receive from having X-rays made is often more than
outweighed by the long-range harm of radiation exposure (entropy increase).

We are also coming to understand how the entropy process
works when it comes to the use of drugs. Every twenty-four to
thirty-six hours, between 50 and 80 percent of all adult Americans swallow a medically prescribed drug.[181] While they might

experience a temporary alleviation of their immediate discomfort or illness, the long-range deleterious effects of the drug on the human physiology are assured to be even greater. Nowhere is this more apparent than with antibiotics. These so-called wonder drugs are prescribed arbitrarily for just about every infectious disease that comes down the pike. The results have been catastrophic. Because antibiotics are indiscriminate killers of bacteria, they destroy many important organisms in the body that are absolutely essential to proper body maintenance. Vaginal thrush, yeast infections of the intestines, vitamin deficiencies, and a host of other disorders result from continued use of antibiotics. Then too, the massive use of these drugs has resulted in the proliferation of new resistant strains of bacteria, which have become so virulent that they can now survive both direct drug intervention and the normal healing activities of the human body. At an international symposium held on the subject in Linberg, West Germany, in 1976, many of the participants agreed that the human race is worse off than it would have been without the introduction of these so-called magic bullets.[182]

Antibiotics are only the tip of the iceberg. According to a detailed study published by a Senate subcommittee in 1962, of the 4,000 drug products legally marketed in the country over the previous twenty-four years, almost half had no scientifically proven value and little has changed since that time.[183] Even more startling is the fact that many of these ineffective products, which are produced by major pharmaceutical houses, are actually dangerous and have caused ill health. In their book *Pills, Profits and Politics,* Milton Silverman, research pharmacologist, and Philip Lee, former assistant secretary of HEW, report that the adverse "secondary disorders" caused by drugs "kill more victims than does cancer of the breast."[184] The problem has become so acute, say the authors, that adverse drug effects now "rank among the top 10 causes of hospitalization and are held accountable for as many as 50 million hospital patient days a year."[185]

It's impossible to know the full extent to which modern medical practices create even greater long-range medical disabilities. We do know, however, that even while patients are being administered treatment in a hospital, one out of five of them acquires an iatrogenic disease. One out of every thirty of these patients ends up dying from hospital-related illness.[186]

The tragedy is that for many patients there is absolutely no reason to be in the hospital in the first place. A congressional report found that, in 1974, doctors performed 2.4 million unnecessary operations, resulting in 11,900 unnecessary deaths, at an unnecessary cost to the public of $4 billion.[187]

Granted, the entropy process is at work. But the skeptic might well argue that modern medicine has at least been responsible for a "temporary" improvement in the health and well-being of people, even if the penalty tax (the entropy increase) is beginning to come due. Statistics on the increase in life expectancy are most often conjured up as proof that modern medicine has produced some impressive results. This myth is tenaciously held onto because it provides society with the evidence it needs to continue to support a mechanical approach to medicine, and to life's other activities as well.

The reality is that modern therapeutic medicine has played only a minor role in the elimination of major death-causing illnesses and has little right to claim the lion's share of credit for improvement in life expectancy. Several studies have shown that the major contributing factors to improved life expectancy in the past 150 years have been better sanitation and hygiene and improved nutrition. One such study was conducted by John and Sonja McKinlay of Boston University and Massachusetts General Hospital. As in an earlier study done by McKeown in Europe, they found that the principal cause of the falling death rate in the United States since 1900 was the disappearance of eleven major infectious diseases: typhoid, smallpox, scarlet fever, measles, whooping cough, diphtheria, influenza, tuberculosis, pneumonia, diseases of the digestive system, and poliomyelitis. With the exceptions of influenza, whooping cough, and poliomyelitis, all of these infectious diseases declined almost entirely before medical intervention came on the scene. Overall, concludes the report:

> Medical measures (both chemotherapeutic and prophylactic) appear to have contributed little to the overall decline in mortality in

the U.S. since about 1900—having in many instances been introduced several decades after a marked decline had already set in and having no detectable influence in most instances.[188]

Up until 1950, the average life expectancy in America continued to climb. After 1950, it began to level off.[189] Today, for men at least, life expectancy has begun to drop. It is interesting that the retreat in life expectancy began to occur around the time that medicine began to take off into high-technology therapeutic health care. The 1950s also mark the early years of America's entry into the petrochemical age. On this last score, even the government now acknowledges a direct correlation between the rise in disease since 1950 and the pollution or high-entropy waste generated by our petrochemical economy:

> The environment we have created may now be a major cause of death in the U.S. Cancer, heart and lung disease, accounting for 12% of deaths in 1900 and 38% in 1940, were the cause of 59% of all deaths in 1976. . . . Growing evidence links much of the occurrence of these diseases . . . to the nature of the environment.[190]

This is the conclusion of a top-level federal government task force composed of representatives of the Environmental Protection Agency, the National Cancer Institute, the National Institute for Occupational Safety and Health, and the National Institute of Environmental Health Sciences.

The problem, according to the medical experts, is the tremendous rise in all forms of pollution at every level of human existence. In entropy terms, the high standard of living—the massive energy-matter flow-through—we have enjoyed in this highly industrial environment is now being paid for with spreading disease and death. Pollution, let us recall, is a by-product of the dissipated energy and material wastes that accumulate from the energy-matter flow of a society. The greater the energy-matter flow, the greater the pollution, and eventually the greater the number of deaths that result.

The deadly effects of pollution on the human physiology are truly staggering. In New York City most taxi drivers have such a high level of carbon monoxide in their blood that it cannot be used for blood transfusions to persons with heart ailments.[191]

Several years ago, scientists told a Senate subcommittee that it was no longer possible to find uncontaminated milk to feed to infants: "Human breast milk increasingly contains pesticides, residues and other carcinogens. Infant formulas contain harmful lead deposits."[192]

In a study conducted several years ago of male university students, nearly one out of every four men had sperm densities below the threshold for reproductive success. The sperm "contained synthetic chemicals including penta-chloropherol (a widely used pesticide and wood preservative), polychlorabiphernyls, and metabolites of DDT."[193]

Several government reports in the past few years conclude that 60 to 90 percent of all types of cancers in the United States are causally related to environmental factors ranging from food preservatives and additives to toxic chemical substances.[194] Secretary of Health, Education and Welfare Joseph Califano shocked the nation's work force in late summer of 1978 by announcing the results of an extensive study showing that between 20 and 40 percent of all cancers are work-related—the result of contact with an entire range of metals, chemicals, and processes that are essential to the continuance of our industrial output. Because there is usually a time lag of from twenty to thirty years between exposure to chemical carcinogens and the onset of the cancer, it is estimated that as many as one out of every three Americans alive today will get cancer in his or her lifetime. In fact, since most of the sharp rise in industrial and commercial uses of synthetics, pesticides, and other chemical substances took place after World War II, many medical experts are predicting a virtual runaway epidemic of cancer by the mid-1990s.

Cancer is by no means the only major disease related to the pollutants of industrial society. The United Steelworkers union reports that "more than a half-million workers are disabled yearly by occupational diseases" of all kinds.[195] A study commissioned by the Environmental Protection Agency concluded that wages lost by American workers suffering from just air pollution alone total a whopping $36 billion per year.[196] Another study, done by the American Lung Association, estimates that the health bill for illness caused by air pollution totals over $10 billion per year.[197] The Office of Technology Assessment says that air pollution may cause 50,000 premature deaths in the U.S. every year.[198]

The health prospects for the immediate future are grim. Homo sapiens are not made for a highly industrialized petrochemical environment. Our anatomy has not changed since human beings first appeared on earth. We were biologically designed for a hunter-gatherer existence. Each successive stage of economic and social development has only increased the physiological strains on the human body and further eroded our chances for long-range survival as a species.

Many diseases are environmentally induced. They are caused by the accumulation of waste (dissipated energy) as the entropy of a given environment increases. This is not hard to understand. We all survive by drawing available energy from the environment. When the environment around us becomes choked and clogged with waste, it blocks the flow of available energy and pushes us closer to an equilibrium state.

Every energy environment creates its own unique form of dissipated energy. That dissipated energy, or waste, is internalized by different groups in society in different proportions depending upon how the energy flow line is set up. While it is true that throughout human history most of the major diseases have occurred within every kind of energy environment, the greater frequency of certain diseases over others can be accounted for by three related factors: the specific type of energy base of a civilization, the way the society's energy flow line has been set up, and the stage of the entropy process itself.

The argument that genetics plays more of a role than environment in the proliferation of certain illnesses is a bit of a misrepresentation. As René Dubos points out in his seminal work on the subject, *Man Adapting*, certain genotypes are less resistant than others to a particular environmental disease and therefore more likely to be affected. But still, it is the nature of the energy base, its state of entropy, and the way the energy flow line is set up that determine the likelihood of specific disease epidemics. For example, infectious diseases were virtually unknown in the hunter-gatherer environment, where the communities were small, extremely mobile, and lived an outdoor existence.

In agricultural environments, where there is a close living relationship between the sedentary populations, domesticated animals and small rodents, microbial agents are the main source of disease. As the energy environments become more depleted by the expansion of agricultural lands, the felling of forests, and the erosion of soil, natural habitats become more and more disrupted, allowing for the spread of certain microbial agents. The kinds of infectious diseases that occur are a result of the types of imbalance created by the energy flow lines.

In the advanced industrial environment, the chief cause of disease is the dissipated energy created by our energy base of nonrenewable resources. As already mentioned, the increased frequency of cancer, heart disease, lung disease, and other chronic and degenerative illnesses is more and more found to have a direct relationship with the nonrenewable energy base. The proliferation of these diseases, in turn, follows directly on the heels of the increase in the entropy of the environment. Finally, the frequency of these types of illnesses is found to vary from group to group in the population depending upon their position in the flow line—that is, the type of work they do, the amount of energy (income) they are compensated with, the places where they live their lives, and the type of life-style they adopt.

As the dissipated waste created by our high flow-through, nonrenewable energy sources continues to build up all along society's energy flow line, causing a dramatic escalation in physical disorders of all kinds, a point will be reached where the population will have no choice but to shift back into a low flow-through, renewable energy base or face disease and death in epidemic proportions.

The warning signs are already up. The increased emissions of CO_2, methane, CFCs, and nitrous oxide—the greenhouse gases—are creating the context for a global medical crisis that is likely to devastate large numbers of our species. The escalating greenhouse phenomenon will be accompanied by a catastrophic rise in cancer and heart and respiratory diseases as billions of people around the world become trapped by the heat and exhaust generated by the burning of fossil fuels and the emission of other industrial gases.

PART SIX

ENTROPY:
A NEW WORLD VIEW

The Greenhouse Transition

There is no easy way to make a transition from a mechanical world view based on the idea of permanent material growth to an entropic world view based on the idea of conserving finite resources. But let there be no mistake about the consequences of holding on to the traditional way of doing things. As the energy crisis and the global greenhouse crisis deepen over the coming decade, the public will begin to demand an effective response by the federal government. There will be no more liberals or conservatives then, no more hawks or doves; only millions of desperate people seeking relief at any cost. That time is not far off in the distant future. It could come at any moment.

Seeking new alternatives to our current energy mode will be difficult. It took thousands of years to make the transition from a hunter-gatherer existence to an agricultural one. It took hundreds of years to move from an agricultural way of life to an industrial one. In both instances there was plenty of time to make the radical adjustment in world views that was necessary to accommodate the new economic circumstances. Today we are being forced to make a transition from the Industrial Age of nonrenewable resources to a new and still undefined age based once again on renewable sources of energy, and we will have to do so in little more than one generation. The radical change in world view required to make this transition will have to be accomplished in a very short period of time. To succeed will require a zealous determination—a militancy, if you will—of herculean proportions.

When we hear proponents of solar energy extol the great benefits of moving our energy base from nonrenewables to sun power, the impression conveyed is that the whole transition can be accomplished without revolutionary changes in our way of life. This is not the case. Different technologies and institutions are designed for different energy environments. The types of transformers that will make up the Solar Age will be completely different from those we now live with in the age of fossil fuels.

We must understand that the Industrial Age is nothing more than a name for the kind of transformers that have been established in response to the nonrenewable energy base we have lived off. While there have been socialist and capitalist flow lines, all industrial countries exist only by the grace of the nonrenewable energy base upon which their economies depend. *The end of the age of nonrenewable energy, then, presages the end of the Industrial Age as well*. As the stored nonrenewable energy runs out, the entire economic superstructure built upon it will begin to crumble. Cracks all along that superstructure are already beginning to appear, and try as we will, there is not enough nonrenewable energy left to mend all of them. This is the hard truth that every person on this planet must ultimately face up to.

The Solar Age we are moving into will function as differently from our Industrial Age as we have functioned differently from the medieval era that preceded us. A formidable journey lies ahead. Making the transition from a nonrenewable to a renewable base of energy represents a monumental task for the whole of civilization. Compounding the problem at hand, is the stark reality of the greenhouse world, which now seriously threatens our chances of making the leap from one great human epoch to another.

The greenhouse global warming trend cannot be effectively reversed in the short run. It can however be slowed down enough to allow our species several more decades of lead time to adjust to the epochal change in the economy and climate of the planet. Buying just a few decades of precious time may well make the difference between survival and extinction for much of life and civilization.

There is no quick technological fix to the greenhouse phenomenon. The only solution is to eliminate the sources of the problem. At both the Bellagio Conference held in Italy in 1987 and the Changing Atmosphere Conference held in Toronto, Ontario, in 1988, scientists from around the world agreed that the first order of business is a radical reduction in the burning of fossil fuels— coal, oil, and natural gas—that produce CO_2 emissions. The goal is a 50 percent or more reduction in fossil fuel use by the year 2015.[1] To reach that goal, governments must begin immediately to devise programs to increase and use efficiency. That initiative should begin with the United States and the Soviet Union, who together account for nearly 45 percent of the fossil fuel burning CO_2 emissions on the entire planet.[2]

Slashing fossil fuel use by half in less than three decades will require an enormous shift in economic, military, and political priorities, a shift so extraordinary in scope that it would require a worldwide mobilization effort on a scale never before experienced in recorded history. The task becomes even more difficult in light of the fact that many economists are currently forecasting a doubling of CO_2 emissions in the coming decades to keep pace with economic development projections.[3]

Improvement in energy efficiency can go a long way toward eliminating unnecessary CO_2 emissions. It is interesting to note that energy efficiency varies widely among industrial countries. The Soviet Union and East European nations rely on an industrial infrastructure that is highly energy inefficient. If these countries were to raise their standard of living to Western levels, they would need to use twice as much energy per capita.[4] Even among the Western industrial powers energy efficiency is not uniform. Japan uses half the energy per capita that the U.S. uses while enjoying a comparable standard of living.

American households are notoriously energy inefficient. The average U.S. home uses two to three times as much energy per square foot as the average Swedish home.[5]

For example, consider the simple replacement of a 75-watt incandescent bulb by a single 18-watt fluorescent bulb. According to Bill Keepin and Gregory Kats of the Rocky Mountain Institute, the fluorescent bulb produces just as much light over its lifetime but its lower power consumption "prevents the burning of 400 pounds of coal, prevents the release of twelve pounds of sulfur dioxide into the atmosphere (which produces acid rain), and saves the American economy \$15."[6]

Current household appliances are also extremely energy inefficient and add to the amount of fossil fuels being burned and to an increase in CO_2 emissions.

As of 1981, fewer than 5 percent of all the air conditioners sold in the U.S. had energy efficiency ratios of at least 9.5 despite the fact that comparable units at competitive costs were available with energy efficiencies of 14.[7] According to a survey conducted by the Pacific Gas and Electric Company, 70 percent of the appliance salespeople in the country do not even broach the question of energy efficiency when making a sale.[8]

Japan is now selling frost-free refrigerators that require half as much energy as current models being sold in the U.S. and air conditioners that are half again as efficient as 95 percent of the air conditioners presently in use.[9]

David Goldstein of the National Resource Defense Council estimates that if a consumer purchased one of the new more efficient refrigerators for \$50 more than the conventional models, the slight additional cost would result in a savings of \$600 in new generating capacity by the local utility company.[10] Several utility companies are now experimenting with special incentive programs, including low-interest loans to encourage the purchase of energy-efficient appliances for the home. Others are investigating the idea of leasing energy-efficient heat pumps, furnaces, water heaters, refrigerators, and air conditioners to customers below market costs.[11]

The federal government can play a major role in encouraging energy efficiency in the home by enacting legislation that would set minimum efficiency standards for appliances, just as was done with auto fuel efficiency standards in 1975. California and some other states have already passed laws requiring minimum energy efficiency standards for household appliances.[12] In 1986 Congress passed the National Appliance Energy Conservation Act requiring major appliances to be 15 to 25 percent more energy efficient in 1990 than they were in 1985. The legislation, which was vetoed by President Reagan, would have cut consumer energy bills by $28 billion by the year 2000, and eliminated the need to generate 22,000 megawatts of electrical generating capacity—greatly reducing the amount of fuel being burned and the amount of CO_2 released into the atmosphere.[13]

As local utilities and state and federal agencies begin to turn their attention to energy-saving programs for the home, particular attention has to be given to the poor. According to a Department of Energy study conducted in 1982, families who make under $5,000 per year spend approximately 15 percent of their income on fuel, while families earning over $35,000 annually spend 3 percent of their income on fuel.[14] The poor are less able to invest in energy-saving appliances and will require outside assistance if we are to establish an effective, society-wide energy efficiency regime.

Increased energy efficiency in the home needs to be matched by similar energy saving programs on the road. By setting Federal standards on automobile fuel efficiency at 40 miles per gallon, it would be possible to greatly reduce CO_2 emissions without suffering adverse economic effects. (Automobiles are currently being tested that can achieve 60 to 100 miles per gallon.) Yet the Department of Transportation recently cut back the vehicle fuel standards from 27.5 to 26 miles per gallon. The 1.5 mpg rollback "resulted in a doubling of oil imports from the Persian Gulf . . . and commits us to higher carbon emissions (about an extra 57 million tons of carbon)."[15] Mass transit and car pooling are also effective means of conserving energy and reducing CO_2 emissions. Commuting to and from work consumes one-third of all the daily gasoline used in the U.S. In 1987, over 110 million people commuted to work. Of that number, only 4.5 million used buses and a mere 2.3 million rode the rails. While 21.7 million commuters used car pools or van pools, an overwhelming 70.8 million chose to drive alone.[16]

Greater attention needs to be focused on improving mass transit, including an expanded federal program of assistance to state and local municipalities to improve bus and intercity rail service.

Public and private employers can and should help coordinate car and van pooling programs for their employees. Incentives can be built into the process. For example, on Route 66 from suburban Virginia to Washington, D.C., the lanes are reserved during rush hours for the exclusive use of cars seating three or more people. These and other innovative programs aimed at the transportation sector are essential if we are to radically reduce our use of fuel oil and cut down on the emission of CO_2 spewed into the atmosphere.

A global program of energy efficiency could save trillions of dollars in unnecessary energy expenditures, and greatly reduce the amount of CO_2 released into the atmosphere.[17] Here in the U.S., a study commissioned by the DOE in 1979 concluded that the implementation of energy efficiency programs could reduce the energy used to heat and cool buildings by 50 percent and reduce energy requirements for industrial processes by 25 percent while doubling vehicle fuel efficiency.[18]

According to a recent article in *Scientific American*, the technology is now available to construct energy-efficient office buildings that would save enough energy in 50 years to avoid building "85 power plants and the equivalent of two Alaskan pipelines." While a nationwide energy efficiency program would cost approximately $50 billion, it could save $110 billion per year in energy expenses, for a net saving of $60 billion each year.[19]

A rigorous national campaign to improve energy efficiency in the home, office, industry, and on the road could reduce the national energy bill from $400 billion to $270 billion, and greatly reduce the burning of fuel and the emission of CO_2 and other greenhouse gases into the atmosphere.[20] Yet as Representative Claudine Schneider pointed out at Congressional hearings on the greenhouse effect, "Less than two percent of the upwards of $50 billion per year in federal energy subsidies goes to promote greater reliance on energy efficiency."[21]

Recycling waste is still another way to reduce fossil fuel use and CO_2 emissions. The laws of thermodynamics tell us that recycling metals and organic material is generally more energy efficient than mining virgin ores or growing biological resources from the seed. For example, recycling just one aluminum can saves the equivalent of a half-can of gasoline, requires only 5 percent as much energy as would be required to produce the same can from bauxite, and reduces air pollution by 95 percent.[22] Recycling paper reduces the energy used per ton produced by up to three-quarters of what would be required for harvesting and processing trees to make new paper, and uses only half the amount of water.[23] Recycling already provides about half of the annual demand for antimony; one-third of the demand for iron, lead, and nickel; and one-fourth of our need for mercury, silver, gold, and platinum.[24]

David Morris, of the Institute for Local Self-Reliance, captures the enormous potential of recycling in addressing both the energy crisis and the global warming of the planet.

A city the size of San Francisco disposes of more aluminum than is produced by a small bauxite mine, more copper than a medium-size copper mine, and more paper than a good-sized timber stand. San Francisco is a mine. The question is how to mine it most effectively and how to get the maximum value from the collected materials.[25]

Several states have initiated comprehensive recycling programs. In New York State, for example, a deposit is required on the sale of all soft-drink and beer cans and bottles—metal, glass, and plastic. (Over 400 million cases of beverage containers are sold each year in the state.) According to a study conducted by the Beer Wholesalers Association, within twenty-four months of enactment of the deposit law, the state had saved $50 million dollars in cleanup costs, $19 million in solid waste disposal, and most important, $50 to $100 million on energy. In addition, the deposit law spawned 3,800 new jobs.[26]

Between 1981 and 1986 more than half of the 300 billion aluminum cans sold in the U.S. were returned for recycling. Consumers received $1 billion in deposit returns and the industry used 22 percent less energy to produce a pound of aluminum.[27]

Recycling paper products and other biological materials also saves energy consumption and reduces CO_2 emissions. In Maryland, an aggressive paper recycling program has been in effect for over a decade. The state government also buys half of its bond stationery and most of its facial and toilet paper from recycled paper compnies. Through this one program alone, the state has saved enough energy to heat 9,000 homes for a year.[28]

Currently, over 200 mills in the U.S. are operating exclusively with recycled paper. While the energy savings are significant, the savings in forests is enormous. The recycling of one Sunday edition of *The New York Times* would allow 75,000 trees to remain uncut.[29] It is estimated that if one-half of the paper used in the world were to be recycled, it would save 8 million hectares of forestland, or about 6 percent of the total forest cover of Europe.[30]

If incentive programs and regulatory procedures for energy efficiency and recycling are not implemented soon or prove to be weak and ineffective, the federal government will be forced to establish a national rationing system to address the issue of fuel shortages and the increased threat to the environment and atmosphere posed by the emission of CO_2, NO_2, and other greenhouse gases. Rationing proved to be an effective tool during World War II and during the short-lived energy crisis of 1973–1974. Many energy experts and environmental scientists are already convinced that rationing policies are inevitable and will likely come into use before the turn of the century.

While conservation is absolutely essential, the fact is that any current conservation proposals will be extremely limited in scope because they have to be implemented within the existing high-energy infrastructure. Any attempt to extend conservation efforts beyond the narrow confines dictated by the current infrastructure can only lead to serious dislocations at various points along the energy flow line.

For example, consider America's legendary addiction to air conditioning. The first air cooler was installed in 1922 in a movie theater. Today, Americans consume more electricity for air conditioning during the three summer months alone than does the entire population of the People's Republic of China to meet all of its annual electrical needs. And China has four times the number of people![31]

During the past three decades, when energy was moving through the flow line at unprecedented rates, buildings in every part of the country—from the World Trade Center in New York to Holiday Inns in California—were designed with windows that do not open. At the time, everyone assumed that there would be plenty of electricity to guarantee yearly air-conditioned comfort in a completely closed environment. Yet, if thermostats are to be set higher, occupants of the buildings need fresh air and occasional breezes. But the only way that can be accomplished is by changing millions of windows in hundreds of thousands of structures— clearly a massive use of energy, resources, time, and people.

This is but one of tens of thousands of examples we could point to. None of this is to deny the absolute necessity of conserving as much as possible. But conservation works to the extent that the system is designed to accept a lower energy throughput. Industrial, urbanized society is specifically designed for just the opposite purpose—to maximize energy flow. Given this basic fact of modern life, conservation measures within the existing high-energy infrastructure can only serve as a transitional adaptation along the road to a low-entropy future.

A New Infrastructure for the Solar Age

While increased energy efficiency in fossil fuel consumption is an important short-run goal, in the long run it will be necessary to make a wholesale transition from nonrenewable to renewable sources of energy. That transition needs to begin in earnest now with the development and expansion of solar, hydro, geothermal, and wind power energy technologies. Unfortunately, between 1980 and 1988 the Department of Energy systematically eliminated 75 percent of the research and development programs in renewable energy technologies, at the very time that such efforts have become vital in addressing what is becoming the greatest environmental crisis in world history.[32] The next oil crisis looms on the horizon and the planet continues to heat up with every gallon of fuel burned. We have no choice but to turn our attention to alternative energy strategies if we are to save civilization and the planet from an apocalypse in the coming century.

Despite a conscious effort by the Reagan administration to scuttle the research and development of alternative energy technologies, public utilities and the private sector have been quietly at work preparing the foundation for a solar infrastructure.

In 1988 scientists at the Solar Energy Research Institute announced that they had successfully increased the efficiency of solar panels from 8 to 11 percent. When solar panels reach 15 percent efficiency they will be cost competitive with conventional fossil fuel energy sources.[33] Already solar powered technologies are being used throughout the U.S. to heat homes and offices and to power small battery operated machines and processes.

Hydropower is also being expanded to fill the vacuum that will be left when oil stocks run dry. Canada, which has 100,000 megawatts of untapped hydropower potential is hoping to develop an energy market in the U.S.[34] In New England, where water is still abundant, it is estimated that new hydropower development could increase electric generating capacity by 7 percent.[35]

The Solar Energy Research Institute projects that 19 percent of the U.S. energy supply could be generated by the various solar-based or soft energy path technologies by the year 2025.[36] Effective energy conservation could fill in much of the remaining vacuum.

The transition to a soft energy path will eliminate much of the CO_2 emissions created by fossil fuel burning technologies. Still, even if we are successful at limiting CO_2 emissions, other greenhouse gases will need to be eliminated if we are to slow the global warming trend. In 1987 thirty-four nations signed the Montreal Protocol on chlorofluorocarbons, which calls for a 35 to 50 percent reduction in CFC emissions by the year 2000. While the press and industry made much of the document, many environmental scientists contend that the agreement falls short of the steps required to effectively address the growing problems of CFC emissions. Then, too, concern is mounting that many nations will simply disregard both the spirit and the letter of the agreement, and will continue to allow CFC emissions within their national boundaries.[37]

Industry has developed efficient alternatives to CFCs that could be eased into the marketplace with minimum inconvenience to consumers and the economy. Phasing out CFC gases, then, is no longer a technical issue, but rather a political one. In order to eliminate the widespread use of CFC gases, public pressure has to be mobilized on a global scale. Industries and nations are likely to take the course of least resistance, continuing to delay the final phasing out of CFC gases, unless the public demands that effective action be taken.

Eliminating CO_2, CFC emissions, and other greenhouse gases will arrest the global warming trend. Reversing it, however, can only be achieved by planting trees. It is more than a bit ironic that the only viable solution to the greenhouse crisis is the reforestation of the planet. The Tree of Life, a long-revered metaphor in Judeo-Christian theology, is now emerging as a symbol of environmental salvation in the coming century. As mentioned earlier, trees absorb carbon dioxide from the atmosphere in the process of photosynthesis. It is estimated that to arrest the effects of the greenhouse crisis, it will be necessary to plant enough trees on the planet to cover an area equal to the entire land mass of Australia.

Governments need to launch ambitious reforestation campaigns over the next several decades if we are to have any hope of reducing the planetary fever and healing the globe. The industrial nations will have to be willing to provide subsidies and direct payments to Third World countries to encourage reforestation programs. Within the developed nations, government-sponsored reforestation projects need to be encouraged. In the U.S., legislation passed in 1985 provides incentives for a modest reforestation effort. The Food Security Act pays farmers to remove erodible cropland from production and maintain it as a conservation reserve. While much of the land will be seeded to grass, the government hopes to seed some 5 million acres with trees. The trees and grass will both store excess atmospheric carbon. In China, where forest cover declined 25 percent between 1949 and 1960 to provide charcoal for the backyard steel furnaces of Mao's Great Leap Forward campaign, plans are now underway to reforest 20 percent of the entire land mass of the country by the year 2001.[38]

Planting trees is more than an ecological requisite. It also provides a vision of hope for the future. When we plant a tree, we are making a commitment to restore the earth to health, to renew the life pulse of the planet. In the coming years, millions of people around the world can join with their governments in reseeding the earth. Reforesting the planet is an essential priority if we are to make a successful transition from a fossil fuel to a solar culture.

Among climatologists and environmental scientists a consensus has emerged regarding the planetary crises brought on by the greenhouse global warming trend. Virtually all of the experts engaged with the issue agree that the world community must radically reduce its reliance on fossil fuels and immediately pursue alternative energy technologies. While most favor solar-based, soft energy technologies, a murmur of support is being voiced for what is euphemistically referred to as a new generation of "safe nuclear power" plants.

Most environmental scientists would consider the term safe nuclear power an oxymoron. Still, the nuclear industry has launched a spirited and aggressive public relations campaign to convince Congress and the country that the peaceful atom is our last hope and best alternative to fossil fuel burning technologies.

At Congressional hearings held in June 1988, on global warming and alternative energy technologies, Bill Keepin and Gregory Kats of the Rocky Mountain Institute presented the results of a study analyzing the feasibility of nuclear power as an energy substitute. Their findings shatter any illusion the nuclear proponents might entertain about the prospects of a nuclear future.

In order to present the most favorable case for the introduction of a large-scale nuclear power program, the authors of the study projected that a new nuclear power plant could be constructed in six years rather than the customary ten to twelve years; that construction costs could be kept to $1,000 per installed KW in contrast to existing construction costs, which average around $3,000 per installed KW; and that the political and scientific objections could be adequately addressed, including the dual problem of guaranteeing the safety of nuclear power plants and the safe storage of nuclear waste.[39]

Even if all of the above conditions were met, it would be necessary to construct a new, 1,000 megavolt-output nuclear power plant "every 1.6 to 2.4 days for the next 38 years" to meet energy demand worldwide.[40] A massive construction schedule of this scale would cost trillions of dollars and would bankrupt civilization well before the switch was triggered on a majority of the plants.

Just to replace the present generation of fossil fuel plants with nuclear plants in the U.S. alone would cost more than $2 trillion dollars, according to Critical Mass, a Washington-based energy organization founded by Ralph Nader.[41]

The Keepin and Kats study compared nuclear power construction to energy efficiency programs and concluded that "each dollar invested in electric efficiency displaces nearly seven times more carbon than a dollar invested in nuclear power."[42]

Solar technologies—the soft energy path—offer the best hope of providing an alternative energy source to fossil fuel burning technologies. Still, a word of caution is in order. The shift in energy base from fossil fuels to solar technologies will not be easy.

Many seem to think that the Solar Age will be just like our own, only cleaner. Cars will be electric, so there will be no smog; cities will run on solar collectors; homes will be inexpensively heated and cooled through sun power; organic material will be converted at biomass plants into energy fuels; quaint windmills will dot the landscape, reminding us of a more tranquil past, even as the pollution-free machines of industry churn on, quietly manufacturing consumer goods to sustain our style of living. In the Solar Age, it would seem, you *can* have your cake and eat it too.

In fact this is far from the truth. The transition period to the Solar Age will require a complete reformulation of economic activity at every level of American society. Once we grasp the enormous implications of shifting the energy base of society from a concentrated stock (fossil fuels) to a diffuse flow (solar), it becomes apparent that our existing industrial structure is completely unsuited to a solar future.

In the most literal sense, highly concentrated nonrenewable energy has shaped today's economy. In order to maintain the existing institutional superstructure, we would have to continue to rely on a highly concentrated flow of energy through the system. Solar energy, however, is not concentrated like nonrenewable energy and is therefore unsuited for a highly centralized industrial life-style.

While there are many different techniques for harnessing energy from the sun—solar thermal projects, photovoltaics, wind power, biomass conversion—and numerous modes of collection, ranging from sophisticated high-tech systems to ancient passive solar systems, all are based on tapping into a diffused flow of energy, rather than a concentrated stock. As a flow, solar power has the obvious advantages of being clean, abundant, and virtually inexhaustible (that is, until the sun burns itself out in billions of years). At the same time, there are inherent disadvantages, at least in terms of trying to maintain our contemporary form of social existence.[43]

Because solar radiation is diffuse, it must be concentrated to do work. Since the laws of thermodynamics tell us that work can only be performed when there is a temperature difference between two places, and since solar energy falls essentially equally on each square foot of land in any given geographical area, the solar flow must be collected. If electricity is desired, the stored solar energy must be transformed from one state into another. The nature of the flow and the economies of scale of solar technologies are most suited to small units, such as those that could provide enough heat and hot water for an individual home. Most solar advocates agree that at this stage of the technology, and for the foreseeable future, converting existing private homes to solar power will only provide 60 percent of the dwelling's energy needs.[44] While far more efficient solar homes could be built from scratch, the conversion will be a slow process; 75 percent of all the structures that will exist in the United States by the year 2000 have already been built.[45]

At the industrial and urban level, solar energy does not lend itself to the complex technological organization required by contemporary society. One estimate, for example, indicates that in order to run our current industrial superstructure we would need to cover between 10 and 20 percent of the total U.S. land area with various types of solar collectors.[46] Another estimate shows that Manhattan daily consumes more than six times the energy that could be provided by a 100 percent efficient collector of all the solar flow that falls on the city.[47] To power New York City through various solar techniques, an area many times the city's mass would have to be given over entirely to solar collectors. While New York is obviously unique in its consumption of energy, other major urban areas will be subject to similar strictures in the Solar Age.

The sheer size of the solar infrastructure that would have to be erected to maintain modern society is mind-boggling. So too is the amount of time and labor that would be required to build and sustain it. For example, to equip just 3 million houses with solar collectors would require a work force of 200,000 people producing and installing 800 million square feet of solar collectors at a cost of $20 billion.[48] To construct a solar energy base for a major urban area would take millions of workers. As E. F. Schumacher wryly noted, "While you can heat a house with solar energy very comfortably, you can't heat Rockefeller Center. In fact, solar energy plus wind power would not push the lifts up and down. And most of the accommodations in Rockefeller Center are inaccessible if there are no lifts: Fancy someone climbing thirty or fifty floors."[49] Schumacher contends that large-scale production and urban living do not fit the model of the Solar Age. Murray Bookchin, the author and ecologist-anarchist, agrees. Bookchin argues that solar power and wind power "cannot supply man with the bulky quantities of raw materials and the large blocks of energy needed to sustain densely concentrated populations and highly centralized industries. . . . Solar devices . . . will produce relatively small quantities of power."[50] Ecologist William Ophuls concurs: "Conversion to exclusive dependence on solar energy would clearly require major changes in our technology and economy in the direction of greater frugality and decentralization."[51]

These statements seem to make sense when viewed in the context of thermodynamic realities. Still, to some they appear heretical. Many solar advocates, for instance, claim that frugality or austerity should not be equated with a sun-powered future. All the energy we require will be available in the coming age, they say. The fallacy in this argument is an unstated myth that solar energy performs work on its own, and since it is nonpolluting and renewable, the more solar power moving through the energy flow lines, the better.

Although the evidence suggests otherwise, let us assume just for the sake of argument that new collecting techniques could be discovered that would allow us to very efficiently concentrate the flow of solar radiation far beyond the capacity now available or even deemed conceivable by many engineers. If this remarkably efficient recovery process were somehow possible, we could then support an urbanized, industrial-technological society through solar flow. But what would be the result? Simply this: we would continue to witness the exponential increase of entropy here on earth as solar energy is used to convert more and more of our limited terrestrial energy resources (matter) into the production process, transforming them from a usable to an unusable state. It is not, then, just the form of energy a society uses that is critical; it is also the amount of energy. If solar energy actually could flow in highly concentrated forms for industrial use, we would experience many of the same economic and social dislocations that result from our high energy use now. That is because *the use of solar energy cannot be divorced from the stock of fixed terrestrial matter that it interacts on and converts. In living and in industrial processes, solar energy must always be combined with other terrestrial resources in order to produce a product. That conversion process always results in the further dissipation of the fixed stock of terrestrial resources on the planet.*

There are many current proposals for diverting as much of the remaining flow of nonrenewable energy as possible into the building of a new infrastructure of institutional and mechanical transformers that would collect, store, process, and direct solar energy. While many of these proposals make sense, it should be made abundantly clear that any such infrastructure is only temporary and can serve as little more than a tiny halfway house to soften the impact of transition. In the long run, a solar infrastructure derived from and dependent on nonrenewable resources cannot be supported on a scale necessary to maintain highly industrialized economies. The nonrenewable resources will simply not be available in the quantities required.

In examining the potential of solar power, environmentalist Howard Odum has developed the concept of *net energy*. Net energy is the energy yield of a technology, minus the energy invested in recovering it. Odum argues that "solar energy can generate some net, concentrated energy in the form of food, fiber and electricity, but the amount per area is small because most of the solar energy is consumed by the various structures that have to be maintained and operated to collect and concentrate the energy."[52]

While Odum is clearly in favor of solar use over coal, uranium, or oil, we must realize, he says, that solar technologies will require vast amounts of nonrenewable energy and material resources to make the millions upon millions of solar devices that will be required. In essence, it will be necessary to construct an entirely new energy infrastructure for society. Although solar techniques may not be as capital-intensive as petroleum refineries and synfuel plants, the volume of scarce resources required is still significant. Converting just 2.5 million homes to 60 percent solar efficiency, for example, would consume fully one-third of all U.S. copper production.[53] If one-half of all U.S. electricity were produced through solar fuel cells—the most efficient converters now available—the building effort would annually require more platinum than is yearly produced worldwide.[54] Truly huge amounts of other nonrenewable resources would also be necessary to build a massive solar infrastructure. Among these are cadmium, silicon, germanium, selenium, gallium, arsenic, and sulfur; as well as megatons of glass, plastics, and rubber; and great volumes of ethylene glycol, liquid metals, and freon. According to one source, "If we settle on cadmium-sulfide cells for direct photovoltaic conversion . . . it would require the entire 1978 world population of cadmium to produce only 180,000 megawatts of installed capacity, or about 10 percent of the capacity the world had in place last year."[55]

Writing in the *Atlantic Economic Journal* in December 1978, Nicholas Georgescu-Roegen pointed out the obvious flaw in current approaches to the harnessing of solar energy:

The truth is that any presently feasible recipe for the direct use of solar energy is a "parasite," as it were, of the current technology, based mainly on fossil fuels. All the necessary equipment (including the collectors) are produced by recipes based on sources of energy other than the sun's. And it goes without saying that, like all parasites, any solar technology based on the present feasible recipes would subsist only as long as its "host" survives. . . . The intensity of solar radiation reaching the ground level being extremely weak, a large material scaffold is needed for its collection. . . . It is highly plausible that the difficulty may not be superable at all, given that the intensity of solar radiation is a cosmological constant beyond our control.[56]

Our future is a solar future, of that there can be no doubt. The question is whether we will continue in our old habits of thinking and futilely attempt to generate a high-technology, resource-intensive solar energy base that will hasten the degradation of the planet, or whether we will generate an energy base that, at every step of its formation and use, seeks to keep the flow of energy and resources at a minimum.

Not surprisingly, the high-tech, resource-intensive mode is favored by big business. Of the nine largest photovoltaics firms (photovoltaics are collectors that store sunlight in batteries for later use as electricity), eight are now owned by large corporations, five of them major oil companies. According to Richard Munson of the Solar Lobby, Exxon and ARCO will soon control more than half the industry between them. Other facets of solar technology are also being gobbled up by big business. For example, twelve of the top twenty-five solar companies are now controlled by corporate giants with annual sales of $1 billion or more. Among them: General Electric, General Motors, Alcoa, and Grumman. Obviously, it is the goal of these companies to ensure that solar power is developed in a highly centralized manner.[57]

The "big is beautiful" solar strategy is already leaving the drawing board and moving into actual production. Aerospace firms, for instance, are lobbying heavily to induce the government to fund "Sunsat," a solar satellite that will be bigger than the island of Manhattan. And in Barstow, California, McDonnell-Douglas, backed by hefty federal funding, is completing work on its "power tower."[58] The $130 million project consists of 2,200 giant mirrors that will focus sunlight on a boiler atop a 500-foot concrete tower.[59] These schemes are obviously solar technologies developed by a fossil-fuel mentality; that is, they attempt to concentrate a diffuse solar flow as much as possible in the hopes of turning it into a centralized energy stock, much like coal and oil. The attempt, however, will only cause greater disorder than any possible value gained. The amount of nonrenewable energy resources that go into constructing the parts of a giant solar satellite and launching it into space where it must be assembled is far greater than the amount of energy the Sunsat could produce for many years. Concentrating solar rays in such high density and beaming them back to collectors on earth will cause microwave radiation pollution that will endanger the health of anyone living or working near the collector. Once the power has been collected at a central location, it must then be shipped as electricity through power lines. This will require the use of more quantities of nonrenewable resources to construct this part of the infrastructure. The "power tower" suffers similar problems. The more concentrated the collection of solar rays, the less net energy that will remain.

Even on a smaller scale, there are important choices to be made. For example, in home units, solar power can be provided through either low or high technology. The higher the technology used, the less net energy that will be provided, because more nonrenewable resources must be used to build and maintain the collecting infrastructure. For instance, in the high-tech—or *active*— home system, sunlight is first concentrated in a collector made of nonrenewable resources; then the solar energy is stored in either air or water housed in containers manufactured of nonrenewables; finally it is moved by fans or pumps to perform the work required. Another high-tech system is one in which photovoltaics concentrate energy and store it in batteries. Once again, nonrenewable materials form the base for the technology. While these systems clearly use a less intensive form of technology than do solar satellites and power towers, small-scale home units of an active nature must still depend ultimately on the supply of copper, platinum, and other diminishing ores out of which the solar utilization equipment is manufactured.

Passive home solar systems tend to be less ecologically damaging and provide the most net energy yield. In a passive system, homes are actually designed and constructed in such a way that they naturally remain cool in summer and warm in winter. Although many workable prototypes of passive solar homes have recently been developed by architects, anthropologists can point to workable systems that were developed hundreds and even thousands of years ago by peoples who had no other way to maintain their homes.

A New Infrastructure for the Solar Age

The Solar Age will require a greater conformity to the ancient rhythms of life. Those wedded to the Newtonian world view and the Industrial Age will no doubt regard these observations about solar technology as pessimistic. Many will consider it inconceivable that urban life, industrial production, and many of the creature comforts that make up the so-called American Dream are antithetical to the Solar Age. However, ecologists and economists like Georgescu-Roegen, Daly, Odum, Bookchin, and Ophuls would argue that to ignore the historical reality in front of us in favor of maintaining false expectations is madness and will lead to an even greater fall for humankind, perhaps an irreversible one. Regardless of which course we follow, the coming transition is sure to be accompanied by suffering and sacrifice. But there is really no other choice. The fact is, the suffering will be minimized if the transition from the existing energy base to the new one is made now in a thoughtful, orderly manner, rather than later, out of desperation, when we finally deplete our existing fossil fuel reserves and heat up the earth to a point beyond adaption and survival.

Third World Development

Trapped in the early stages of industrial development, Third World nations are going to experience the brunt of the transition into the greenhouse world and the Solar Age. Already the deepening energy crisis and global warming trend are forcing Third World countries to reappraise conventional economic development models and the set of assumptions that underlies them.

According to the prevailing wisdom, the more the industrial economies grow, the more the rest of the world will benefit. This assumption rests on the idea that the faster we can convert raw resources into economic goods, the more permanent value or wealth we create that can be divided among the peoples of the earth. With this as the central principle of international economic development, it is no wonder that advances in technology are viewed as the source for creating more and more "permanent" wealth. The laws of thermodynamics, however, provide a very different frame of reference. The fact is, the faster the developed nations convert raw resources into economic goods, the less is available in nature's storehouse for other countries and for future generations. Advances in technology, for the most part, serve to speed up the conversion of more resources in a shorter period of time, depleting nature's stock and creating even greater waste and disorder in the process.

As this reality begins to sink in, it is important to recognize the

fact that the remaining reservoirs of untapped nonrenewable resources are primarily in the hands of the poor Third World
nations. These resources are their only remaining trump card to
bargain for a more equitable redistribution of wealth between the
industrialized countries and their own. The Middle East oil-
producing countries have used this leverage effectively in the
past. Their cartel arrangement to control the terms and the flow of
oil exports is now being copied by other Third World countries
dealing in other nonrenewable resources. Cartels have now been
established to regulate the price of bauxite, copper, iron, chromium, and lead. Says *Fortune* magazine, "If the material export-
ers succeed in this endeavor, the days of sustained improvement
in living standards in the advanced industrial countries may well
come to an end."[60]

To those of us who have lived for decades on huge quantities
of energy and resources provided by the Third World, it is easy to
resent the squeeze that cartels will put on our economic system. A
popular country-and-western song of the summer of 1979 summed
up the frustration many Americans felt over escalating OPEC oil
prices: "No crude, no food." In other words, if the Third World
won't sell us its petroleum, then we should withhold food exports
from the world's hungry. This kind of jingoistic attitude on our
part is not only morally and politically indefensible, but also
threatens our very survival. The choice is ours. We can either
accept the new terms presented by Third World nations and cut
back dramatically on our energy flow and material consumption,
or we can intervene militarily to seize the resources we need.
This latter choice would not go unresisted by the Soviet
Union and other world powers. Competition over scarce resources could well lead to a superpower confrontation in the
years ahead.

Most of us simply do not understand what is taking place in the
Third World. While we pay lip service to the tragedy of squalor,
hunger, and overpopulation in the Southern Hemisphere of the
globe, we really have no conception of the misery in which over
half the planet lives. Fully 800 million human beings are barely
surviving in what the World Bank calls "absolute poverty" on an

annual income of $200 or less.[61] Fifteen to twenty million Third
World deaths annually—three-fourths of them children—directly
result from malnutrition. As you read this, twenty-eight people
are dying in our world each minute as a consequence of hunger.[62]
Eighty percent of the world's population, mostly living in villages, have no system of health care.[63]

Yet, as long as we in the United States continue to consume
one-third of the world's resources annually, the Third World can
never rise to even a semblance of a standard of living that can
adequately support human life with dignity. Those who are irate
over the formation of resource cartels as an economic weapon to
be used against rich nations like our own had best ask themselves
what they would do if they were living in the Third World. Any
Third World leader who continues to allow the industrialized
nations to plunder his country's natural resources is likely to lose
popular support in his own country.

To Third World people, talk of the era of limits, curbing
material expectations, establishing no growth economic policies,
appears to be just one more attempt by the industrialized nations
to keep poor countries in their place of international subservience.
Third World countries, just beginning their own industrial output,
see the ecological concerns of the rich as little more than an effort
by countries like the United States to hold on to their wealth by
hindering economic growth among the poor. In a paper presented
before the World Council of Churches' 1979 Conference on
Faith, Science and the Future, C. T. Kurien spoke for many when
he offered a Third World perspective on the "limits to growth"
thesis:

> It is a small affluent minority of the world's population that
> whips up a hysteria about the finite resources of the world and
> pleads for a conservationist ethic in the interests of those yet
> to be born; it is the same group that makes an organized effort
> to prevent those who happen to be outside the gates of their
> affluence from coming to have even a tolerable level of living.
> It does not call for a divine's insight to see what the real
> intentions are.[64]

Kurien's point is well taken. As long as we continue to devour a disproportionate share of the world's resources, squandering the great bulk of them on trivialities while the rest of the world struggles to find its next meal, we have no right to lecture other peoples on how to conduct their economic development. Therefore, if we are truly committed to preventing our planet from being turned into a giant industrial sewer, we must begin, now, voluntarily, to substantially limit our own material wealth. We must show our own willingness to accept hard sacrifices in the name of humanity.

However, Third World nations should not harbor hopes that they can ever reach the material abundance that has existed in America over the past few decades. According to economist Herman Daly:

> If it requires roughly one-third of the world's annual production of mineral resources to support that 6% of the world's population residing in the U.S. at the standard of consumption to which it is thought that the rest of the world aspires, then it follows that present resource flows would allow the extension of the U.S. standard to at most 18% of the world's population, with nothing left over for the other 82%. Without the services of the poor 82%, the "rich" 18% could not possibly maintain their wealth. A considerable share of world resources must be devoted to maintaining the poor 82% at at least subsistence. Consequently even the 18% figure is an overestimate.[65]

It is thus impossible for the rest of the world to develop as the United States has. In fact, as we have already seen, resource scarcity makes it impossible for even the United States to continue at anything near its present level of energy flow. This is not, however, to dismiss the absolute necessity of fostering economic development in the Third World. The question is: What kind of development is appropriate to poor nations?

When Western-style progress comes to a Third World nation, "instant underdevelopment" is usually the result. In other words, the masses of people of these countries actually become poorer than before development began. The major reason for this is that

Western industrialism favors cities over rural areas and highly centralized, energy- and capital-intensive production over human labor. As nations seek to industrialize, jobs actually diminish because production is automated. At the same time, mechanized agriculture promoted by the much-vaunted Green Revolution has the effect of forcing peasant farmers off the land. This is so because mechanized agriculture requires expensive inputs of energy into the farming process. Because of this, small farmers are squeezed out of the market. Dislocated peasant farmers are forced to move to the city to try to find jobs. This process is taking place all over the Third World. By the year 2000, it is estimated that 1 billion more people will be jammed into Third World urban areas than lived there in 1975.[66] As forced urbanization proceeds, greater poverty ensues. Further, as agriculture around the world follows the U.S. model, the world's food situation becomes more precarious because farming becomes increasingly reliant on non-renewable resources. If the entire world converted to our style of agriculture, up to 80 percent of all energy conversion would go into food production, and we would exhaust all petrochemicals within a decade.[67]

High-energy industrial development also brings with it other disruptions to traditional patterns of living. In the 1880s, it is said, a Saudi Arabian sheikh discovered oil bubbling out of the sand in a remote desert. He ordered the hole filled in, and forbade anyone to reveal what they had seen. Why? Because he feared that Westerners would come barreling in with their technology and contempt for tradition. The sheikh's motives might well be suspect, but he was certainly correct in his fears. As high-energy technology is exported to the Third World, it brings with it a unique ideology. Third World leaders continue to naively assume that they can bring in the wealth and technique of a country like the United States but not bring with it a set of modern technological values that are destructive to the traditional culture.

Unfortunately, many Third World countries are using their newfound wealth to industrialize their economies along the same line as the United States and other so-called developed nations. Their ill-conceived economic policies can only lead to tragedy for both their own nations and the planet as the entropy process escalates even faster toward a watershed. First of all, at a time when the world is running short of nonrenewable resources it is foolish to develop an economic infrastructure based on a high energy flow of nonrenewable resources. Third World nations like Brazil and Nigeria will have built a massive industrial infrastructure by the year 2000, only to find that they can no longer secure adequate amounts of nonrenewable energy to keep the economic machinery running.

Second, the escalating greenhouse crisis is going to force a global transition away from fossil fuels in the coming decades. Third World nations will find it exceedingly difficult, if not impossible, to justify increased reliance on nonrenewable sources of energy, knowing that it is contributing to the global warming trend that threatens the very survival of our species.

It is clear that Third World nations must seek different forms of development from those used in the industrialized West. High-energy, centralized technology should be eschewed in favor of intermediate technology that is labor intensive and can be used in local villages. This new approach to technology is essential if we are to reverse the mass migration of people from rural communities to squalid, overcrowded cities. Agriculture will still have to form the base of Third World societies. Because of its current development pattern, Arab nations now import 50 percent of their food. By the year 2000, they will be importing 75 percent.[68] For these and other Third World countries any sound policy of development should refocus on the establishment of a labor-intensive farming base that can provide society with a self-sustaining food source.

Several appropriate models for Third World development already exist. Although fraught with environmental problems, the People's Republic of China has at least organized itself in a way that maintains the rural base of the society and favors labor-intensive production. China is not a rich society, but very few people are jobless or homeless. More attention should also be turned to the Gandhian economic model in India. During the anticolonial movement led by Gandhi, the symbol of the struggle became the hand-operated spinning wheel, a simple piece of appropriate technology that allowed each Indian to have some control over his or her own economic livelihood in even the poorest or the most remote village. Gandhian economics favor the country over the city, agriculture over industry, small-scale techniques over high technology. Only this general set of economic priorities can lead to successful Third World development. But once again, it must be said that high-energy-flow nations like the United States must be willing to undertake sacrifices.

Domestic Redistribution
of Wealth

In the next several decades, the cost of nonrenewable energy is going to rise dramatically along with the environmental cost of adjusting to the worsening greenhouse crisis. Together, these two factors are going to seriously compromise the American economy. For the first time in our country's history we will have to deal with the ultimate political and economic question—redistribution of wealth. In the past this question has always remained on the periphery of our national agenda. As long as the economy was continuing to expand, there were always enough marginal gains—or leftovers—to pacify or buy off those at the bottom of the economic pyramid. As the economy begins to contract in the 1990's the call for distribution of the remaining share will be heard from many quarters: Not only the poor, but the working class and middle class as well are likely to join in demands to redistribute both wealth and power.

Today, the top one-fifth of the American population consumes over 40 percent of the nation's income.[69] This is also the class that exercises control over the institutional machinery, that is, the energy flow line of the nation. The battle between this class and the poor is going to intensify in the years ahead; the outcome is likely to hinge on how successful each of these two groups is in recruiting the large middle-income sector to its side.

The stock market crash of 1987 may have signaled the end of the fast-track lifestyle of the 1980's. Many economists are now predicting a deep recession or even a world-wide depression sometime in the 1990's. As economic conditions worsen, the disparity between rich and poor will increase, forcing American society to address the issue of redistribution of wealth and power. Without that redistribution, the poor and working classes in America will rightly condemn any talk of austerity or economic sacrifice in much the same way as Third World nations inveigh against the wealthy countries preaching the gospel of limits.

In nature, whenever one element of an ecosystem multiplies or grows out of proportion to its proper functioning relationship with the rest of the elements in the system, it robs other life forms of the negative entropy (available energy) they need to survive. By doing so, it threatens the continued existence of the entire system. This is also the case in human society. When certain individuals or institutions capture an inordinate amount of the society's energy for themselves, their gross accumulation of wealth and power robs the rest of the members of society of the available energy they need to survive. History shows that whenever a society's energy (wealth) becomes so concentrated in the hands of a few individuals or institutions that the rest of the society suffers energy deprivation so great as to imperil their own survival, the society either crumbles or moves to revolution or both. While nature relies on self-regulating biological laws to restore balance, society must rely on agreed-upon principles of economic justice to achieve the same ends.

Slowing down the entropy process requires both minimizing energy flow-through and redistributing the smaller amounts of energy more equitably among all members of society. Unless both are done at the same time, it is unlikely that the social order could survive intact during the transition period to a new energy base.

Without a fundamental redistribution of wealth, any talk of lowering energy flow and heeding our planet's biological limits will result in the rich locking the poor forever into their subservient status.

Values and Institutions in an Entropic Society

In a high-entropy culture, the overriding purpose of life is to use high energy flow to create material abundance and satisfy every conceivable human desire. Human liberation is thus equated with the accumulation of greater wealth. A primary value is placed on transforming the environment to extract its riches.

Having banished God from society, the high-entropy, materialist value system attempts to provide a heaven on earth. In so doing we have placed man and woman at the center of our universe, and defined the ultimate purpose of our existence as the satisfaction of all possible material wants, however frivolous. We have reduced "reality" to that which can be measured, quantified, and tested. We have denied the qualitative, the spiritual, the metaphysical. We have entered into a pervasive dualism—our minds separated from our bodies, our bodies divorced from the "surrounding" world. We have gloried in the concepts of material progress, efficiency, and specialization above all other values. In the process, we have destroyed family, community, tradition. We have left behind all absolutes, except for our absolute faith in our ability to overcome all limits to our physical activity.

Now our world view and social system are falling victim to the very process of their creation. Everywhere we look, the entropy of our world is reaching staggering proportions. We have become creatures struggling to maintain ourselves in the midst of growing chaos. Each day we experience the truth that biologists have long known: an organism cannot long survive immersed in its own waste.

There is no doubt that we are in need of a massive institutional realignment. Our social structure, geared as it is for a maximum energy flow, is no longer sustainable. Our institutions—their configuration, their purpose, their method of operation—need to be radically transformed. But before we can even begin to broadly outline the nature of agriculture, industry, and commerce in a low-entropy society, we must turn our attention to first principles, those underlying values that give meaning and direction to our lives.

On his 1977 lecture tour of the United States, social critic E. F. Schumacher noted: "The most urgent need of our time is and remains the need for metaphysical reconstruction, a supreme effort to bring clarity into our deepest convictions with regard to the questions What is Man? Where does he come from? and What is the purpose of Life?"[70] These are the big questions of human existence, questions that have absorbed people for thousands of years. Today, in our nine-to-five existence, they are not much discussed and are, in fact, dismissed as being "prescientific" because they do not fit into the neat little standardized explanations of the world offered us by the Newtonian world view. Nonetheless, the big questions of the past are destined to reemerge in the low-entropy world that awaits us. For a low-entropy energy environment provides a completely different orientation to the goals of humanity. The governing ethical principle of a low-entropy world view is to minimize energy flow. Excessive material wealth is recognized as an irreversible diminution of the world's precious resources. In the low-entropy society "less is more" becomes not a throwaway phrase but a truth of the highest magnitude. A low-entropy society deemphasizes material consumption. Frugality becomes the watchword. Human needs are met, but whimsical, self-indulgent desires—the kind pandered to in every shopping center in the country—are not.

The traditional wisdom, as embodied in all the great world religions, has long taught that the ultimate purpose of human life is not the satisfaction of all material desires, but rather the experience of liberation that comes from becoming one with the metaphysical unity of the universe. The goal is to find "the truth that will set us free"; to find out who we really are; to identify with the Absolute Principle that binds together all of existence; to know God. In Sanskrit, it is put most succinctly: *Tat tvam asi* (That art thou). To know this in the very ground of our being and to conduct our life in accordance with this transcendent reality: this is the human development that comes from an adherence to traditional wisdom.

Unwarranted consumption, possessions, and a general attachment to material things have been discouraged by all the great religious teachers of the past:

> The cultivation and expansion of needs is the antithesis of wisdom. It is also the antithesis of freedom and peace. Every increase of needs tends to increase one's dependence on outside forces over which one cannot have control, and therefore increases existential fear. Only by a reduction of needs can one promote a genuine reduction in those tensions which are the ultimate causes of strife and war.

This point has been emphasized again and again in all traditional wisdom. The early Christian mystic Meister Eckhart wrote, "The more we have, the less we own." A Sufi religious teacher has been traditionally described as "he who neither possesses nor is possessed." Mahatma Gandhi believed that "the essence of civilization consists not in the multiplication of wants but in their deliberate and voluntary renunciation."[71]

It is important to understand that the great religious teachings do not promote abject, forced poverty. In fact, the moral and spiritual necessity to redistribute wealth so that all may live decently is proclaimed by all traditional wisdom. What is promoted, however, is restraint, simplicity, voluntary poverty, limits. For if our purpose is to transcend the merely material through contemplation of the divine, possessions and consumption can only clutter our lives by focusing our attention on the transitory, the energy of the world that is constantly degrading. More often than not, the goods we own come to own us. We become attached to them. We fear they will be taken from us. We define ourselves not by who we are but by what we own. In the *Bhagavad-Gita* it is written: "Thinking of sense-objects, man becomes attached thereto. From attachments longing, and from longing anger is born. From anger arises delusion; from delusion, loss of memory is caused. From loss of memory, the discriminative faculty is ruined and from the ruin of discrimination, he perishes."[72] Or, to put it in modern terms: If you don't own an automobile, you don't need to worry about steel-belted radials, gas lines, traffic tie-ups, and car thieves.

In a low-entropy culture the individual is expected to live a much more frugal or Spartan life-style. Consumption ceases to be regarded as an end of human existence and reverts to its original biological function. In the new age, the less production and consumption necessary to maintain a healthy, decent life, the better.

The low-entropy and high-entropy cultures also differ in their approach to labor and production. In a high-energy environment, human labor has no real positive value. The goal of the system is to increase energy flow by eliminating human labor and automating all steps in the production process. Productivity and economic growth become the sole ends of the economy. Where human beings must be involved in the production of goods and services, scientific management is used to remove creativity and individual decision-making by standardizing the method of production. Work, especially physical labor, is considered demeaning, something to avoid. Our society is engrossed with "labor saving" devices that can remove from human hands all work functions. Pay scales reflect our attitudes toward work: those who labor with their backs and their hands are almost universally at the bottom of the scale; white-collar executives who spend their worktime behind desks are at the top.

In the modern scheme of things, work is a necessary evil, a burden that has to be borne in order to make the money that will allow us to do what we really enjoy. Whenever anyone wins a large sum of money in a lottery, the first thing the press asks is, "Are you going to quit work now that you're rich?" They are dumbfounded if the recipient of the sweepstakes returns to his job. As for what is produced, that hardly matters at all. The only guiding principle is "the more the better." No one takes responsibility for determining whether something should be produced or not. As long a market for the item can be developed, it will be provided. Thus, society is deluged by a plethora of material effluence—microwave ovens, hair dryers, automobiles that poison the air, and prescription drugs that poison the body.

Whereas industrialism views the end of production as consumption, and work as merely a means to reach that goal, in a low-entropy society work becomes an essential component in our efforts to reach an enlightened state of consciousness. Work in a high-entropy society is secularized; it is divided and measured by the clock and the output; and it is a burden because it has no transcendent significance. In a low-entropy society, human labor is sanctified as any activity that helps us "know who we really are." Thus, there is a positive value inhering in work. In his essay "Buddhist Economics," E. F. Schumacher suggests that this value is threefold: "To give a man a chance to utilise and develop his faculties; to enable him to overcome his ego-centredness by joining with other people in a common task; to bring forth the goods and services needed for a becoming existence."[73]

In low-entropy culture, work is understood to be an activity as necessary for the proper life-balance as sleep, contemplation, or play. Without work, man is incomplete. The person who is engrossed with "saving labor" and endless indulgence in leisure can no more comprehend the true nature of reality than the person who is lost in the jungle of illusions that comes from an attachment to consumption and possessions.

But not just any kind of work can be considered appropriate. It must be designed, first and foremost, to provide dignity and purpose for the worker. The work must have a human scale to it, a certain type of organization, in order that it can "give a man a chance to utilise and develop his faculties." In practice, this means that the type of technology used in work becomes a critical issue in a thermodynamic, as well as a metaphysical, sense. The Entropy Law shows us that the larger the work tools—the machines, the factories—the more capital and energy intensive and the more entropic they become. From the metaphysical point of reference, the scale of the work tools is also critical, for the larger and more centralized they become, the more the role of the human is reduced to just another factor of production. On an automobile assembly line, for instance, the workers must essentially do what the machine "wants" because the production process is centered on the machine, not the individual. The human loses importance in the work process, and as this occurs, human self-sufficiency is diminished: the worker necessarily becomes dependent on the machines for a livelihood.

Along with the size and type of technology, the organization of production and decision-making also takes on renewed importance. As we have seen, specialization of human activity at the workplace is an outgrowth of a high-entropy economy. The techniques of scientific management, the systematic separation of thoughts from action, of conception from performance, is designed to maximize productivity by making nonthinking automatons of workers. Once again, we see that work itself is not valued, only the product of that work.

Likewise, the authoritarian structure of the workplace robs the individual worker of a chance to join in a community with his fellows to make decisions and develop his talents. Unable to join with others to explore his potential and creativity, the individual is forced to retreat into a shell in which he has neither meaningful rights nor responsibilities at his work. All he is left with is a job, a place to make money, and a degrading environment to which he must submit, eight hours of every day.

In terms of governing—both economic and political—a low-entropy culture emphasizes the notion that "that government is best which governs least." Popular democracy is favored over rule by the few, and economic arrangements are emphasized in which each person exercises an equal vote and voice in the affairs that affect his life both at the workplace and in the community. Self-managed, worker-run enterprises and small democratically run city-states are the preferred economic and political forms. Decentralized participatory democracy is preferable, not just on a moral or philosophical basis, but also because it minimizes energy flow-through and, as a consequence, reduces the accumulation of disorder. As we have already seen over and over again, highly centralized economic and political institutions only increase the energy flow and the buildup of disorders. Therefore they have no place in an entropic culture based on the limited flow of renewable sources of energy.

In a low-entropy culture the concept of private property is retained for consumer goods and services and family real estate but not for large tracts of land and other renewable and nonrenewable resources. The long-accepted practice of private exploitation of "natural" property is replaced with the notion of public guardianship. The orthodox economic view that each person's individual self-interest when added together with the self-interest of everyone else always serves the common good of the community is regarded with suspicion or, more appropriately, with outright derision. Individual rights are protected, but they are no longer regarded as the sole reference point from which to judge society. Instead, the notion of public duties and responsibilities once again gains ascendancy as a dominant social motif, as it has been throughout most of history.

In a low-entropy society, the modern view of man and woman divorced from the workings of the ecosystem gives way to a post-modern comprehension of the interrelatedness of all phenomena. A low-entropy culture emphasizes man and woman as a part of nature, not apart from it. Nature becomes not a tool for manipulation, but the source of life that must be preserved in its entire workings. Once it is understood that human beings are an integral part of nature, then an ethical base is established by which the appropriateness of all human activity can be judged. For instance, a low-entropy society would view as an obscenity any economic policy that contributed to the destruction of another species. Every species must be preserved simply because it has an inherent and inalienable right to life by virtue of its existence. The first law of ecology tells us that "everything is connected to everything else." Any destruction of one part of nature will affect all other parts, including human beings.

In a low-entropy society the notion of "conquering" nature is replaced by the idea of harmony with other creatures and the environment as a whole. Individual humans have a responsibility to preserve nature to the maximum extent possible, so that those yet to come—both people and other creatures—may enjoy life in their own day.

All the great teachers of traditional wisdom have embraced the values inherent to a low-entropy life. Buddha, Jesus, Muhammed, the prophets of Israel, and the mahatmas of India all led exemplary lives of simplicity, voluntary poverty, and communal sharing. Their teachings expressed similar values for all of society. In our own century, Mohandas Gandhi generated an entire liberation movement based on a low-entropy value system.

Above all else, the low-entropy world view shows us the physical limits we face—the limits of our planet's resources and the limits we must impose on the use of technology.

We stand today at the edge of a historic entropy watershed. As we begin the transition from the age of nonrenewable resources to the Solar Age, we will experience much more than a mere shift in the type and amount of energy we use. The movement from a high-entropy to a low-entropy system will transform our values, our culture, our economic and political institutions, and our day-to-day lives. The harbingers of these vast changes are already with us. Although at this time the signs remain fragmentary, and sometimes contradictory, millions of people are already beginning to conduct their lives in ways that are reflective of the emerging entropy watershed. A 1976 report from the Stanford Research Institute, for instance, estimated that between 4 and 5 million adult Americans have chosen to reduce their incomes drastically and have withdrawn from their former positions as active participants in the high-entropy, industrial, consumer economy. These people have embraced what might most accurately be called "voluntary simplicity"—a low-entropy form of existence based on frugal consumption; a dominant concern with personal, inner growth over materialism; and a growing ecological awareness. According to SRI, another 8 to 10 million Americans have already adapted parts of this simpler life-style.[74]

Even those more thoroughly wedded to consumerism, industrialism, and urbanism are beginning to make personal adjustments in their lives that seem reflective of the entropy crisis. Whether out of sheer necessity, or choice, these life-style changes are significant steps toward institutionalizing the new world view. We could point to many small examples: a significant growth in urban gardening; farmers' markets reopening and prospering in cities around the country; wood-burning stoves, a few years ago novelty items, now selling faster than they can be produced; bicycle sales soaring as this transportation vehicle becomes a serious alternative to auto travel; the growth of ecologically minded architectural firms that design passive solar homes; alternative-technology corporations springing up around the country; a burgeoning cottage handicraft industry; and a growing preventive health movement. All of these are only fragments of the new world order, but they point the way.

It would be misleading, however, to read too much into these hopeful signs. The transition to the Solar Age will not be accomplished easily. Because our society has been designed to maximize energy flow, the dawning of the new energy environment will disrupt our way of life. Sacrifice and hard work will be necessary to make it through the transition period. Writing of another empire at another time, C. W. Hollister, professor of medieval history at the University of California at Santa Barbara, has perhaps outlined elements of our own fate. The fall of Rome, he notes, "brought disorganization and savagery, but it also gave Europe the chance for a new beginning, an escape from old customs and lifeless conventions, a release from the stifling prison that the Roman Empire, for most of its inhabitants, had come to be. . . . Life in the post-Roman West was hazardous, ignorant, foul and deeply insecure, but such was the price of the new beginning. Periods of momentous change are seldom comfortable."[75]

As we look ahead to the emerging order, we are naturally eager to see how our society will be arranged and how our lives will be changed. We cannot, of course, divine all of the specifics, any more than Bacon, Locke, and Adam Smith could have forecast how their philosophies would come to fruition centuries later in the modern technological society of twentieth-century America. Nonetheless, using the general principles of the low-entropy paradigm, we can already foresee the bare outline of the tremendous social reformation that awaits us.

In the Solar Age, agriculture will be transformed into diversified organic farming. Organic farming uses no chemical fertilizers and pesticides, but relies instead on natural manures and natural pest enemies. Studies done comparing organic farming with chemical farming show that while the yield per acre is roughly the same, organic farming uses two-thirds less energy. Organic farms use 6,800 BTUs of energy to produce a dollar of output, whereas conventional farms use over 18,400 BTUs. One study found that while the cost of conventional farming—using highly mechanized farm machinery and massive doses of chemical fertilizer and pesticides—averaged $47 per acre, the cost per acre on an organic farm was only $31.[76] As the cost of energy skyrockets in the years ahead, organic farming will prove to be an even more economically viable alternative; not to mention the fact that organic farming produces crops of higher nutritional value and creates less pollution in the environment.

Making a global transition away from chemical farming and toward organic agriculture will be one of the great challenges of the coming decades. As already mentioned, chemical fertilizers used in green revolution agriculture emit NO_2 into the environment, one of the principle greenhouse gases polluting the atmosphere of the planet. New research programs to promote sustainable agricultural alternatives to chemical fertilizers need to be funded. Unfortunately, the USDA eliminated a small pilot program in organic agriculture in the early 1980s and only reluctantly initiated a new program after Congress passed legislation mandating that agency do so.

Researchers around the world are now actively searching for plants that fix nitrogen effectively and can be used to enrich soil, in order to lessen the reliance on artificial, chemical-based fertilizers. In Asia farmers are experimenting with a nitrogen-fixing blue-green algae that coexists with the *Azolla microphylla* fern. Philippine farmers who have grown *Azolla microphylla* in their rice paddies were able to reduce their reliance on fertilizers by 50 percent without adversely affecting their yields.[77] In Africa, the International Institute of Tropical Agriculture in Nigeria is experimenting with an African shrub, *Sesbania rostrata,* as a potential source of nitrogen for enriching native soil.[78]

In West Africa farmers have traditionally planted *Acacia albida* trees alongside their sorghum and millet crops to enhance the nitrogen content of the soil.[79]

The Land Institute in Salina, Kansas, is experimenting with permaculture, a form of agriculture based on planting a variety of perennial grasses, sunflowers, legumes, and grain crops together in the same field rather than planting a single species. The goal, according to Wes Jackson, the founder of the institute, is to mimic the natural conditions of the prairie. In a wild prairie environment a range of plants flourish under extreme climatic fluctuations, from drought to floods, intense heat to cold. Prairie soils are also very effective at storing water and sustaining nutrients. At the Land Institute, scientists are planting together native species like Illinois bundle flower, maximillan sunflower, eastern gamma grass, and wild Senna, sorghum, and legumes.

> The bundle flower, a legume, is high in protein and is able to draw nitrogen from the atmosphere to produce natural fertilizer in the soil. Legumes and gamma grasses produce broad networks of roots and are highly resistant to drought. All the plants are resistant to diseases and appear to be capable of producing good yields of seeds.[80]

These innovative approaches to what might be called a postmodern agriculture combine age-old agricultural practices that have been all but abandoned during the short reign of the Green Revolution with new highly sophisticated ecological experimentation. By combining traditional wisdom with the latest developments in the ecological sciences, it is possible to envision a regenerative agricultural development program that can gradually wean the world away from its addiction to petrochemical-based agricultural practices.

Greater reliance on nitrogen-fixing plants, increased emphasis on organic manuring and composting, and experimentation with radical agricultural alternatives like permaculture will significantly improve the nutrient quality of soil and provide sustainable alternatives to petrochemical energy inputs.

The global warming trend is also renewing interest in new plant strains and foodstuffs that can adapt to a radically changing atmospheric environment. Anthropologists have identified over 3,000 plants that have been used as food sources by various cultures over history. Yet, today the human population relies almost exclusively on only sixteen major crops.[81] Many of these staples require heavy irrigation, artificial energy inputs, and can only grow within a narrow climate band. The radical shift in climatic conditions, especially in the mid-latitudes of the planet, is going to seriously compromise the yield and even threaten the survival of these traditional crops. Already, agricultural research institutes are searching for alternative foodstuffs that can prolong life under radically different climatic regimes. In the U.S., the Rodale Research Center in Pennsylvania is experimenting with a drought-resistant grain called amaranth, which is native to the American continent and was used as the primary grain by the ancient Aztec civilization in Mexico.[82]

As we move into the Solar Age, large-scale centralized farming will be increasingly challenged by small-scale bio-regional farming in the United States. The energy costs in transporting agricultural products across the country to distant markets will soon be so high that local and regional farming will in some instances provide a less costly economic alternative. Farmers' markets, which once existed in towns and cities nationwide, are already making a comeback. Squeezed by the escalating middle-man costs in food processing, farmers and consumers are beginning to deal with each other directly.

While urban life will not disappear in the Solar Age, the reign of the megalopolis will come to an end. "Large" cities will need to gradually scale down to a preindustrialized size of 100,000 or so. This reduced scale will be in keeping with the ability of the surrounding environment to produce both food and solar power. Moreover, numerous studies in recent years have indicated that when urban centers grow to more than 100,000 residents, disorders also grow at an alarming rate. As we saw earlier, large cities are disproportionately costly to run and have a much higher incidence of crime, mental illness, pollution, and other forms of disorder. In the Solar Age, big cities will simply be too large a drain on precious resources.

Along with the scaling down of cities, transportation systems are also going to be vastly reoriented in the years to come. The high cost of energy is going to force a fundamental shift in the pattern of travel away from automobiles and trucks and toward greater mass transit and long-distance rail use.

Bicycling is also going to become an increasingly popular mode of travel. Between 1978 and 1988 the number of bicycle commuters quadrupled in the United States. Transportation experts say that if communities provide safe bicycle paths along regular thoroughfares and allow bicycle commuters to ride on rail and bus transport, the bicycle could offer a competitive alternative for millions of Americans, as it already does in other nations like China, the Netherlands, and Sweden. Many cities are already beginning to pay serious attention to the bicycle commuter. In Santa Barbara over 40,000 bicyclists a year use the special bus trailer system. More than 30 percent of them switched from automobile commuting to bike commuting because the bus trailer system was available to augment their travel. Providing free bicycle parking at public transit facilities will also encourage more commuters to use bicycles and public transport rather than relying exclusively on the automobile.

Our social and economic life will undergo radical changes reflecting the change in transportation. Less recreational time will be spent in travel, and more near and around the home. Increasingly places of business will be located within a short travel radius of available labor pools.

Community developers are beginning to heed the demand for new commercial and residential modes of working and living that reflect a low-entropy lifestyle. The "neo–traditional" town has become the new prototype of development in small cities like Seaside and Charleston Place, Florida, and the Mashpee Commons on Cape Cod, Massachusetts. Planners have begun copying many of the salient features of 19th century towns in restoring existing communities and building new ones. The "neo-traditional" movement is based on the idea of closely integrating offices, shops, and housing in compact areas, allowing people to live, work, and socialize in a self-contained environment. It is a movement that is in sharp contrast to the planning that took place for three decades following World War II, when planners and architects separated homes, offices, and shops into sprawling suburbs, concentrated downtown business districts, and giant shopping malls connected only by freeways. Writing in the March, 1988 issue of *Atlantic Monthly*, Philip Langdon summed up the appeal of this movement by observing that many American families are no longer able to cope with the time demands of a bumper-to-bumper freeway culture. As a result, many people are beginning to seek out communities where the various amenities of life can be enjoyed within walking distance of home, in a setting that is village-oriented and in scale with human needs.

In keeping with the character of the low-entropy economy as one of necessities, not luxuries or trivialities, production will center on goods required to maintain life. To recognize the extent to which production will be diminished, we have only to take a tour through a suburban mall and ask ourselves, "How many of these products are even marginally useful in sustaining life?" Any honest appraisal is sure to conclude that most of what is manufactured in our economy is simply superfluous.

The production that does continue should take place within certain guidelines in keeping with the low-entropy paradigm. First, production should be decentralized and localized. Second, firms should be democratically organized as worker-managed companies. Third, production should minimize the use of nonrenewable resources. All of these points are consistent with both the energy and ethical requirements of the entropic world view. Of course, adhering to these guidelines will necessarily mean that certain items will become impossible to produce. Thus, a new ethic will have to be adopted as the litmus test of what should be produced in the low-entropy society: if it cannot be made locally by the community, using readily available resources and technology, then it is most likely unnecessary that it be produced at all.

The uses of technology will also change drastically in the future. Once technology is recognized as being essentially a low-entropy transformer of energy from a usable to an unusable state, we will come to understand that the less we use complex energy-consuming technologies, the better off we are.

In a low-entropy society, big, centralized, energy- and capital-intensive technologies will be discarded in favor of what is called appropriate or intermediate technology. Futurist-author Sam Love defines appropriate technology as "locally produced, labor-intensive to operate, decentralizing, repairable, fueled by renewable energy, ecologically sound, and community-building."[83] E. F. Schumacher, credited as the father of the intermediate-technology movement, says that this low-entropy form of technique is "vastly superior to the primitive technology of bygone ages but at the same time much simpler, cheaper, and freer than the super-technology of the rich. One can also call it self-help technology, or democratic or people's technology—a technology to which everyone can gain admittance and which is not reserved to those rich and powerful."[84]

Finally, the low-entropy age we are moving into will require a great reduction in world population. The massive explosion in world population is really only understandable when viewed in thermodynamic terms. Picture our world at its beginning, before life began its development and evolution. The planet was covered with seas, mountains, and valleys. Then, 3 billion years ago, life began—growing literally out of the energy resources contained within the earth and emanating from the sun. Like all other forms of life, when Homo Sapiens appeared on the planet some 3 million years ago, he sustained himself by receiving energy from the renewable resources of the sun. Because life was based on this decentralized flow of solar power, the absolute numbers which could be sustained remained relatively low. Population density increased quite slowly. It took the entire period of human existence until roughly 1800 to reach the first billion people.

From that point on, the explosion began in earnest. As we saw earlier, the second billion humans took only a hundred years. The third billion took only thirty years, between 1930 and 1960. The fourth billion took only fifteen years. At current growth rates, the world's population will double once again to 8 billion by the year 2015 and to 16 billion by the year 2055. This explosion in population corresponds exactly to the world's shift from an agricultural economy (based on solar flow) to an industrialized system (based on the extraction of a nonrenewable stock of energy from the earth's capital). In other words, it is not only our buildings, cars, and other artifacts that are made from fossil fuels and nonrenewable resources: in a sense, the 5 billion additional people on earth today have been made possible by the conversion of billions of years of stored solar energy. It should come as no surprise that the industrial era based on nonrenewable resources comprises less than .02 percent of human history, and yet "80 percent of the increase in human numbers has occurred during this period."[85]

The thermodynamic implications of population growth are staggering. In the preindustrial age, the carrying capacity of the world was only 1 billion people. Even at that number, the world's resources were being severely strained. As a direct result of a higher energy flow of stored nonrenewable resources, 4 billion additional people were added to the world's load. Without this energy flow, these people could not be sustained. Yet, as we have seen, the finite limit of our planet's resources makes it impossible that the energy flow of the past 200 years can long continue. Because of this, it is essential that the world begin with renewed vigor a serious program aimed at reducing the earth's population in the decades to come. The world must once again move back toward a sustainable, Solar Age population.

The world's population will diminish, of that there can be no doubt. The question is how. There have been many specific proposals: licensing parents to have no more than two children; changing tax laws so that people who have children are penalized severely for each additional offspring; programs of force such as that in which 11 million Indians were sterilized under Indira Gandhi's rule. All of these programs are distasteful at best, because they are externally applied by society. The only other alternative is a full internalization of the entropy paradigm, so that we voluntarily limit our population by exercising restraint in our individual desires to have children. Once we fully comprehend that each child we bring into the world places a burden on succeeding generations by denying them their own share of resources to sustain their own lives, then we can develop a set of values that will lead to a humane program of population control.

For most Americans, any discussion of population control immediately conjures up Malthusian visions of India, and other overcrowded Third World nations. It is, of course, urgent that these poorer countries move to substantially curtail their own populations. But lest we think that the population problem is endemic to the Third World alone, let us remember that it is not just the numbers of people who physically exist that are important, but also the amount of energy consumed by each individual. As we have seen before, in the United States we are using as much of the earth's fixed energy resources as 22 *billion* people. A population map of the planet based not just on human numbers but on energy consumption would show that the greatest population problem in the world today, in terms of energy depletion, exists right here in the United States. Thus, we must not only move to limit the absolute numbers of individuals in our country, but we must also limit our energy consumption drastically.

Our list contrasting high-entropy and low-entropy social systems could go on and on. In even this brief overview of the general nature of the emerging entropic society, it should be clear that vast transformations are impending. From our perspective, the coming changes may not appear desirable. Let's face it: most of us, having lived in an era of unparalleled material affluence, and indoctrinated by education, television, and advertising, are hedonists to one degree or another. Nicholas Georgescu-Roegen wonders whether we will be able to wrest ourselves from our existing world view:

> Will mankind listen to any program that implies a constriction of its addiction to exosomatic comfort? Perhaps the destiny of man is to have a short, but fiery, exciting and extravagant life rather than a long, uneventful and vegetative existence. Let other species— the amoebas, for example—which have no spiritual ambitions, inherit an earth still bathed in plenty of sunshine.[86]

If the task ahead seems impossible to accomplish it is only because we continue to view what needs to be done with Newtonian eyes. Our existing world view cannot provide us with the confidence and zeal we need to overcome the present historical crises, because it is bound up with the existing energy environment. Only the entropy paradigm provides a scythe that is both sharp enough to cut through the tangled debris of this death-bound culture and broad enough to clear a path for the dawn of a new age.

Only when we have revised some of the old way of thinking and behaving and take onto ourselves the new entropic world view will we be ready to go forth and remake our culture. The new order of the ages must begin with a revolution in science, education, and religion. In each area, the old mechanical constructs must be tempered and modified by new constructs cast to the requirements of the second law.

Reformulating Science

It is a curious fact that, just when the man in the street has begun to believe thoroughly in science, the man in the laboratory has begun to lose faith. When I was young, most physicists entertained not the slightest doubt that the laws of physics give us real information about the motions of bodies, and consist of the sorts of entities that appear in the physicists' equations.[87]

These words come from Bertrand Russell. If the people knew what the physicists now know, the bottom would fall out from the mechanical world paradigm. The assumptions of classical physics upon which we have confidently erected our entire way of organizing life turn out to be largely fallacious, say today's scientists.

Take, for example, the idea first expounded by Bacon and Descartes that the world could be understood and then organized by the "scientific method," that is, the separation of things into subjects and objects that could be precisely measured and quantified by mathematical formulas. Quantum theory contradicts this overly simplistic premise. Early in the twentieth century, scientists began peering farther and farther into the microworld of life, trying to locate, isolate, and measure the most elemental particle of matter in the universe. They found that as they probed deeper and deeper, locating more minute elements along the way, there seemed to be no end in sight. Then it dawned on them that the whole procedure was like a giant cosmic joke unfolding at their expense. The scientific community was surprised when the German physicist Heisenberg discovered that the "objective observation of atomic particles was an impossibility, the very nature of atomic particles being such that the very act of observation was interfering and altering, instead of fixing and preserving, the object."[88] Heisenberg and those who followed him into the microworld of quantum physics learned, with each new observation they made, that precise measurement of matter—the very basis of classical physics—is impossible because it calls for being able to determine both the velocity and location of an object at a given moment in time. To their chagrin, they realized that every time they observed the tiniest of particles, the electron, their act of observation was influencing what they saw. That is because "you can only see an electron when it emits light, and it only emits light when it jumps, so that to see where it was, 'you' have to *make it* go elsewhere."[89] That being the case, you can't have it both ways. You can measure either its location or its velocity but never both at the same time. The point is, "If you know where you are, you can not tell how fast you are moving, and if you know how fast you're moving, you cannot tell where you are."[90]

Heisenberg's discovery was given a name: the Heisenberg uncertainty principle. His discovery marked the darkest day in the history of classical physics. For all intents and purposes he pulled the rug out from under the ironclad determinism that had surrounded the laws of physics for nearly 300 years. In science, only one uncompromising exception is enough to invalidate a law. Heinsenberg broke the back of Newtonian science and the world view that was built upon it.

Heisenberg's uncertainty principle, however, was only the opening salvo of a long and protracted scientific assault that has left much of classical physics in shambles. Newton's claim that he had found the scientific key for unlocking the secrets of the universe is now treated as little more than the bravado of an infant science, unencumbered by the paradoxes and complexities that ultimately accompany the process of growth in knowledge.

Up to a hundred years ago, physics rolled along self-assured by its own claims that any set of initial conditions can lead to one, and only one, final state. Today, the causality principle of classical physics has become so qualified that it could hardly claim the status of a law. Scientists now acknowledge that a given set of initial conditions can lead to several possible alternative states. They distinguish between the early deterministic laws and the newer indeterministic laws. In the latter case, probabilities are assigned to each of the possible outcomes of an initial set of conditions as the best that can be hoped for in terms of measurement. But even the indeterministic laws are now being challenged by what some scientists refer to as "a second stage of indeterminism," in which the assignment of probabilities for the various outcomes of an event are virtually impossible to establish. The renowned physicist Max Born summed up the frustration of his colleagues over the direction in which their own research has led: "We have sought for firm ground and found none. The deeper we penetrate, the more restless becomes the universe; all is rushing about and vibrating in a wild dance."[91]

The scientists have learned that every event is unique; its own occurrence distinguishes it from all other events. For that reason, each event not only claims a place all its own in the world but cannot be said to share an objective reality with any other phenomenon. Its subjective occurrence, in turn, is not the result of a particular initial set of conditions. Rather, it owes its occurrence to the entire labyrinth of all past subjective occurrences whose collective configuration gave rise to its own particular unfolding. The idea that specific phenomena can be isolated from the rest of the universe they are a part of and then connected in some kind of "pure" causal relationship with other isolated phenomena is just plain wrong thinking. The Newtonian paradigm of precise measurement, of dividing matter into neat quantities that can then be linked to each other and rearranged without regard to either their effect on the rest of the cosmos or the effect of the rest of the cosmos on them, has led to the wanton manipulation and destruction of nature at the hands of modern science.

Everything in this world is connected with everything else in a delicate and complex web of interrelationships. The best computer ever designed by humankind still cannot calculate even a tiny fraction of all the relationships that exist in the ecosystem of a simple pond. Scientists have tried it and despaired after realizing the complexity and detail involved.

The old Newtonian view that treats all phenomena as isolated components of matter, or fixed stocks, has given way to the new idea that everything is part of a dynamic flow. Classical physics, which recognized only two kinds of classifications, things that exist and things that do not exist, has been challenged and overthrown. Things don't just "exist" as some kind of isolated fixed stock. This static view of the world has been replaced by the view that everything in the world is always in the process of becoming. Even nonliving phenomena are continually changing. This process of becoming is really nothing more than the Entropy Law at work. Every single thing is energy and that energy is continually being transformed. Every transformation affects everything else that is in the process of becoming. The life and death of every blade of grass affects the total change in the energy in the world. The Entropy Law tells us the direction in which the energy flow moves, but not the speed. The speed fluctuates. There is nothing smooth about the ebb and flow of the becoming process. It moves along in jumps and spurts.

Ilya Prigogine, who received a Nobel Prize for his work on nonequilibrium thermodynamics in 1977, says that the entire notion of causality and precise measurement, the hallmarks of classical physics, are about to give way to a redefinition of science based on the imperative of the second law. Every occurrence in the world is unique, argues Prigogine, and for that reason it is impossible to make precise predictions about the future based on scientific observations. The most that science can do is predict likely scenarios. The old security provided by classical physics was an illusion from the beginning, say Prigogine and his colleagues. It is not possible to know nature in the sense that Bacon, Descartes, and Newton had in mind. The idea that human beings can separate themselves from nature, discover its inner secrets, and then use them as a "fixed body of truths" to manipulate and change the natural world has proven to be erroneous. First, as scientist Niels Bohr once remarked, we are all actors as well as spectators in the unfolding of the natural order. We cannot separate ourselves from the world around us no matter how hard we try. Second, the notion of fixed bodies of truths, in the deterministic sense of classical physics, no longer holds up as we now experience a universe of continual fluctuation and instability. Prigogine captures the essence of the new reformulation of science when he says that "instead of the classical description of the world as an automaton we go back more to the Greek paradigm of the world as a work of art."[92]

In the final analysis, every science is nothing more than a methodology for predicting the future. At the same time, every scientific methodology is involved in a constant search to define the upper limits of what is possible. A scientific law remains valid as long as it satisfactorily predicts the future and no exception can be found that undermines the limits it establishes. The Entropy Law satisfies both objectives. More than any other concept yet discovered, the Entropy Law provides a comprehensive methodology for predicting the future and establishes the supreme limits within which things can take place in this world.

The Entropy Law will likely supersede Newtonian mechanics as the ruling paradigm of science because it, and only it, adequately explains the nature of change, its direction, and the interconnectedness of all things within that change process. The Entropy Law may someday be invalidated and overthrown. But for now it remains the one law of science that seems to make common sense out of the world we live in and provides an explanation of how to survive within it.

Reformulating Education

Our entire learning process is little more than a twelve- to sixteen-year training program for the Newtonian world view. In school, emphasis is placed on quantities, distance, and location but rarely on qualities, relationships, or context. Think of all of the countless tests where the only questions asked were those concerning names, dates, and places—things that could be precisely measured and that involved no ambiguities. The tests themselves are cut directly from the mold of classical physics. True, false, fill in the blanks, multiple choice, and matching answers are all based on the concept of causality: that for every set of initial conditions there is one and only one correct final state.

If a poll were taken, it is likely that just about everyone who has gone through school will recall a time when he or she questioned the testing procedure itself. How many of us have had the experience of taking a test and looking at a specific question, and all of the specific answers, and feeling somehow compromised by having to pick one of them. Our common sense told us that it wasn't as simple as all that. We told ourselves that other things needed to be considered, and that it was just plain foolish to try to isolate this particular phenomenon from everything else around it. Still, after a bit of quiet mumbling, we allowed ourselves to succumb to the process. If we had to pick one answer, then so be it. We might even rationalize our surrender by musing that even if there was no right answer, at least we could select the one best answer.

At this very moment children all over America are taking examinations. The kind of tests they are taking are preparing them to think in terms of causality and quantification, the basics of the Newtonian world paradigm. Of course, few teachers are consciously aware that they are promulgating a particular ideology when they teach. They would probably protest that their only concern is to teach the child how to think "objectively."

The thinking process is only important if it produces results, and that means learning facts. Our educational system places its highest priority on facts. The more bits of information a student can collect and recall, the better grades he will receive. Facts are valuable, it is argued, because they help one to better understand the world and to better organize one's own life. The amount of *facts* we know about the world around us is doubling every few years. Yet one would be hard pressed to claim that humankind is becoming twice as knowledgeable about our proper role in the larger scheme of things.

Finally, our educational process is devoted to specialization. Every time we learn something new and different about the world, a new academic or professional discipline is set up to collect and interpret the new data. Learning has become fragmented into tinier and tinier frameworks of study on the Newtonian assumption that the more we know about the individual parts, the more we will be able to make deductions about the whole those parts make up.

Our academicians and professionals become like the proverbial blind men poking their sticks at different parts of the elephant, each with a different notion of what the beast must look like. The more they poke at the little space reserved for them, the more convinced they are that they know what they are poking at, and the more wrong they become.

Our educational process is designed to accommodate the needs of an industrial society. Industrial society, in turn, is designed to suit the needs of a nonrenewable energy base. As we begin to make the transition to a solar energy environment, our current approach to education and learning will be rendered increasingly obsolete. The Newtonian style of learning will be forced to give way to an entropic approach to education.

The new emphasis in learning will be dramatically different from the way we go about things today. For example, education will stress process over measurement. The notion of collecting, storing, and exploiting *stocks* of isolated facts will be replaced with the idea of examining the *flow* of interconnected phenomena. Testing will focus on conceptual abilities over empirical ones; and essays, oral discourse, and practical experience will be the standard forms reflecting the need to think in terms of process. The external world will be examined not as a series of isolated causal relationships, but as a web of interrelated phenomena expressing many possible scenarios for movement and change.

Education will be more concerned with the *why* of things as opposed to the *how*. The shift from the empirical to the metaphysical will mean less attention on manipulating the environment and more on understanding our relationship to it. Learning, then, will not be seen as a tool to carve up the world and fashion it into something else, but as a method to better know how to live within the limits of the world we have inherited from nature and of which we are a part. Learning as progress will be replaced with learning as stewardship.

While some specialization will be required, even in the Solar Age, the educational process will be centered on a holistic approach to knowledge. Unlike today's educational system, which separates students into either trade or academic tracks in high school and afterward, the new emphasis will be on combining mental and manual skills, teaching each person to become self-sufficient in the world.

The artificial separation between human culture and nature, characteristic of the Newtonian era, will give way to a new reunification of the two in the coming Solar Age. The concept of "man against nature" will be replaced by the concept of "people in partnership with nature." The educational process will reflect this basic change. In contrast to the current academic process, which separates students from the outside world for twelve to sixteen years in a hermetically sealed, artificial environment, the educational experience in the entropic era will emphasize learning integrated with day-to-day experiences in the world. Apprenticeship will once again take on the importance it has had in previous periods of history. At the same time, the large, centralized learning complexes typical of the last stages of the age of nonrenewables will give way to the notion of "learning environments." In the Solar Age, going to school will include going into the community to learn.

Some of the knowledge accumulated during the Industrial Age will become increasingly irrelevant in the coming Solar Age, and will eventually be discarded altogether. However, it is important to emphasize that much of the Newtonian paradigm will remain useful and will be retained and passed on through the educational process. Every major shift in world view incorporates significant fragments of the old schematic within the new order. While many of the distinguishing features of the old world view will survive as a part of the new paradigm, their role and importance will be radically redefined to fit the new set of governing assumptions.

Although the emerging educational process is likely to evolve in many new and as yet unimaginable directions, it will be guided, from beginning to end, by the overriding principles of the first and second laws of thermodynamics.

A Second Christian
Reformation

The emerging entropy world view is already being accompanied by a radical reformulation of Christian theology. The Protestant Reformation, which provided an expansionary theology ideally suited to the expansionary economic era of the past 400 years, is giving way to a new theological construct, one reflecting the requirements of the Entropy Law and the new Solar Age.

Over the past fifteen years there has been a great deal of experimentation in this country with Eastern religions. Today, over half a million Americans are adherents of Buddhist theology, and 4 to 5 million more practice meditation, yoga, and other mental and physical exercises whose source of inspiration is found deep in the religious experience of the East.[93] At the same time, the United States is experiencing a massive religious revival, which pollsters like George Gallup are claiming represents the early stage of a third great awakening in America.[94]

America has experienced two other great religious awakenings in the past. The first great spiritual revival, in the 1740s, helped unite the colonies and served as a catalyst in the political movement against the crown. The second such awakening, a century later, helped spawn the abolitionist movement and set the stage for the Civil War. Today, the evangelical fervor is spreading across the land once again, and there is every reason to believe that this third great awakening will help spark a profound change in the social and economic life of the nation, just like the first two revivals.

The growing interest in Eastern religions and the mushrooming evangelical movement represent the unconscious search for a new religious synthesis that can accommodate the new age we are moving into. Each brings with it an essential ingredient for a new theological reformulation.

Adherents of the Eastern religions—and especially the Buddhists—have long understood the value of minimizing energy flow-through. The practice of meditation is designed to slow down the wasteful expenditure of energy. The state of Nirvana or truth is reached when the individual is expending the least energy necessary to support his outward physical survival. The Eastern religions have long claimed that unnecessary dissipation of personal energy only adds to the confusion and disorder of the world. Ultimate truth, according to Eastern doctrine, is arrived at only by becoming one with the world around you. This can only be accomplished by entering into a unified relationship with the rest of nature.

Westerners have always had a hard time understanding the Eastern approach to truth and wisdom. We have believed that only by constantly doing can we unlock all the hidden secrets of the world. So we are perpetually engaged in collecting and piecing together bits and fragments of information and manipulating and rearranging the world around us, convinced that our efforts will lead to increased wisdom and eventually bring us face to face with the supreme architect of the universe. The Eastern theologians would say that our frenetic activity is only increasing the disorder and confusion and removing us further from the divine revelation we seek.

While the Eastern religions have understood the value of minimizing energy flow and lessening the accumulation of disorder, it is the Western religions that have understood the linear nature of history, which is the other important factor in synthesizing a new religious doctrine in line with the requirements of the Entropy Law. Unlike Eastern theology, which emphasizes recurring worlds and history as cycles, the Judeo-Christian tradition has always taught that earthly history has a distinct beginning and end.

On the other hand, the traditional Christian approach to nature had been a major contributing factor to ecological destruction.[95] The overemphasis on otherworldliness has led to disregard and even exploitation of the physical world.[96] This view holds that the only things of true value are those found in the heavenly world of God. Our world, the world of people and nature and the flesh, is seen as low, depraved, and unworthy and therefore of little concern or consequence to those seeking to live a holy life. The natural world is merely a stopover on our journey to the next world. Therefore, the less attention placed on it and the more attention placed on God's kingdom, the better.

The other shortcoming of Christian doctrine over the centuries has been the interpretation of the concept of dominion in the account in Genesis of the Creation: "Be fruitful and multiply and fill the earth and subdue it; and have dominion over the fish of the sea and over the birds of the air and over every living thing that moves upon the earth." The concept of *dominion* has been used by people to justify the ruthless manipulation and exploitation of nature. Now, however, a major reformulation of Christian doctrine is beginning to take shape. For the first time, Christian scholars are beginning to redefine the meaning of dominion, and in so doing they are creating the theological foundations for an entropic world view.[97]

The new interpretation of Genesis begins with the idea that since God created the heavens and the earth and everything in this world, that all his creations take on importance and an intrinsic worth because they are of his making. Since this creation of God's has a purpose and order to it, that purpose and order is to be revered just as God's creations are to be revered. It follows from this, argue the new theologians, that anything that exploits or harms God's creations is sinful and an act of rebellion against God. Likewise, anything that undermines the purpose and order that God has given to the natural world is also sinful and an act of rebellion. This is no small theological point. Every other religious conviction flows from these central truths of creation, contend the new theologians. Either God created the world or he didn't. Either God gave purpose and order to the world or he didn't. If one believes in these truths, then one believes in God. If one doesn't believe in these truths, one can't possibly believe in God. This thesis is the beginning point for all Christian believers.

It follows, then, that sin is people's hubris in believing that they can treat God's creations differently than God does; namely, manipulate and exploit them for purposes other than what they were created for. Sin is also people's hubris in believing that they can reorder this world and redefine its purpose to suit their own whims and fancies. The Christian life must be one of conserving wholeness over fragmentation, balance over imbalance, and harmony over disharmony. A Christian must love God's creation and treat it with respect because God created it with love.[98]

Dominion, then, does not mean the right to exploit nature. Far from it, say the scholars. Dominion means stewardship over nature. Henlee H. Barnett, in his book *The Church and the Ecological Crisis,* points out that the Biblical view of humankind "is that of a keeper, caretaker, custodian . . . of the household earth." Stewardship, says Barnett is "the New Testament term for this role of human beings in relation to the natural order." The first requisite of a steward, according to Barnett, "is faithfulness, because he handles that which belongs to another."[99] The concept of stewardship leads directly to the Biblical notion of covenant. In Genesis, God says, "I established my Covenant with you [humankind], and with your seed after you and with every living created thing."

God, then, has a covenant with humanity. Men and women are to act as His stewards on earth, preserving and protecting all of God's creations. This covenant puts human beings in a special relationship to God. Since people are a creation of God, just like all of God's other creations, they are equal to them in their finite nature; only God is infinite. While all creations are equal in that they owe their existence to the same source—God—human beings are nonetheless different. The difference, as Francis Schaeffer points out in his book *Pollution and the Death of Man,* is that human beings are made by God in his image and are given the responsibility to act as stewards over the rest of God's creation. Therefore, people are both part of nature, equal to and dependent on all other living creatures, and at the same time separate from nature with a responsibility to protect and take care of it. As long as people accept both relationships, they are faithful to God's purpose and are carrying out the covenant God made with them. However, when people take advantage of their special relationship by taking over God's creation as their own, using it for their own ends rather than God's glory, they have broken the covenant and are rebelling against God.[100]

The new stewardship doctrine and the laws of thermodynamics, when combined with more orthodox theology, set the tone for a new, reformulated Christian doctrine and covenant suited to the ecological prerequisites of an entropic world view. Most of all, the stewardship doctrine provides an answer to the ultimate question, "Why should I take the responsibility of caring for and preserving the natural order?" Because it is God's order. God created it and God entrusted human beings with the responsibility of overseeing it. It comes down to a question of serving God or rejecting Him.

The new stewardship doctrine turns the modern world view upside down. The rules and relationships that are used to exploit nature are diametrically opposed to those that are necessary to conserve nature. For example, private ownership of resources, increased centralization of power over nature, the elimination of biological diversity, the refusal to set limits on production and consumption, the fragmentation of human labor into separate and autonomous spheres of operation, the reductionist approach to understanding life and the interrelationships between phenomena, and the concept of progress as a process of continually transforming the natural world into a more exploitable human-made environment have long been considered as valid pursuits and goals in the modern world. Every single one of these items and scores of others that make up the operating assumptions of the age of growth are inimical to the principles of ecology, a low-entropy economic framework, and, most important, the newly defined stewardship doctrine.

Stewardship requires that humankind respect and conserve the natural workings of God's order. The natural order works on the principles of diversity, interdependence, and decentralization. Maintenance replaces the notion of progress, stewardship replaces ownership, and nurturing replaces engineering. Biological limits to both production and consumption are acknowledged, the principle of equitable distribution of resources is accepted and the concept of wholeness becomes the essential guideline for measuring all relationships and phenomena. In reality, the new stewardship doctrine represents a fundamental shift in humanity's frame of reference. It establishes a new set of governing principles for how human beings should behave and act in the world.

If the Christian community fails to embrace the concept of a New Convenant vision of stewardship, it is possible that the emerging religious fervor could be taken over and ruthlessly exploited by right-wing and corporate interests. The evangelical awakening could end up providing the essential cultural backdrop that a fascist movement in the United States would require to maintain control over the country during a period of long-range economic decline.

Even a thoughtful and respected evangelical theologian of the stature of Francis Schaeffer believes that fascism is a very real possibility for the United States in the troubled economic years that lie ahead. In reflecting on America's inability to find a solution to the problem of worsening inflation and recession cycles, Schaeffer concludes: "I cannot get out of my mind the uncomfortable parallel to the German's loss of confidence in the Weimar Republic just before Hitler, which was caused by unacceptable inflation. History indicates that at a certain point of economic breakdown people cease being concerned with individual liberties and are ready to accept regimentation."[101]

Schaeffer is pessimistic about the prospect for the United States. He believes that the overriding value Americans place on their own "personal peace and affluence" will likely lead to a fascist-type order as the economy continues to contract: "I believe the majority . . . will sustain the loss of liberties without raising their voices as long as their own lifestyles are not threatened."[102]

What Schaeffer fails to say is that there are already many disturbing signs within the evangelical movement pointing to just such a possibility. For example, many middle-class Christians are falling back more and more on the old notion of the "gospel of wealth," equating Biblical doctrine with rugged individualism, free enterprise, and unlimited material accumulation. This kind of expansionist theology is still very much a dominant motif in American Christianity. The "gospel of wealth" theme will likely continue to be used by individual Christians to justify a lack of concern or involvement with the pressing economic needs ahead, needs that require a communal and not merely an individual or free-enterprise response. For these Christians, the evangelical movement will serve as a sanctuary for withdrawal from the turmoil around them. If economic conditions become so bad that they begin to threaten even this last refuge of the middle class, chances are good that withdrawal will quickly translate into active support of right-wing and capitalist interests even to the point of accepting whatever authoritarian measures are deemed necessary by the state to maintain social order.

By radically redefining humanity's relationship to the rest of God's creation, contemporary Christian scholars are challenging our expansionist epoch. The new concept of dominion as stewardship and conservation rather than ownership and exploitation is at loggerheads with both traditional Christian theology and the mechanical world view of the past several hundred years. By refocusing the story of Creation and humanity's purpose in the world, Christian theologians have committed an act of open rebellion against their own doctrinal past. The Christian individual who for hundreds of years sought salvation through productivity and the subduing of nature is now being challenged by a new Christian person who seeks salvation by conserving and protecting God's creation. *The Christian work ethic is being replaced by the Christian conservation ethic*. This new emphasis on stewardship is providing the foundation for the emergence of a new Christian Reformation and a New Covenant vision for society.

Facing the Entropy Crisis

There is no way to escape the Entropy Law. This supreme physical rule pervades every facet of our existence. Because everything is energy, and because energy is irrevocably moving along a one-way path from usable to nonusable forms, the Entropy Law provides the framework for all human activity. As we have seen, the entropy world view challenges our most treasured, and commonplace, assumptions about our environment, our culture, our very biological being. The trappings of modern culture—our great urban areas, our mechanized agriculture, our massive production and consumption, our weapons, our education, and our medical technologies—are all revealed in a radical new light. The Entropy Law shatters our view of material progress. It reorients the very foundation of economics. It transforms the notion of time and culture, and strips technology of its mystique.

Once we begin to understand the vast social and economic implications of the second law of thermodynamics, we come to understand that our existing world view bears little relationship to the way the world actually works. Our daily lives—our work, our play, our consumption, our very thoughts—lose their certainty, their grounding. We become strangers in a strange land. All of a sudden what used to be a clear and solid reality becomes fantasy, no better contrived than the Wonderland of the looking-glass world visited by Alice.

And yet, we resist the new orientation placed upon the world and our lives. Even as we are lured by the wisdom that emanates from an entropic world view, we struggle to keep our minds from being subverted by a vision whose import we can scarcely fathom. This is only natural, for we are being challenged to discard the safe and familiar myths that govern our existence. For many, of course, the prevailing myths have already lost their allure. Millions of Americans, some out of choice, others of necessity, are already adopting bits and pieces of the low-entropy philosophy and life-style. Increasingly, high-entropy concepts such as "material progress at any cost" and "bigger is better" no longer command the allegiance of as many inhabitants of the modern technological state as they once did. Some of these alienated heirs of the Newtonian world view will thus naturally welcome the liberation that comes from a shift in reality toward the entropy world view.

At the same time, it is also true that many others will struggle to deny the coming of the new age, preferring decaying familiarity to uncharted opportunities. Trapped within the framework of a philosophy they barely comprehend, these people will turn their attention to finding some mechanism that will provide them with an escape. This too, is only natural. We have been trained to think that there is always an out, that no force is beyond the human's ability to manipulate. We have been taught that there are no limits, that only narrow minds that have lost their nerve will give in to limits. But twist and turn as we might, there is no escape.

In some ways we are like the man who refuses to believe in gravity. To prove its nonexistence—or at least his ability to overcome it—he climbs to the top of a large skyscraper and jumps. Gravity, of course, couldn't care less whether the man believes in it or not, and so it proceeds to administer a lesson to the skeptic by pulling him inexorably toward the ground. But the man, grasping at any straw to preserve his intellectual and physical survival, hurtles past the fortieth floor proclaiming, "So far, so good."

If we, like the man who denies gravity, choose to deny the consequences of the Entropy Law, then we too will be taught an ultimate and shattering lesson. And, no doubt, like that man, we will continue to say, "So far, so good," even as the world around us disintegrates into chaos as a result of our high-entropy culture. Already we can anticipate at least three generalized responses from those who cannot bring themselves to cast off the prevailing world view.

First, there will be the *optimists*. They will pin their hopes on the assumption that somewhere, just over the next hill, or in the next laboratory, a technological solution will come along that will allow us to continue in our ways. Their faith soundly rooted in the values of modern society and the benefits of progress, they will unite under the well-worn banner of "there's always a way." They will tell us that "you can't stop progress," and that "the American standard of living is the envy of the world." Tying these hackneyed phrases to the assumption that the more material wealth a society has, the better off it is, these people will seek any possible measure to overcome our planetary limits.

The optimists are likely to concentrate their efforts on finding new ways to exploit renewable energy sources. While there is no question that we are about to shift from an energy base of nonrenewables back to renewables, what still remains in doubt is the type of energy transformers and flow line that will be set up. The technological optimists reject the notion of returning to a low-entropy flow and a greater accord with the natural rhythms and processes of the earth's ecosystems. Instead, they are placing their hopes on new genetic engineering technologies which they say will enable us to speed up the process of biological evolution and provide us with an increasing flow-through of matter-energy. If we are running out of petrochemical-based fertilizers necessary for mechanized agriculture, then we will develop a genetic engineering technique to construct plants that can fix their own nitrogen directly from the air. If oil is running out, we will genetically engineer and then mass-produce microorganisms that can substitute for depleted nonrenewable stocks. If the greenhouse crisis worsens, we will develop genetically engineered plants and animals that can survive in extreme weather conditions.

It is even likely that the optimist will advocate the "ordering" of the individual's biology. It is no coincidence that genetic engineering is moving out of the laboratories and into the region of applied science at this moment in our history. As entropy builds, our bodies internalize the disorders in the form of cancer, birth defects, diminished IQ in infants, and so on. The technological optimist, realizing that such disorders can seriously affect the nation's desire and ability to continue ever-greater economic growth, thus seeks solutions in bioengineering. If radiation and synthetic organic chemicals cause cancer and birth defects, then modern technology will cure us by rearranging our genes. With genetic engineering the concept of high-energy, high-performance industrial production will be integrated directly into the blueprints of our species. In his never-ending quest for efficiency in all things, the optimist will likely seek to make life itself more "biologically efficient."

The optimists argue that we are not only moving from the age of nonrenewables to the age of renewables, but equally from the age of physics to the age of molecular biology. They point to the incredible scientific breakthroughs in genetic engineering in recent years and claim that within the next two decades our existing industrial technostructure will begin to give way to an entirely new set of technological transformers derived from bioengineering. Just as applied physics was used to transform a nonrenewable energy base into the accoutrements of the Industrial Age, applied genetic engineering will now transform a renewable energy base into an entirely new way of life, the biotechnical age.

It is interesting to observe that as the system attempts to shift from a nonrenewable energy base to a renewable one, and from applied physics as the transforming process to applied molecular biology, a new scientific paradigm is likewise emerging, one that the optimists hope will provide the basis for a new world view for the genetic age they are preparing for. The paradigm is called the *theory of dissipative structures* and its chief architect is Ilya Prigogine, the Belgian physical chemist whose work in nonequilibrium thermodynamics won him the Nobel Prize in chemistry in 1977. *Dissipative structures* refers to open systems that exchange energy with their environment. All living things, and some nonliving systems, are dissipative structures. They maintain their structure by the continual flow of available energy through their system. Prigogine points out that the more complex the dissipative structure, the more integrated and connected it is and thus the more energy flow-through it requires to maintain itself. Noting that the flow of energy through a dissipative structure causes fluctuation, Prigogine rightfully concludes that if the fluctuations become too great for the system to absorb, it will be forced to reorganize. Prigogine then asserts that the reorganization always tends toward a higher order of complexity, integration, and connectedness and greater energy flow-through. Each successive reordering, because it is more complex than the one preceding it, is even more vulnerable to fluctuations and reordering. Thus, complexity creates the condition for greater reordering and a speedup of evolutionary development and energy flow-through. Prigogine, then, equates instability with flexibility. Using complicated mathematical formulas, he attempts to show that the more complex and energy-consuming the system is, the more flexible it is and the better able it is to change and readapt to new circumstances.

No matter that this theory flies in the face of our everyday common sense. We experience a world where increased complexity is narrowing our options, creating greater inflexibility, and increasing the likelihood of collapse and fragmentation. The theory of dissipative structures is an attempt to provide a growth paradigm for an energy environment based on renewables, just as Newtonian physics provided a growth paradigm for a nonrenewable energy environment.

It should be remembered that Newtonian physics was tailormade for "nonliving" energy resources. It deals with dead matter in motion, with pure quantity. Therefore, it is an entirely inappropriate paradigm for an energy environment that is alive, renewable, and flowing. In contrast, the theory of dissipative structures provides a convenient scientific basis for the manipulation of "living" energy sources, and it is for that reason that it is being heralded as a revolutionary breakthrough commensurate in scale with Newton's laws. As an overarching paradigm, the theory of dissipative structures provides a perfect rationalization for the age of bioengineering. It places a positive value on increased biological complexity and the continued reordering of living matter into new structures, which is what genetic engineering is really all about. With dissipative structures we move from viewing the world as an industrial machine to viewing it as an engineered organism.

In the next few years there will be a mad scramble to embrace renewable resources as the new energy base, genetic engineering as a new technological transformer, and the theory of dissipative structures as the new scientific paradigm. Greater energy flow-through, unlimited growth, and material progress without end will continue to dominate the thinking of those in power.

In an effort to ignore the Entropy Law, the experts will attempt to convince the rest of us that with a renewable energy base we will never run out of resources, and that growth will go on forever. In the short run, new genetic technologies might greatly increase the matter-energy flowing through the system, just as the first industrial transformers did with nonrenewables. For a time at least, it may well appear that we have overcome the fixed limits of the earth's ecosystems. That time span will be short-lived. In terms of its intimate effect on our day-to-day lives, the age of physics lasted less than a hundred years. If we proceed into the age of molecular biology, we can expect the span from beginning to end to be greatly reduced: the entire age may run its course in less than half a century. That is because the increased flow of matter-energy through the system will create disorders equal to those produced by the massive flow of nonrenewable energy through the system.

First, by "hot-wiring" the flow of living matter through society's energy flow line, we deplete, in absolute terms, the available stock of living matter. In a literal sense, renewable resources are really nonrenewable. That is, while they continue to reproduce, each blade of grass or microorganism produced today means one less in the future. In the words of Georgescu-Roegen, "Matter, matters." While the solar flow is virtually unlimited, the matter-energy that makes up the earth's crust is not. The earth's matter is continually degrading and dissipating. Natural recycling only reclaims for future use a part of whatever matter-energy is used up. The rest is irretrievably lost. Thus, the faster we speed up the flow of matter-energy through the system, the faster we will run out of renewable resources, regardless of how long the sun shines.

At the same time, the effect that the escalating entropy is likely to have on the gene pool and the earth's fragile ecosystems could well be cataclysmic, doing much greater damage to the planet than was wrought during the entire age of nonrenewable energy flow.

The theory of dissipative structures, like the earlier Newtonian paradigm, completely ignores the Entropy Law, concentrating only on that part of the unfolding process that creates increasing order. By refusing to recognize that increased ordering and energy flow-through always creates ever greater disorder in the surrounding environment, those who advocate bioengineering technology as the transforming apparatus for a renewable energy environment are doomed to repeat the same folly that led us to the final collapse of our nonrenewable energy environment and the age of physics that was built upon it.

As entropy, in its various forms, continues its dramatic rise within the high-energy culture so gloried in by the optimist, it will become necessary to attempt to maintain rigid order amid the developing chaos. A true believer in the existing world order, the optimist will more and more condone practices and techniques that will become increasingly repressive and dehumanizing. For example, unable to admit that the high-entropy, megamillion city is simply not a viable living pattern, he will likely support the imposition of whatever police-state techniques are deemed necessary to maintain social order. Similarly, to maintain our nation's role as the planet's chief energy user, the optimist will encourage higher defense budgets and further weapons development in an attempt to protect a dwindling empire.

Of course, all this activity is doomed to failure. Each attempt at forcing order with new high-energy technologies will only speed up the chaos. Genes will be manipulated to create new forms of renewable energy or to cure disease, but in the process, the evolutionary wisdom of billions of years will be irreversibly destroyed. Attempts to stem rising social disorders such as crime with new high-energy surveillance and weapons technologies will drain off precious energy from the rest of society and only create new forms of repression and antisocial behavior. The optimist will not be able to win in his megalomaniacal quest for order, but he may succeed in taking all of humanity down with him.

The second general response to the Entropy Law can be called the *pragmatic*. Less of a true believer than the optimist, and far less grandiose in his schemes, the pragmatist will attempt to tinker with the existing structure in an effort to make it reflect at least some of the implications of the entropic world view. By nature, the pragmatist has a limited view of the world. He will comprehend part of the entropic paradigm but will miss its overall import. He will be willing to admit some of the shortcomings of the present system, but, after all, he will continue, that's the way the world is. New York City won't just go away; we can't sustain urban life unless we have mechanized agriculture and food processing; Americans will never give up their love affair with the automobile. Let's be realistic, he will say.

Of course, being a pragmatist, he will not deny that there is considerable room for improvement. "Let's get more out of less" becomes his motto. Fine-tuning the existing high-energy structure will become his lifelong occupation. City planners will busy themselves developing thermodynamically sound transportation systems, well-insulated buildings, and neighborhood advisory councils to encourage greater conservation. Auto makers will give us more miles to the gallon and cars that run on gasohol or electricity. Politicians will herald the virtues of "lowered expectations" and "planetary realism." They will be careful, of course, to leave the overall technostructure in place.

Even the most established powers will become engrossed with fitting their institutional imperatives into some kind of loosely defined entropy framework. In August 1979, for instance, the Department of Energy sponsored a three-day conference on the second law of thermodynamics. Papers at the conference carried such weighty titles as "Thermodynamic Analysis of Energy Efficiency in Catalytic Reforming" and "The Reduction of Product Yield in Chemical Process by Second Law Penalties" and "A Second-Law Taxonomy of Combustion Processes."

In the future, we can no doubt expect heated technical debate from the pragmatists over the question, "Given that entropy is always rising, what rate of increase is acceptable?" Theirs will be an effort at quantification, an attempt to take existing systems and make them more "efficient" in the narrowest of senses. Thus, a world view will be converted in their minds into another cost-benefit tool. Unable to grasp the supreme reality of the Entropy Law, the pragmatist will miss the point entirely. Rather like a Christian asking, "How much sin can I get away with and still make it to Heaven?" the pragmatist will be very good at adopting bits and pieces of the entropy vocabulary, all the time missing the essential message of the Entropy Law.

This is not to dismiss entirely the value of thermodynamic systems analysis. But before we can arrive at a point where such analysis has real meaning, we must first recognize that the Entropy Law tells us that a society's energy flow must be reduced to as low a point as possible in order to sustain the unfolding of all of life as far into the future as possible. The entropy economy is one of necessities, not luxuries. Once this is understood, then a basis is established that allows us to selectively use thermodynamic concepts as a tool to help organize the low-entropy society.

Compare, for example, the way a thermodynamic pragmatist (of the fine-tuning, get-more-from-less school) would tackle a set of problems, as opposed to the way these problems would be viewed by someone who has fully internalized the overarching importance of the Entropy Law. A pragmatist would look at an automobile and ask questions such as, "How do we use the second law to redesign the motor so that we can get more work out of it?" and, "What is the most thermodynamically sound design for a car's body?" A person who has fully comprehended the entropic world view would ask a far different set of questions. These might include: Are automobiles really necessary for sustaining human life? Does the automobile enhance our well-being, our health, our culture? Do today's automobiles rob succeeding generations of their own ability to sustain life?

The person who has internalized the low-entropy world view will always ask these comprehensive questions before getting down to specifics. He will understand that if something is not worth doing in the first place, then it really doesn't matter whether or not it is done well. If automobiles are not worth having, then it makes very little difference whether we have cars that get twenty or fifty miles to the gallon.

The third type of response to the Entropy Law might be called the *hedonistic*. The hedonist's motto is, "Let's go out with a bang!" with the subtheme, "What has posterity ever done for me?" These individuals will likely agree that, in an overall sense, things are indeed getting worse. They will complain about air pollution, poisons in their food, the destruction of open spaces. But in a kind of last-days-of-Rome syndrome, they will argue that there is really nothing that can be done. Human nature is simply greedy and destructive, they will claim. Every time someone tries to change the system, they will point out, things just stay the same, unless they get even worse. What can the little person do except look out for number one; eat, drink, and be merry; and wait for the approaching doom?

The optimist, the pragmatist, and the hedonist all share one thing in common—they each regard human beings before the modern age as being little more enlightened than beasts of burden. Because they did not know about subatomic particles, computers, and stereos, our ancestors must have been less human than we are now. These stalwart supporters of the Newtonian paradigm do not understand that we simply possess a different *kind* of knowledge from that which people held 500 or 5,000 years ago. From our reductionist viewpoint, we seem to know more and more. At the same time, we seem to comprehend less and less of what is happening to us. Completely divorced from nature, our urbanized intellects really have no insight into our true relationship to our environment. Our high-energy culture has, in fact, so fragmented our minds that we are no longer in harmony with the source of life. Divorced as we are from nature, we have no real chance to become enlightened, as that word has been understood by peoples throughout history. True, our ancestors had no scientific understanding of and explanation for the phenomena around them, but perhaps they had a better intuitive grasp of what was really important in life.

Our ancestors, at least, were self-sufficient. They knew how to provide for their needs. We, on the other hand, are the complete captives of our high-energy environment. We cannot grow our own food, provide our own entertainment, clothe ourselves with our own hands. We are like helpless infants whose every need must be serviced. In a marvelous passage, Wendell Berry, farmer and author, portrays our modern dilemma:

[An American] is probably the most unhappy citizen in the history of the world. He has not the power to provide himself with anything but money, and his money is inflating like a balloon and drifting away, subject to historical circumstances and the power of other people. From morning to night, he does not touch anything that he has produced himself, in which he can take pride. For all his leisure and recreation, he feels bad, he looks bad, he is overweight, his health is poor. His air, water, and food are all known to contain poisons. There is a fair chance that he will die of suffocation. He suspects that his love life is not as fulfilling as other people's. He wishes that he had been born sooner, or later. He does not know why his children are the way they are. He does not understand what they say. He does not care much and does not know why he does not care. He does not know what his wife wants or what he wants. Certain advertisements and pictures in magazines make him suspect that he is basically unattractive. He feels that all his possessions are under the threat of pillage. He does not know what he would do if he lost his job, if the economy failed, if the utility companies failed, if the police went on strike, if the truckers went on strike, if his wife left him, if his children ran away, if he should be found to be incurably ill. And for these anxieties, of course, he consults certified experts, who in turn consult certified experts about *their* anxieties.

Berry concludes, "In living in the world by his own will and skill, the stupidest peasant or tribesman is more competent than the most intelligent workers or technicians or intellectuals in a society of specialists."[103]

From Despair to Hope

Our generation faces a unique moment in human history. As this book has argued time and again, the energy environment influences the culture, values, politics, and economics that a society establishes. Now that we are witnessing the transition from an energy environment built upon nonrenewable resources to one built on solar flow and renewable energy sources, great personal and institutional changes will sweep over our society. The questions that confront us are: How long will the transition take? How will it be accomplished? What will be our individual roles?

The question of timing is the most difficult to speculate upon. The energy crisis in the 1970s, and the public's concern about the global warming trend and the destruction of the environment in the late 1980s have already set the stage for the rudimentary emergence of the entropic paradigm. No doubt, in the decades to come, bits and pieces of the entropic society will continue to develop, even as many vestiges of the old order linger on. Much the same process unfolded in Europe during the transition period between the medieval and the modern eras. Even today, visitors to European countries can observe remnants of feudal culture perpetuating themselves centuries after the disappearance of the system. In this sense, the transition to the Solar Age will likewise be an evolutionary development that will gain added momentum with each new entropy crisis.

At the same time, we should not delude ourselves into believing that the process of changing energy environments will be so gradual that business-as-usual will continue with only minor disruptions. The transition period will not extend over hundreds of years, as happened during the shift of previous energy environments. Our high-energy social and economic system is so fragile, so absolutely dependent upon continued inputs of nonrenewable resources, that monumental collapse could come any time. Certainly, we can anticipate that the next twenty to thirty years represent the key period in launching the shift in energy environments. For this reason, we must begin to prepare, now, to minimize the possible shock waves that will naturally occur during this period of the entropy watershed.

A previous section outlined some of the broad, long-term institutional changes that will accompany the shift in energy environments. Some might think such changes utopian (and impossible to achieve); others might well regard them as oppressive (and therefore undesirable). To both groups it can only be said that if the low-energy future that has been outlined is unachievable or undesirable, what is the alternative? The scarcity of nonrenewable resources and the escalating greenhouse crisis make it clear that we can no longer maintain our existing high-energy industrial infrastructure. As we move from a nonrenewable energy base to a renewable one, it is equally unrealistic to expect that we can support, for very long, a continuing high matter-energy flow-through with bioengineering technology.

Like it or not, we are irrevocably headed toward a low-energy society. It is up to us whether we get there because we want to, because we understand both the necessity for our own survival and the vast opportunities for a better existence, or whether we try desperately to hang on to our existing world view and, finally, painfully, are forced into the future.

The longer we put off the necessary transition from a high- to a low-entropy society, the bigger the greenhouse bill becomes and the more difficult the turnaround becomes. If we wait too long, we will find that the price that must be paid is beyond the ability of the human race to absorb.

The alternative to the wholesale squandering of available energy and the overheating of the planet is an internalization of the values and dictates of the entropic paradigm. Unless we, individually and in unity with others, modify our Newtonian world view, there is no hope that a movement will develop that can revolutionize our society. The first step in this historic process is to fully comprehend what it is, as people, we believe. We must voluntarily reformulate our lives so that they reflect the new paradigm. But that is not enough. We must also join together, in a popular, grassroots social force, to begin the dismantling of the existing high-energy infrastructure. At the same time, we must build our new society based on a new set of values which reflect our awareness of the entropy process.

Perhaps all of this defies imagination. The task seems so great, the possibility of success so small. Once having come in contact with the Entropy Law, many will feel there is no hope. At first, the new world vision may seem profoundly depressing, and they will be left with nothing but despair. Where is hope? How can anyone be hopeful for a better future when, no matter what we do, we will leave the world in a more degraded form than it was when we were born? Where is hope when it appears that almost everything humanity has done in the past several hundred years has had a result exactly opposite to what was intended?

If we continue to base our hope on maintaining the existing order, then, truly, we will have only despair for our companion, for there is no hope that the modern age as we know it can long continue. On the other hand, what is so desirable about even entertaining such a hope? Why should we hope for more complex technology and more wasteful economic growth, when it only serves to rob us of our future as a species? Continuing to have faith in our high-energy environment is not a hope but an illusion. We should not despair of relieving ourselves of this illusion. Rather, we should rejoice that our generation has the opportunity to begin a planetary transformation that will move our world from the brink of annihilation into a new order of the ages.

There is great beauty in the Entropy Law. It guides us through the cosmic theater with authority, assured of the ultimate fate that lies ahead but leaving to us the decision of how to proceed.

Up to this point in history the human race has driven relentlessly forward, conquering everything in its path. Now that it has succeeded in capturing and exploiting virtually every major ecological niche on the planet, humanity finds itself at the crossroads of its own history. The colonizing mode is taking its toll. As humankind continues to try to maximize its energy flowthrough, the world's total energy environment depletes faster and faster, the dissipation and disorder mount to higher and higher levels and the global warming continues unabated. The only hope for the survival of the species is for the human race to abandon its aggression against the planet and seek to accommodate itself to the natural order.

Our transformation to a climactic mode, if it is to occur at all, must be the result of a conscious choice by the human race. The fact that we are now becoming aware of that choice means that we have the power to effect a decision. That awareness of choice comes from an understanding of the Entropy Law.

After a long, futile search to find out where we belong in the total scheme of things, the Entropy Law reveals to us a simple truth: that every single act that occurs in the world has been affected by everything that has come before it, just as it, in turn, will have an effect on everything that comes after. Thus, we are each a continuum, embodying in our presence everything that has preceded us, and representing in our own becoming all of the possibilities for everything that is to follow.

Because every event that ever was or will be is interconnected, we share an ultimate responsibility for the infinite past and future. What we do in this world reverberates into the remotest corner of the universe, affecting everything else that exists. How we choose to live our lives is not only our own individual concern. It is of concern to everything, because our actions touch everything.

The Entropy Law is a concept to behold with wonder. Yet it strikes terror in most of us. We cannot accept the fact that our physical world will one day complete its journey and cease to exist, any more than we can accept the fact that our own individual sojourns on earth are of a fixed duration. The Entropy Law, however, tells us that every occurrence in the world is a unique experience; it is the uniqueness of every event that makes us aware of the respect we owe to everything that exists around us. The whole world is temporary. In its finiteness, we experience our own. In its vulnerability we experience our own. In its fragile nature we experience our own.

Yet we desperately search for immortality in this finite world while knowing there is none. There is a nihilism to our search. The finiteness of the world is a constant unpleasant reminder of our own. We tear into everything around us, devouring our fellow creatures and the earth's treasures even while telling ourselves that it is progress we are after. It is, in truth, our own immortality we seek. It is as if we were determined to destroy every last reminder of this finite world in the hope of ridding ourselves of the painful awareness of our own temporary nature. Our violent actions only bring us faster to our own demise and to the demise of the fixed endowment bequeathed to all future living beings. Meanwhile, we remain unconcerned about the carnage and affliction because we believe that modern science and technology can develop a substitute for everything we use up in nature's storehouse.

Only when we learn to accept the finite nature of the world can we begin to appreciate how precious this gift called the earth really is. Only then will every occurrence take on a special meaning and will life itself be something worth cherishing and conserving. As Wilhelm Ostwald, the great philosopher and scientist, once remarked, "The responsibility for every act has sense only if the act cannot be repeated, if what is done is done forever."[104]

There are those among us who are willing to accept the finiteness of the physical world but who believe that the entropic flow is counterbalanced by an ever-expanding stream of psychic order. To these people, the becoming process of life is synonymous with the notion of an ever-growing consciousness. In the Newtonian scheme, human consciousness is perceived as moving on an uphill grade against the downward journey of the entropy flow. Eventually, it is believed, humanity's collective consciousness will expand to a point where it will escape the physical plane altogether, overcoming the Entropy Law in a kind of cosmic metamorphosis. Piercing through the physical veil of existence, the collective human consciousness will then begin a steady ascent into the ethereal world of spiritual enlightenment.

It is not hard to understand, then, why people also harbor the unstated belief that in a nongrowth or low-energy flow-through environment, consciousness will atrophy or be prevented from developing. The idea lingers on that consciousness must be constantly watered and cultivated by accelerated physical activity if it is to grow. Taken to its logical conclusion, this line of reasoning would suggest that greater energy flow-through and greater disorder and dissipation in the world create a more conducive environment for the nourishing of consciousness.

This just is not so. Speeding up the physical flow does not insure greater spiritual development; quite the contrary. Transcendence comes out of quietude and the recognition of the beauty in "being," not out of discord and the travails of "doing." Hermann Hesse's Siddhartha had to sit down by the river and listen quietly to the flow in order to become one with it and to reach enlightenment. Human development in the modern era however, has been bound up with resistance to the natural flow of things. The hallmark of the colonizing mode is the attempt to conquer and subdue. We continue to think of enlightenment as something to "achieve" when it is really something to "experience." As long as we frantically struggle for enlightenment, we will continue to resist the natural rhythm of the unfolding process and slide farther away from the enlightenment we seek.

Modern man and woman have also mistakenly associated technological prowess with higher forms of consciousness. In reality, the more sophisticated we have become in engineering our environment, the less attentive we have been to our spiritual needs. Our secular pursuits and spiritual advancements can only begin to converge once again when humanity surrenders its will to dominate and begins to adjust to a world not of our own making but for which we were made.

We also make a mistake when we confuse the becoming process with progressing or evolving toward some future perfect state. We experience a rose becoming but do not perceive it as an imperfect predecessor of some more perfect flower that is likely to unfold sometime in the far-off future. Nor do we question the value of a particular rose existing. Its very existence is enough to justify it. The perfection of the rose is in its being. Why shouldn't it be the same with humanity? People have not changed in terms of physical and mental capacity for tens of thousands of years. Just as each rose is a rose and is therefore perfect in itself, that is, in its own subjective occurrence, so too with every human life.

It is ironic then, that we continue to hold on to the belief in the progressive unfolding of a collective human consciousness that will culminate in total enlightenment sometime in the far-off future, whereas in truth, the perfect state is ever present. Until we recognize that revelation and cosmic consciousness is available to everyone at all times, we will never accept full responsibility now for our every action and our relationship to the world around us. Instead, we will continue to rationalize our errors and omissions as being the result of our less than enlightened state in the collective becoming process. In other words, because we are not yet totally conscious, therefore, we do not yet have to be totally responsible.

Once we fully accept the Entropy Law, however, we can never again hide from our total responsibility for everything that happens in the world we live in and affect. Total responsibility, in turn, is a precursor to the experiencing of total consciousness and spiritual enlightenment.

The Entropy Law answers the central question that every culture throughout history has had to grapple with: How should human beings behave in the world? While it has been generally agreed that people should act in a way that preserves and enhances life, there have been countless prescriptions for exactly how to go about achieving such ends. Finally, the Entropy Law provides an answer that is all-embracing. Preserving and enhancing life, in all of its forms, requires available energy. The more energy available, the greater the prospects for extending the possibilities of life into the future. But the second law also tells us that the available store of energy in the world is continually being depleted by every occurrence. The more energy each of us uses up, the less is available for all life that comes after us. The ultimate moral imperative, then, is to waste as little energy as possible. By so doing, we are expressing our love of life and our loving commitment to the continued unfolding of all of life.

Therefore, when we speak of love in the universal sense, we are speaking of that deep spirit of oneness that acknowledges that we are each an inseparable part of the total flow that is the becoming process of life itself.

Love is not antientropic, as some would like to believe. If love were antientropic, it would be a force in opposition to becoming, for the entropic flow and becoming go hand in hand. Rather, love is an act of supreme commitment to the unfolding process. That is why the highest form of love is self-sacrifice—the willingness to go without, even to give one's own life, if necessary, to foster life itself.

Love is a gentle, subtle force that conveys a feeling of total awareness and integration with the universal rhythm that is the becoming process. By its expression, love acknowledges a master plan for the unfolding of the physical sojourn in the universe, even as it acknowledges the impossibility of ever fully understanding the mysteries that lie behind it. It is at once a statement of faith in the ultimate goodness of that cosmic process and an act of total, unconditional surrender to the natural rhythmic flow that carries all physical reality along its course.

Love, then, is a savoring experience. It attempts neither to speed up nor to arrest the becoming process because in its pure form it is simply the embodiment of that universal cosmic rhythm that is meant to be respected and adhered to.

In the end, our individual presence rests forever in the collective soul of the unfolding process itself. To conserve as best we can the fixed endowment that was left to us, and to respect as best we can the natural rhythm that governs the becoming process, is to express our ultimate love for all life that preceded us and all life that will follow. To be aware of this dual responsibility is the first step toward our transformation from a colonizing to a climactic mode. We are all stewards of the world.

Postscript

The human species is entering into the Greenhouse World. The emerging energy crisis and global warming trend represent the greatest challenge to the survival of our species in recorded history. To effectively meet that challenge, the human race will need to develop a new world view that takes into account the underlying tenets of the laws of thermodynamics and especially the Entropy Law. There are seven things every reader should bear in mind, then, when examining the laws of energy.

First, the earth is virtually a closed system. In thermodynamics, consideration is given to three types of systems: isolated systems, which exchange neither matter nor energy with the outside world; closed systems, which exchange energy but not matter; and open systems, which exchange both matter and energy with the external environment. The earth is virtually a closed system in relation to the solar system. It exchanges energy with the sun, but for all practical purposes, does not exchange matter with the rest of the solar system. With the exception of an occasional meteorite that falls to earth, the spraying of small amounts of cosmic dust, and an occasional satellite sent into space, no significant amount of matter enters or leaves the earth.

Second, in the short run and in isolated geographic pockets around the planet, entropy watersheds are experienced. That is, the particular matter-energy base that a society is using becomes depleted, as a result of natural forces at work or as a result of people consuming resources faster than nature can reproduce them. This forces a change to a new matter-energy base. This essay in no way suggests that the final heat death of the planet is imminent. It does suggest that our current matter-energy base of fossil fuels and a combination of specific metals is becoming depleted, requiring the shift to a new matter-energy field.

Third, every new matter-energy base becomes the context for the development of a new set of technologies to collect, exchange and discard that particular matter-energy environment. Along with the new modes of technology come new institutions, values, and world views. While the matter-energy base sets the context, it does not rigidly determine the specific ordering process that a society chooses to utilize in transforming the environment into the economic utilities of life. The types of technologies, institutions, values, and world views can vary considerably, but they must at least remain compatible with the matter-energy base they are processing.

Fourth, the world economy is in the early stages of an historic transition from an extractive energy base of fossil fuels and rare metals to a solar age with renewable resources as the primary energy source. Already two competing methodologies are developing, each with a very different approach to organizing biological resources in the coming solar age. The first method can be loosely defined under the rubric of ecological technology. This approach puts a premium on compatibility with the speed of the production process in nature. The overriding principle is to balance our economic budget with nature. In other words, an effort is made not to consume faster than nature can produce. Emphasis is placed on decentralized institutions, labor intensive skills, greater diversity and regional self-sufficiency along with frugal and equitable use of nature's resources. An ecological technology approach and infrastructure is already developing in a fragmented fashion in communities across the country.

At the same time, an entirely different approach to organizing renewable resources is emerging as we enter the Solar Age. It is called genetic engineering. Corporations are pouring billions of dollars into developing genetic engineering because they are beginning to recognize that the historic transition from fossil fuels to solar and renewable energy is upon us. Believing that the ecological technology approach to organizing renewable resources is too slow and inefficient to maintain existing "growth" patterns, it is argued that engineering the biology of the planet is essential in order to speed up the conversion of living matter beyond nature's own tempo, providing an ever-expanding growth curve as we enter the Solar Age.

In the next two decades critical decisions will be made as to which of these two very different methods of organizing renewable resources will eventually dominate.

An understanding of the Entropy Law and the laws of thermodynamics is essential if we are to avoid the folly of a genetically engineered solar age. For a more detailed analysis of the grave danger of a genetically engineered solar age, the reader might wish to refer to three of my books, *Algeny, Declaration of a Heretic* and *Who Should Play God?* These works examine the ecological, economic, political, and moral issues raised by genetic engineering and the artificial creation of life.

Fifth, in the very long run, when the sun ultimately dies out, the earth will become a cold, barren planet, and eventually be only dust swirling through the cosmic theatre. In the past, scholars have equated entropy with the final heat death of the solar system and then concluded that it is not of great concern to human life since that eventuality is so far off into the distant future. *In contrast, this essay focuses attention on entropy as a process rather than a final state.* It examines the great shifts in matter-energy environments here on earth and the relationship of human beings to the laws of thermodynamics and the entropic flow. Its goal is to provide a framework for analysis. The political, cultural and economic struggles that unfold as people and civilizations adjust to a radical shift in their resource environment is examined, but not explored in depth. Hopefully, this emerging conceptual framework based on the laws of thermodynamics will encourage others to look at the political, cultural and economic dimensions of change with a new perspective.

Sixth, there will be those who find the Entropy Law utterly depressing. This is indeed strange since it is merely a physical law. When Copernicus announced that the universe does not revolve around the earth, many people were similarly depressed, but humanity somehow managed to adjust to reality. Physical laws merely tell us the way the physical world operates. How we choose to relate to those laws determines our frame of mind. It is curious to hear people lament that if the physical world is truly finite and is moving toward death with each passing moment, of what good is it to even try? Why not just give up? Yet our own personal lives also obey the Entropy Law. We go from birth to death. Our physical sojourn is finite and try as we will, there is simply no way to overcome that reality. As we first come to recognize our own finite existence, we do not generally say to ourselves, if it's all downhill (from birth to death) why bother trying at all? Instead, for most of us, the profound recognition of our own mortality usually propels us, for at least brief moments, to consider using every experience in life judiciously and with respect and reverence, knowing there is no substitute, alternative, or reversal for anything we do in our personal lives. Unfortunately these moments of profound recognition of our own personal mortality are usually few and far between, the rest of our time taken up with the scramble to overcome the Entropy Law. What is true for our personal experience is equally true for the rest of the physical world around us. Just as it is often difficult to accept our own physical mortality and the irreversibility of our life's experiences, it is difficult to accept the irreversible and finite nature of the world around us.

The entropy process is neither optimistic nor pessimistic. It is just a description of how the physical world unfolds. How we choose to come to terms with that process philosophically, determines our outlook individually and as a society. Coming to terms means understanding that entropy itself is neither good nor evil. It is true that entropy represents decay and disorder, but at the same time also represents the unfolding of life itself. Values come into play when we make decisions as to how to interact with the entropic flow.

Finally, like all scientific constructs, entropy and the laws of thermodynamics are anthropocentric in nature. All scientific laws represent our need to use symbolic abstractions to try to understand, as best we can, the way the physical world operates.

Knowledge of the Entropy Law can help us understand our relationship to the physical sojourn of which we are a small, but significant part. Like gravity, entropy is only a physical law, and this should be understood by those who would either deny its relevance altogether or who would turn it into an all embracing ideology. As an anthropocentric concept, entropy can help define the physical rules within which the game of life unfolds. How that game is played, however, is determined by the values and visions, whims and caprices, ideologies and "isms" that emanate from the human mind as people interact with each other and their environment.

Afterword

The history of thermodynamics has been—and still is—unusually agitated mainly because of the unique nature of the Entropy Law. Although the basic facts with which thermodynamics is concerned have very likely been known to humankind since the dawn of civilization, they were incorporated into the edifice of science only a hundred years ago. Before that time, men of science paid no attention to one of the most elementary facts, namely, that heat always passes by itself from the hotter to the colder body, never by itself in reverse. Today, this truth constitutes the most transparent formulation of the second law of thermodynamics, alias the Entropy Law.

The first interesting thing about this law is that it was established long before the other, less intriguing, laws—the first and the zeroth. The first law states that energy can be neither created nor annihilated (which implies the theoretically sensitive point that work of any kind is a form of energy). The zeroth law, the last to be added as a necessary theoretical pillar of classical thermodynamics, simply says that if two bodies are each in thermal equilibrium with a third, the two will also be in thermal equilibrium when brought in contact with each other.

Curiously, it was the acceptance of the first law that met with great difficulties. One can speculate that the human mind was somewhat reluctant to give up the hope that one day we may construct an engine that can perform work without using energy, that is, a perpetual motion of the first kind. One need only look up the first issue of *Science* to see that as late as 1880—hence, after thermodynamics had become a legitimate branch of natural science—the belief that electricity represents an endless free source of motor power was going strong.

As far as the march of science is concerned, it was the Entropy Law that struck the first blow to the mechanistic dogma which reigned supreme ever since the spectacular successes achieved in astronomy by Newtonian mechanics. According to that dogma, processes can proceed both forward and backward, and, as Laplace emphasized in his celebrated apotheosis of mechanics, all in nature consists of simple qualityless motion. To the crisis, purists replied—and a few still do—that thermodynamics is not a legitimate natural science because some of its concepts are anthropomorphic (as if any human concept can have any other root). The Entropy Law indeed implies a distinction rooted in the structure of humans. One of its formulations calls for distinguishing between two qualities of the quantitatively invariable energy. There is the available energy, the quality that we can use for our own purposes, and the unavailable energy that, in the words of Lord Kelvin, is "irrevocably lost to man . . . although not annihilated." The point is a consequence of a principle first brought to light by N. L. S. Carnot (in a famous memoir of 1824): "For a heat engine operating in cycles to perform mechanical work, we must use two bodies of different temperatures."

Just as a weight can produce mechanical work only if it can fall from a higher to a lower level, so thermal energy cannot drive an engine operating in cycles unless it can "fall" to a lower level of temperature (a parallel that Carnot wrongly interpreted as an analytical identity). Just as a weight cannot supply any mechanical work once it reaches the lowest available level, so thermal energy is "irrevocably lost to man" after it reaches the lowest available temperature.

What is denied here is the perpetual motion of the second kind: that is, an engine operating in cycles and using only the thermal energy of a single source. But we must not fail to note that this denial would not apply if we were creatures that would not necessarily be confined to a finite space, so that we could also use engines that do not operate in cycles; as well as creatures for which time did not matter, so that we could use engines that, moving with infinitesimal speed, encounter no friction. The only reason that sets perpetual motion of the second kind out of bounds for us is the finitude of the human condition. Only on this basis can one say that thermodynamics smacks of anthropomorphism.

Because Rudolf Clausius defined entropy as a relative index (relative to temperature) of the unavailable energy in an isolated system, we speak now of the irrevocable increase of entropy, thus leaving the impression that the increase comes mysteriously from nowhere. What is overlooked is that the increase corresponds to a decrease in the available energy. For a simple representation of this otherwise complex phenomenon I liken the isolated system to an hourglass that cannot be turned upside down yet marks the true passage of time.

Because of the mysterious way the Entropy Law is usually formulated and because the great physicist A. S. Eddington hailed it as the supreme law of nature, that law has had an unusually strong appeal. The concept of entropy has also been translated into virtually all other domains—communications, biology, economics, sociology, psychology, political science, and even art. The culprit for opening the door on this situation is Claude Shannon. On finding in his pathbreaking contribution of 1948 that the average number of messages per signal in a vernacular code is given by the same algebraic formula as that proposed by Boltzmann for entropy, Shannon referred to that average as "the entropy of information." The term has stuck ever since. A muddled semantic metamorphosis has then led even to the identification of knowledge with low (negative) entropy. But Shannon, at least, showed his scholarly stature by denouncing in his 1956 article "The Bandwagon" the absurdity of the trend that has "ballooned [the entropy information] to an importance beyond its actual accomplishments." Not surprisingly, however, the parade with the naked emperor still marches on.

In view of the irreversibility proclaimed by the Entropy Law, it was quite natural that this law should create great stirring around the eternal issue: What is life? The establishment of the Entropy

Law threw that issue onto the horns of a dilemma. If the material universe is constantly subject to irrevocable degradation, how can life-bearing structures develop, survive, and even expand? This thought, no doubt, prompted some of the great pioneers in thermodynamics to have reservations on the universal validity of the Entropy Law. Quite early, Hermann von Helmholtz questioned whether the reversal of unavailable into available energy "is also impossible for the delicate structures of the organic living tissues." Still more interestingly, Lord Kelvin's first formulation of that law ran as follows: "It is impossible *by means of inanimate material agency,* to derive mechanical effect from any portion of matter by cooling it below the temperature of the coldest of the surrounding objects" (emphasis added).

The open conflict sprang from an epistemological clash. Long before the Entropy Law was established, Karl Ernst von Baer (1792–1876) refuted the prevailing dogma that eggs are miniatures of developed creatures by discovering the mammalian ovum. He was thus led to proclaim that the heterogeneous emerges from the homogeneous. Later, Herbert Spencer raised this idea to the level of the most important law of nature. Still later, some scholars (such as George Hirth and Felix Auerbach) and philosophers (such as Henri Bergson and Alfred North Whitehead) insisted on the unique property of life to run counter to the downgrade movement of inert matter. The accusations of mysticism cast at this philosophy crumble if one simply observes the following:

First, the Entropy Law applies only to completely isolated systems, whereas a living organism, being an open system, exchanges both matter and energy with its environment. There is thus no contradiction to the Entropy Law as long as the increase in the entropy of the environment more than compensates for the decrease in the entropy of the organism.

Second, the Entropy Law does not determine the speed of the degradation; this may be accelerated (as by all animals) or slowed down (as by green plants).

Third, the same law does not constrain the types of structures that may emerge from the entropic whirlpool. For a clarifying analogy: geometry constrains the size of the diagonals in a square, but it does not constrain the color of the square. To be sure, how a square happens to be "green," for instance, is a different and almost impossible question.

Thermodynamics teaches what Boltzmann and, quite recently, Erwin Schrödinger said, namely, that any organism needs to continuously suck low entropy from the environment; otherwise, it would very quickly degrade entropically. But no loophole has yet been discovered in the Entropy Law to justify the impressive claim that the existence of life-bearing structures is a necessary conclusion of thermodynamic laws. The truth as we know it today is that life is not a conclusion of the whole body of chemicophysical laws and that it is the *behavior* of any chemical compound or biological organism that must be listed among the properties of every element composing that compound or organism.

This brief story has recently been completed with a very important episode. Either because the Western intellect is dominated by a flow complex or because energy, being a homogeneous "substance," is analytically far more tractable than heterogeneous matter, thermodynamics (or any other theoretical branch of physics for that matter) paid no attention to what happens to the material scaffold of engines. Matter is mentioned in thermodynamics only in relation to the waste of available energy through the nonuseful work against friction. Yet the fact that available matter (to retain Lord Kelvin's expressive term) also becomes unavailable is just as elementary and transparent as the similar transformation to which energy is subjected. That is not all. Transparent and elementary also is the fact that, again because of the finitude of our existence, we cannot recycle the rubber molecules dissipated from automobile tires, the copper molecules dissipated from coins, the phosphorus molecules dissipated from chemical fertilizers, and so on down the line. These are "irrevocably lost to man." We can recycle only matter that is still available but is no longer in a useful shape: broken glass, worn-out tools, etc.—in a word, "garbojunk."

A new law, the fourth law of thermodynamics (not a very fortunate terminological choice) must, therefore, complete our description of the entropic transformations. It may be stated in several equivalent formulations:

A. Unavailable matter cannot be recycled.
B. A closed system (i.e., a system that cannot exchange matter with the environment) cannot perform work indefinitely at a constant rate.

This law proclaims for matter what the Entropy Law proclaims for energy. One difference is that in an isolated system, instead of tending toward heat death (when all energy is unavailable), it tends toward chaos (when all matter-energy is unavailable). However, we must refrain from speaking of the entropy of matter as a measurable entity. There is a measurable entropy for energy because energy is homogeneous; matter in bulk is instead heterogeneous, as is plainly evidenced by the Mendeleev table. The factors that dissipate matter, therefore, vary greatly from one material substance to another; hence, we cannot (at this time) subsume all material dissipations into one general formula—which does not mean that such dissipations do not take place irrevocably or that we cannot speak of the general degradation of available matter-energy into the unavailable form.

In this new light, the entropic predicament of our species emerges as far more complicated than we all now think in reacting to the present energy crisis. First, the recipe of a steady state can no longer be considered an ecological salvation (which does not mean to repudiate also the ethical and social merits that Herman Daly invokes in its support). Second, a valid technology must be able to maintain its material scaffold as long as its specific fuel is available. Considering only the energy flows, as is now the general practice, may mislead. Notwithstanding continuous claims to the contrary, the direct use of solar energy does not yet constitute a viable technology. The presently known recipes are certainly feasible (as the recipe for putting a man on the Moon is), but (like this other recipe) they are parasites of the current technology. Not to recognize this fact overtly fosters false and, hence, dangerous hopes in the public mind.

A still more interesting turn in the history of thermodynamics is the heated controversy, often exaggerated beyond reason, that grew around irreversibility; that is, around the unique direction of time as the stream of human consciousness. It was the peculiar attachment of our minds to the mechanistic explanation that burst to the surface again. As we may recall, in his Baltimore Lectures (1894), Lord Kelvin acknowledged that only if he was able to represent a process by a mechanical model was he able to understand it. Naturally, the Entropy Law, which expressly denied that thermal energy can move by itself in both directions between two bodies, was not accepted wholeheartedly by the scholarly world. So, apart from a few protesting voices, all physicists were delighted when Boltzmann set forth the idea that thermodynamic phenomena are the result of the movements of the molecules of a gas according to the deterministic laws of classical mechanics combined with a random factor.

The mechanistic dogma thus triumphed again. That it has ever since remained the fundamental password in thermodynamics should not surprise us. But the flaws caused by the probabilistic viewpoint in our *Weltbild* and, finally, in our *Weltanschauung* should not pass unnoticed.

As long as the logical foundation of thermodynamics rests also on probability (in whatever formulation), the spontaneous turning of unavailable into available energy is only a very improbable but not impossible event. We can therefore hope to think up a sharper's trick by which to cause this possible transformation to happen almost at will and thus increase our supply of available energy. It is not unreasonable to think that this sanguine hope is responsible for the rather frequent belief that the Entropy Law will be refuted someday.

Unfortunately, this belief bears on mankind's entropic predicament mentioned earlier. It stems from the fact that the human species transcended the slow and uncertain biological pathway to ecological progress when it began producing exosomatic (detachable) organs out of mineral resources. The root of economic scarcity lies not only in the finitude of these resources but also in the irrevocable entropic degradation. It is for this reason that, fifteen years ago, in my analysis of the entropic nature of the material side of the economic process, I felt it necessary to expose in detail the fallacy of the marriage between probability and the strict laws of mechanics. That my effort was worthwhile finds proof in the outburst with which Peter L. Auer, a professional physicist, once prefaced his claim that the Entropy Law does not prevent continuous economic growth. This is the same position as that of the economic profession as a whole: "Come what may, we shall find a way."

It is rather hard to explain how this view was reached. True, the founders of neoclassical economics were infatuated with the mechanistic dogma dominant at that time. Economists have taken notice of the first law. Alfred Marshall, for one, explicitly recognized that we can produce neither matter nor energy; we can produce only "utilities." Modern economists, however, have failed to take notice of the Entropy Law; so none has come to ask how we can produce utilities. Briefly, standard economics (the economics prevalent nowadays) has completely ignored the special role of depletable natural resources in mankind's mode of life, a role that transpires through the main actions of history, especially through the history of warfare. Not only are depletable natural resources completely absent from standard economic theory, but only economic growth is "the grand objective" of the economic science, as Sir Roy Harrod proudly proclaimed. Indeed, some of the greatest palms have been won by economic models in which continuous exponential growth is taken for granted. Naturally, to claim that to bring about growth is the economist's expertise constitutes the surest way to induce a general admiration for the profession.

After the oil embargo of 1973–1974 a few economists stealthily shifted their old positions somewhat. Walter Heller—an exception— even admitted that economists "have been caught with their parameters down." (It would have been more correct to say "up in the air" than "down.") Yet most economists stubbornly cling to the position that the price mechanism can prevent any scarcity calamity. The simple fact, noted by William Miernyk, is that the price of oil at the time when one could get free drinking glasses with each gasoline fill-up pointed the United States technology and economy in a direction we all now regret. Because of the general growth mania and the economists' unchallenged faith in the price mechanism, some people now crave such utterly absurd gadgetry as the golf cart, while numberless others go through a very short life of sufferings beyond imagination.

Afterword

Although the haves care, albeit marginally, for their contemporary have-nots, mankind as a whole does next to nothing to protect future generations from possible catastrophes. Programs such as my bioeconomic one have been variously proposed. The only reason why they have remained virtually ignored is the difficulty of changing values concerning intranational and, especially, international relations. It is therefore imperative for us all to realize the dangers for our whole species created by a behavior based on individual self-interest and on maximizing personal utility instead of minimizing future regrets.

The Entropy Law in its extensive form sets material limits to the specific mode of life of the human species, limits that tie together present and future generations in an adventure without parallel in our knowledge. Because the importance of these limitations has come into plain view only recently and because the entropic abundance of the last two hundred years or so is rapidly approaching its end, we must reassess and remodel our approach to economic, political, and social evolution. Jeremy Rifkin is especially qualified to set this entire problem in a convincing light, not cluttered by unsubstantial technical details. This volume is written with the same masterly human penetration that has won great acclaim for his earlier essays. In writing about the Entropy Law, one runs the risk of falling victim to the fashion of seeking to impress by complex but empty exercises. Jeremy Rifkin steered clear of the frequent exercises about the formal parallelism imagined to exist between entropic transformations and social phenomena: thermodynamics sets a limit to these phenomena but does not govern them. For its timely educative value and for its pronouncedly human underpinning this volume should have an honored place on any individual or public bookshelf, to spread the commandment suggested by the present turning point in mankind's life on this planet: "Love thy species as thyself!"

Nicholas Georgescu-Roegen
Vanderbilt University
February 1980

Notes

PART ONE
WORLD VIEWS

1. Irving M. Mintzer, "A Matter of Degrees: The Potential for Controlling the Greenhouse Effect," World Resources Institute, Research Report #5 (April 1987), Foreword, i.
2. A. M. Solomon, "The Global Cycle of Carbon," R. M. Rotty and C. D. Masters, "Carbon Dioxide from Fossil Fuel Combustion: Trends, Resources, and Technological Implications," and R. A. Houghton, "Carbon Dioxide Exchange Between the Atmosphere and Terrestrial Ecosystems," cited in John R. Trabalka, *Atmospheric Carbon Dioxide and the Global Carbon Cycle* (Washington, D.C.: U.S. Government Printing Office, 1985).
3. Ramanathan, "Trace Gas Trends and their Potential Role in Climate Change," 90 *Journal of Geophysical Research* (pp. 5547–66 (1985).
4. Ibid.
5. Anthony Ramirez, "A Warming World," *Fortune*, July 4, 1988, p. 104.
6. "A Gaping Hole in the Sky," *Newsweek*, July 11, 1988, p. 22.
7. National Aeronautics and Space Administration, "Knowledge of the Upper Atmosphere," January 1986; Environmen-

tal Protection Agency, "Analysis of Strategies for Protecting the Ozone Layer," prepared for Working Group Meeting, Geneva, Switzerland (January 1985).

8. "A Gaping Hole in the Sky," op. cit., p. 21.

9. Ibid., p. 22.

10. Ibid., p. 23.

11. Ibid.

12. "Knowledge of the Upper Atmosphere," op. cit.; "Analysis of Strategies for Protecting the Ozone Layer," op. cit.

13. Gordon J. Macdonald, "Climate Change and Acid Rain," The MITRE Corporation, McLean, Virginia (December 1985).

14. National Research Council, *Global Change in the Geosphere-Biosphere,* (Washington, D.C.: National Academy Press, 1986).

15. Macdonald, op. cit.

16. "The Heat Is On," *New York Times*, June 26, 1988.

17. *Allegemeine Forst Zeitschrift*, Munich, West Germany, No. 46 (1985) and No. 41 (1986); G. H. M. Krause, "Forest Decline in Europe: Possible Causes and Etiology," paper presented at the International Symposium on Acid Precipitation (Ontario, Canada, September 1985).

18. *Allegemeine Forest Zeitschrift*, op. cit., No. 46 (1985) and No. 41 (1986).

19. Krause, op. cit.

20. Bryon W. Bachel, "The Acidification of Soils," and B. Ulrich, "Production and Consumption of Hydrogen Ions in the Ecosphere," in T. C. Hutchinson and M. Havas, eds., *Effects of Acid Precipitation on Terrestrial Ecosystems* (New York: Plenum Press, 1980).

21. "Acid Rains," *East-West Journal*, p. 23 (October, 1977).

22. D. W. Schindler, "Long-Term Ecosystem Stress: The Effect of Years of Experimental Acidification on a Small Lake," *Science*, June 21, 1985.

23. H. J. Ewers, "Zur Monetarisierung der Waldschaden in der Bundesrepublik Deutschland," paper presented at Symposium on Costs of Environmental Pollution, Bonn, West Germany (September 12–13, 1985).

24. A. H. Moore, "A Warming World," *Fortune,* July 4, 1988, p. 104.

25. Ibid,; Mintzer, op. cit., Foreword, i.
26. "The Greenhouse Effect: Impacts on Current Global Temperature and Regional Heat Waves." Testimony of James E. Hansen before the Senate Committee on Environment and Natural Resources, June 23, 1988.
27. Ibid.
28. Jill Jaeger, *Developing Polices for Responding to Climate Change* (Stockholm, Sweden: The Beijer Institute's World Climate Programme—Impact Studies, April 1988) [Bellagio Report], p. 11.
29. Ibid., p. 10.
30. Ibid., p. 11.
31. Andrew C. Revkin, "Endless Summer: Living with the Greenhouse Effect," *Discover*, September 27, 1988, p. 50.
32. Ibid.
33. Ibid.
34. Ibid.
35. Ibid.
36. James Hansen, NASA's Goddard Institute for Space Studies, quoted in "The Endless Summer?" *Newsweek*, July 11, 1988, p. 20.
37. Ibid., pp. 18–19.
38. W. R. Rangeley, "Irrigation and Drainage in the World," presented at the International Conference on Food and Water, Texas A & M University, (May 26–30, 1985).
39. Ibid.
40. Ramirez, op. cit., p. 107.
41. Walter Roberts, president emeritus of the National Center for Atmospheric Research (NCAR), quoted in ibid., p. 105.
42. Ramirez, op. cit., p. 105.
43. Bellagio Report, op. cit., p. 12
44. Erik Eckholm, "Disappearing Species: The Social Challenge," *Worldwatch Paper 22* (Worldwatch Institute, June 1978), p. 7.
45. "Report Urges Greenhouse Action Now," *Science*, July 1, 1988, p. 23.
46. Bellagio Report, op. cit., pp. 1–2.
47. Ramirez, op. cit., pp. 104–105.

48. Ibid., p. 104.
49. Bellagio Report, ibid.
50. J. B. Bury, *The Idea of Progress: An Inquiry into Its Origin and Growth* (New York: Macmillan, 1932), pp. 11–12.
51. Pardon E. Tillinghast, *Approaches to History* (Englewood Cliffs, N.J.: Prentice-Hall, 1963), p. 9.
52. Ibid., p. 11.
53. John Herman Randall, *The Making of the Modern Mind* (Cambridge, Mass.: Houghton Mifflin, 1940), p. 34.
54. Dante Germino, *Modern Western Political Thought: Machiavelli to Marx* (Chicago: Rand McNally, 1972), p. 166.
55. Francis Bacon, *Novum Organum,* Book 1, Aphorism 2.
56. Ibid., Aphorism 71.
57. Randall, op. cit., p. 223.
58. Ibid., p. 224.
59. Theodore Roszak, *Where the Wasteland Ends* (Garden City, N.Y.: Doubleday/Anchor Books, 1973), pp. 144–45.
60. Randall, op. cit., p. 224.
61. Jean Houston, "Prometheus Rebound: An Inquiry into Technological Growth and Psychological Change," in *Alternatives to Growth I,* Dennis Meadows, ed. (Cambridge, Mass.: Ballinger, 1977), p. 274.
62. Randall, op. cit., p. 241.
63. Ibid., pp. 241–42.
64. Ibid., p. 259.
65. Ibid.
66. Alfred North Whitehead, *Science and the Modern World* (New York: New American Library, 1925), p. 50.
67. Leo Strauss, *Natural Rights and History* (Chicago: University of Chicago Press, 1953), p. 258.
68. John Locke, "Second Treatise," in John Locke, *Two Treatises of Government,* ed. Peter Laslett (Cambridge University Press, 1967), p. 315.
69. Ibid.
70. Ibid.
71. Ibid., p. 312.
72. Ibid.
73. Ibid.

74. Adam Smith, *An Inquiry into the Nature and Causes of the Wealth of Nations,* ed. Edwin Cannon (London: Methuen, 1961), 1:475.

PART TWO
THE ENTROPY LAW

1. Theodore Roszak, *Where the Wasteland Ends* (Garden City, N.Y.: Doubleday/Anchor Books, 1973), p. 139.
2. Isaac Asimov, "In the Game of Energy and Thermodynamics You Can't Even Break Even," *Smithsonian,* August 1970, p. 9.
3. Ibid., p. 6.
4. Herman Daly, *Steady-State Economics* (San Francisco: Freeman, 1977), pp. 21–22.
5. Nicholas Georgescu-Roegen, "The Steady State and Ecological Salvation," *Bio Science* (April 1977): 268.
6. Ibid.
7. Bertrand Russell, *The Scientific Outlook* (New York: Norton, 1962), p. 114.
8. Stanley Angrist and Loren Hepler, "Demons, Poetry and Life: A Thermodynamic View," *Texas Quarterly* 10 (September 1967): 27–28.
9. Ibid.
10. Ibid., p. 29.
11. Russell, op cit., pp. 90–91.
12. Nicholas Georgescu-Roegen, *The Entropy Law and the Economic Process* (Cambridge, Mass.: Harvard University Press, 1971), pp. 6–7.
13. Angrist and Hepler, op. cit., p. 30.
14. G. Tyler Miller, Jr., *Energetics, Kinetics and Life* (Belmont, Calif.: Wadsworth, 1971), p. 46.
15. Philip P. Weiner, ed., *Dictionary of the History of Ideas* (New York: Scribner's, 1973), 2:113.
16. P. A. Y. Gunter, ed., *Bergson and the Evolution of Physics* (Knoxville, Tenn.: University of Tennessee Press, 1977), p. 63.
17. William Thompson (Lord Kelvin) in *Proceedings of the Royal Society of Edinburgh* 8:325–31 (1874). Cited in *American Scientist,* October 1949, p. 559.

18. Harold F. Blum, *Time's Arrow and Evolution* (Princeton, N.J.: Princeton University Press, 1968), p. 94.

19. Erwin Schrodinger, *What Is Life?* (New York: Macmillan, 1947), pp. 72, 75.

20. Leslie A. White, "Tools, Techniques and Energy," in *Cultural and Social Anthropology,* ed. D. Hammond (New York: Macmillan, 1964), p. 28.

21. Miller, op. cit., p. 291.

22. Ibid.

23. White, op. cit., p. 28.

24. Alfred J. Lotka, "Contribution to the Energetics of Evolution," *Proceedings of the National Academy of Science* (1922): 8:149. Also see, Lotka, "The Law of Evolution as a Maximal Principle," *Human Biology* 17 (September 1945): 186.

PART THREE

ENTROPY: A NEW HISTORICAL FRAME

1. Harry Rothman, *Murderous Providence: A Study of Pollution in Industrial Societies* (New York: Bobbs-Merrill, 1972), p. 34.

2. Lynn White, Jr., "Technology in the Middle Ages," in *Technology in Western Civilization,* ed. Melvin Kranzberg and Carroll W. Purrell, Jr. (New York: Oxford University Press, 1967), p. 72.

3. William McNeill, *Plagues and People* (New York: Doubleday/ Anchor Books, 1976), p. 147.

4. Lewis Mumford, *Technics and Civilization* (New York: Harcourt, Brace, 1934), pp. 119–20.

5. Ibid., p. 120.

6. Eugene Ayres, "The Age of Fossil Fuels," in *Man's Role in Changing the Face of the Earth,* ed. William L. Thomas, Jr. (Chicago: University of Chicago Press, 1956), p. 368.

7. Edmund Howes, ed., *Stow's Annals* (London, 1631), quoted in W. H. G. Armytage, *A Social History of Engineering* (London: 1961).

8. Richard Wilkinson, *Poverty and Progress* (New York: Praeger, 1973), pp. 90, 102.

9. Friedrich Engels, *The Condition of the Working Class in England* (Oxford University Press, 1958), pp. 78–79.

10. Jacques Ellul, *The Technological Society* (New York: Random House/Vintage Books, 1964), p. 105.

11. Ibid., p. 116.

12. Eugene S. Schwartz, *Overskill: The Decline of Technology in Modern Civilization* (New York: Quadrangle, 1971), p. 72.

13. "Innovation: Has America Lost Its Edge?" *Newsweek,* June 4, 1979, pp. 58–59.

14. *Environmental Quality,* Ninth Annual Report of the Council on Environmental Quality (Washington, D.C.: U.S. Government Printing Office, 1978), p. 437.

15. *Environmental Quality*, Fifteenth Annual Report of the Council on Environmental Quality (Washington, D.C.: U.S. Government Printing Office, 1984), p. 614.

16. Information available from the National Petroleum Institute.

17. "Innovation," ibid., p. 59.

PART FOUR

NONRENEWABLE ENERGY AND
THE APPROACHING ENTROPY WATERSHED

1. Fred C. Allvine and Fred A. Tarpley, Jr., "The New State of the Economy: The Challenging Prospect," in *U.S. Economic Growth from 1976 to 1986: Prospects, Problems and Patterns,* Studies for the Joint Economic Committee of the U.S. Congress (Washington, D.C.: U.S. Government Printing Office, 1976), p. 58.

2. Wilson Clark, *Energy for Survival* (Garden City, N.Y.: Doubleday/Anchor Books, 1975), p. 70.

3. Resources for the Future, *Annual Report*, Washington, D.C.: 1972, p. 12.

4. "Annual Energy Review 1987," United States Department of Energy, Office of Energy Markets and End Use, Energy Information Administration, 1987, p. 5.; "International Energy Outlook 1987, With Projections to the Year 2000," United States Department of Energy, Office of Energy Mar-

kets and End Use, Energy Information Administration, 1987, p. 22.

5. Clark, op. cit., p. 70.
6. "International Energy Outlook 1987, With Projections to the Year 2000," op. cit., p. 1.
7. Statistics from Frank H. Oram, Associate Director, World Population Society, Washington, D.C., August 1978.
8. "Our Population Predicament: A New Look," from Population Reference Bureau Inc., vol. 34, no. 5, December 1979.
9. Lester R. Brown, "State of the World 1988," World Watch Institute, Washington, D.C., p. 23.
10. Robert L. Heilbroner, "Boom and Crash," *The New Yorker,* August 28, 1978, p. 70.
11. William Ophuls, "The Scarcity Society," *Skeptic,* July–August 1974, pp. 50–51.
12. Lee Schipper, "Energy: Global Prospects 1985–2000," *Bulletin of the Atomic Scientists,* March, 1978, p. 58.
13. Ibid.
14. Hobart Rowen, "Oil Supply Adequate, Possibly to 1990s, Trilateral Commission Study Concludes," *Washington Post,* June 14, 1978, p. D9.
15. Emile Benoit, "The Coming Age of Shortages, Part I," *Bulletin of the Atomic Scientists,* March 1978, p. 9.
16. Lester R. Brown. *The Twenty-Ninth Day* (New York: Norton, 1978), pp. 99–100.
17. Brown, op. cit. p. 57.
18. Complex Systems Research Center (CSRC) Study (University of New Hampshire, 1982).
19. Ibid.
20. Hall, C. J. Cleveland, and R. Kaufmann, *Energy and Resource Quality: The Ecology of the Industrial Process* (John Wiley and Sons, 1986).
21. Ibid.
22. Benoit, op. cit., p. 9.
23. Worldwatch Institute, op. cit., p. 33.
24. U.S. Department of Energy, *Strategic Plan for the Civilian Reactor Development Program* (October 1985).

25. "Turning Down the Heat: Solutions to Global Warming," a publication of the Safe Energy Communication Council and Public Citizen, Washington, D.C., 1988, p. 17.
26. David Dickson, "Nuclear Power Uneconomic Says Congressional Committee," *Nature*, May 11, 1978, p. 91.
27. Helen Caldicott, *Nuclear Madness* (Brookline, Mass.: Autumn Press, 1978), p. 43.
28. U.S.S.R. State Committee on the Utilization of Human Energy, "The Accident at the Chernobyl Nuclear Power Plant and its Consequences," information compiled for the International Atomic Energy Agency Experts' meeting, Vienna (August 25–29, 1986).
29. Ibid.
30. Bureau Europeen des Unions De Consommateurs, *Chernyobyl: The Aftermath*.
31. "Swiss Plan Nuclear Meeting," European Energy Report (Financial Times Business Information), September 19, 1986.
32. Francis X. Clines, "Chernobyl Shakes Reindeer Culture of Lapps," *New York Times*, September 14, 1986.
33. "Cost of Chernobyl," *European Energy Report;* "Chernobyl Costs Put at $3 Billion," *Journal of Commerce*, September 22, 1986.
34. Stuart Diamond, "Two Experts Foresee Deaths of 24,000 Tied to Chernobyl," *New York Times*, August 27, 1986.
35. Worldwatch Institute projections.
36. Andrew Holmes, "The Ratchet Turns Again on Safety and Economics," *Energy Economist* (Financial Times Business Information), June 1986.
37. Caldicott, op. cit., p. 51.
38. Ibid., p. 23.
39. Office of Technology Assessment, *The Effects of Nuclear War* (Washington, D.C.: U.S. Government Printing Office, 1979).
40. Luther J. Carter, "Radioactive Wastes: Some Urgent Unfinished Business," *Science*, February 18, 1977, p. 61.
41. *Transportation of Hazardous Materials*, Office of Technology Assessment, U.S. Congress, p. 221 (July, 1986).
42. "Turning Down the Heat," op. cit., p. 24.

43. "Surveying the Radioactive Waste Dilemma: An Overview," Critical Mass Energy Project, Washington, D.C., August 1978, p. 5.
44. Worldwatch Institute estimates.
45. Sandia National Laboratory, "Estimates of the Financial Consequences of Nuclear Power Reactor Accidents," prepared for the Nuclear Regulatory Commission (Washington, D.C., 1982).
46. James Cook, "Nuclear Follies," *Forbes,* February 11, 1985.
47. W. Jackson Davis, *The Seventh Year: Industrial Civilization in Transition* (New York: Norton, 1979), p. 65.
48. Wilson Clark, *Energy for Survival* (New York: Doubleday/ Anchor Books, 1975), p. 320.
49. Malcolm W. Browne, "Fusion Power: Is There Still an Eldorado for Energy?" *New York Times,* April 15, 1979, p. E9.
50. Ibid.
51. Amory Lovins, "A Light on the Soft Energy Path," in *Sun: A Handbook for the Solar Decade,* ed. Stephen Lyons (San Francisco: Friends of the Earth, 1978).
52. Sam Love, "The New Look of the Future," *The Futurist* 11 (April 1977): 80.
53. Richard England and Barry Bluestone, "Ecology and Social Conflict," in *Toward a Steady State Economy,* ed. Herman E. Daly (San Francisco: Freeman, 1973), p. 196.
54. Preston Cloud, "Mineral Resources in Fact and Fancy," in *Toward a Steady State Economy,* ed. Herman Daly (San Francisco: Freeman, 1973).
55. Ibid.
56. *U.S. Long Term Economic Growth Prospects: Entering a New Era,* Studies for the Joint Economic Committee of the U.S. Congress (Washington, D.C.: U.S. Government Printing Office, January 25, 1978).
57. Edward Goldsmith, "Settlements and Social Stability," in *Alternatives to Growth I,* ed. Dennis Meadows (Cambridge, Mass.: Ballinger, 1977), p. 331.
58. Lester R. Brown, "Resource Trends and Population Policy: A Time for Reassessment," Worldwatch Papers, no. 29, May 1979.

59. Benoit, op. cit.
60. Ophuls, *Ecology and the Politics of Scarcity,* op. cit., p. 87.
61. S. L. Blum, "Tapping Resources in Municipal Solid Waste," *Science* 191 (1976): 669–75.

PART FIVE
ENTROPY AND THE INDUSTRIAL AGE

1. Barry Commoner, *The Poverty of Power* (New York: Bantam Books, 1977), p. 200.
2. Ibid., p. 200.
3. John Geier, et. al., *The Threat to Food and Fuel in the Coming Decades,* "Beyond Oil" (Cambridge, Mass: Ballinger Publishers, 1986), p. 55.
4. Commoner, op. cit., p. 201.
5. "Survey of Current Business," United States Department of Commerce, August 1988, p. 85.
6. Commoner, op. cit., pp. 208–9.
7. Ibid, p. 207.
8. Leslie Ellen Nulty, *Understanding the New Inflation: The Importance of Basic Necessities* (Washington, D.C.: Exploratory Project for Economic Alternatives, 1977), pp. D19–20.
9. Ibid., pp. D26–30.
10. "Economic Report of the President 1988," U.S. Government Printing Office, 1988, p. 299. Figures given for total private non-agricultural average weekly earnings.
11. *Environmental Quality,* 1984, p. 614.
12. *Environmental Quality,* Ninth Annual Report of the Council on Environmental Quality (Washington, D.C.: U.S. Government Printing Office, December 1978), p. 270.
13. Bureau of Labor Statistics, October, 1988.
14. Herman Daly, *Steady State Economics* (San Francisco, Calif.: W.H. Freeman Co., 1977).
15. Herman Daly, "The Economic Thought of Frederick Soddy," in *History of Political Economy,* vol. 12, no. 4, (Durham, N.C.: Duke University Press, 1980), pp. 469–488.
16. Ibid., p. 475.

17. Ibid., p. 475.
18. Dennis Hayes, *Rays of Hope* (New York: Norton, 1977), p. 91.
19. Derived from "The 1988 Industrial Outlook," U.S. Department of Commerce, International Trade Administration, 1988, pp. 7–2, 7–4, and 7–5.
20. Orville Schell, "Inside the Food Technology Bazaar," *Mother Jones,* February–March 1979.
21. Institute for Local Self-Reliance, Washington, D.C., 1988.
22. Jackson W. Davis, *The Seventh Year* (New York: Norton, 1979), p. 126.
23. Barbara Ward, *The Home of Man* (New York: Norton, 1976), p. 49.
24. G. Tyler Miller, Jr., *Energetics, Kinetics and Life: An Ecological Approach* (Belmont, Calif.: Wadsworth, 1971), p. 306.
25. *The Works of Jonathan Swift,* ed. Walter Scott (Edinburgh, 1814), 12:176.
26. "Agricultural Statistics 1987," U.S. Department of Agriculture, U.S. Government Printing Office, Washington, D.C., 1987, p. 1.
27. Wilson Clark, *Energy for Survival* (Garden City, N.Y.: Doubleday/Anchor Books, 1975) p. 170.
28. Fred Warshofsky, *Doomsday: The Science of Catastrophe* (New York: Pocket Books, 1979), p. 223.
29. *Environmental Quality,* op. cit., p. 270.
30. Peter Farb, *Humankind* (Boston: Houghton, Mifflin, 1978), pp. 181–82.
31. Clark, op. cit., p. 179.
32. Fred Harris, *The New Populism* (New York: Saturday Review Press, 1973), p. 85.
33. *Food: Green Grow the Profits,* ABC television.
34. Ibid.
35. Clark, op. cit., p. 171.
36. "Agricultural Statistics 1987," p. 414.
37. Miller, op. cit., p. 300.
38. *Environmental Quality,* op. cit., p. 276.
39. Clark, op. cit., p. 172.
40. "Commercial Fertilizer Consumption Report," U.S. De-

partment of Agriculture, U.S. Government Printing Office, Washington, D.C., 1988.

41. "Agricultural Statistics 1987," p. 1.
42. "Presticide Industry Sales and Usage: 1986 Market Estimates," Economic Analysis Branch, Benefits and Use Division, Office of Pesticides Programs, Environmental Protection Agency, August 1987.
43. *Environmental Quality*, op. cit., p. 278.
44. Ibid., p. 277.
45. Clark, op. cit., p. 173.
46. *Environmental Quality,* op. cit., p. 274.
47. Lester R. Brown, *The Twenty-ninth Day* (New York: Norton, 1976), p. 49.
48. Clark, op. cit., p. 174.
49. Worldwatch Institute, *The Global Environment and Basic Human Needs,* A Report to the Council on Environmental Quality (Washington, D.C., 1978).
50. *Facts and Trends,* 12th ed. (Washington, D.C.: Transportation Association of America, 1976), p. 3.
51. Emma Rothschild, *Paradise Lost* (New York: Random House, 1973), p. 18.
52. "Annual Energy Review 1987," Energy Information Administration, Office of Markets and End Use, United States Department of Energy, Washington, D.C., 1988.
53. Clark, op. cit., p. 162.
54. Ibid., pp. 157–61.
55. Ibid., p. 160.
56. Ibid.
57. Commoner, op. cit., p. 165.
58. A. Q. Mowbray, *Road to Ruin* (Philadelphia: Lippincott, 1969), p. 15.
59. K. R. Schneider, *Autokind v. Mankind* (New York: Schocken, 1972), p. 123.
60. "Highway Statistics," Department of Transportation, Federal Highway Administration, 1988. Income figure used as median annual family income provided by the Federal Reserve.
61. R. L. Polk & Company, Taylor, MI. According to Polk,

there were 27,732 new registrations every day in 1987, and there were 28,158 cars sold every day.

62. Mowbray, op. cit., p. 15.
63. Helen Leavitt, *Superhighway: Superhoax* (New York: Ballantine, 1971), p. 13.
64. "National Safety Council Facts 1987," U.S. Government Printing Office, 1987.
65. Leavitt, op. cit., p. 257.
66. The United States Department of Transportation, Federal Highway Traffic Safety Administration.
67. Leavitt, op. cit., p. 20.
68. "Federal Highway Statistics," U.S. Department of Transportation, 1988.
69. Clark, op. cit., p. 158.
70. Brown, op. cit., p. 2.
71. Mowbray, op. cit., p. 14.
72. Ibid., p. 12.
73. Leavitt, op. cit., p. 6.
74. Mowbray, op. cit., p. 68.
75. John Dillin, "Potholes, Ruts Crumbling Asphalt Mark Interstate Highway," *The Christian Science Monitor,* September 4, 1987.
76. Ridley, op. cit., p. 4.
77. Eighth Annual Report to Congress: Highway Bridge Replacement and Rehabilitation Program," Federal Highway Administration, Office of Engineering Bridge Division, p. 9 (1987).
78. Mowbray, op. cit., p. 33.
79. Robert Goodman, *After the Planners* (New York: Simon & Schuster, 1971), p. 79.
80. "The Clean Air Act: A Briefing Book For the Members of Congress," The National Clean Air Coalition, Washington, D.C., 1985, p. 120.
81. Mowbray, op. cit., p. 71; Clark, op. cit., p. 110.
82. Harold M. Schmeck, Jr., "Lower Level Lead Exposure Tied to Child Brain Damage," *New York Times,* March 29, 1979, p. A18.
83. Ibid.

84. Irving M. Mintzer, "A Matter of Degree: The Potential for Controlling the Greenhouse Effect," Report #5, (World Resources Institute, April, 1987).

85. "Drift Away from Big Cities Goes On," *U.S. News and World Report,* November 15, 1976.

86. Davis, op. cit., p. 229.

87. Murray Bookchin, *The Limits of the City* (New York: Harper & Row, 1974), p. 92.

88. Kirkpatrick Sale, "The Polis Perplexity: An Inquiry into the Size of Cities," *Working Papers,* January–February 1978, p. 75.

89. "Drift Away from Big Cities Goes On," op. cit.

90. "USA By Numbers: a statistical portrait of the United States," Susan Weber, Ed., Zero Population Growth, Washington, D.C., 1988, pp. 12, 13, and 26.

91. Sale, op. cit., p. 66.

92. Ward, op. cit., p. 4.

93. Population Reference Bureau, *1986 World Population Data Sheet.*

94. Lewis Mumford, "The Natural History of Urbanization," in *Man's Role in Changing the Face of the Earth,* ed. William L. Thomas, Jr. (University of Chicago Press, 1956).

95. Bookchin, op. cit., p. 33.

96. A. Wolman, "The Metabolism of Cities," *Scientific American* 213 (1965): 178–90.

97. Mary Thornton, "Food Exports Threatened by Loss of Farmland in U.S.," *Washington Star,* November 26, 1979, p. 2.

98. Woldman, op. cit.

99. Clark, op. cit., p. 197.

100. Ibid.

101. Kirby and Prokopovitsch, "Technological Insurance Against Shortages in Minerals and Metals," *Science* 191 (1976): 713–19.

102. Nancy Humphrey et al., *The Future of Cleveland's Capital Plant* and *The Future of New York City's Capital Plant* (Washington, D.C.: Urban Institute, 1979).

103. *Inadvertent Climate Modification,* Sponsored by the Royal Swedish Academy of Sciences and the Royal Swedish Academy of Engineering Science (Cambridge, Mass.: MIT Press, 1971), p. 12.

104. Sale, op. cit., p. 67.

105. Ibid., pp. 68–69.

106. Ward, op. cit., p. 254; Sale, op. cit., p. 70.

107. Neil Seldman, "Who Takes Out the Garbage in D.C.?" *Building System Design,* October–November 1975; Kathy Sylvester, "Monumental Garbage Problem," *Washington Star,* August 14, 1979, p. B1.

108. Sale, op. cit.

109. Leopold Kohr, *Breakdown of Nations* (New York: Rinehart, 1957).

110. *Environmental Quality,* op. cit.; "Drift Away from Big Cities Goes On," op. cit.

111. Committee For a Sane Nuclear Policy, Washington, D.C., 1988.

112. Source: Center for Defense Information, Washington, D.C., 1988.

113. Seymour Melman, "Beating Swords into Subways," *New York Times Magazine,* November 19, 1978.

114. Ibid.

115. John K. Cooley, "Oil Crunch Worries U.S. Military," *Christian Science Monitor,* May 17, 1979, p. 17.

116. Ibid.

117. Tristram Coffin, "Conversion, the Answer to Inflation and Recession," *Washington Spectator,* February 1, 1979.

118. Marion Anderson, Michael Frisch, and Michael Oden, "The Empty Porkbarrel: The employment cost of the military buildup of 1981 to 1985," by Employment Research Associates, Lansing, Mich., 1986, 16pp.

119. Marion Anderson, *The Impact of Military Spending on the Machinists Union,* Washington, D.C., International Association of Machinists, January 1979.

120. Coffin, op. cit.

121. Source: *The Bulletin of Atomic Scientists,* available from SANE, Washington, D.C., 1979.

122. Source: Center for Defense Information, Washington, D.C., 1979.

123. Ibid.

124. Coffin, op. cit.

125. John Hooper, "MX Missile Raises Specter of Massive Land Grab," in *Wilderness Report* (Washington, D.C., Wilderness Society, January 1979).

126. Letter from Robert F. Bennett to President Jimmy Carter, October 2, 1978.

127. *Congressional Record,* June 27, 1979, pp. S8740–43.

128. Telephone interview with Earl Ravenal, October 1979.

129. *Your Taxes, Your Choices,* pamphlet issued by Coalition for a New Foreign and Military Policy, Washington, D.C., 1979.

130. Source: National Defense Clearing House, 1979.

131. Eugene Schwartz, *Overskill: The Decline of Technology in Modern Civilization* (New York: Quadrangle, 1971), p. 216.

132. Hayes, op. cit., p. 209.

133. *What Could Your Tax Dollars Buy?* (Washington, D.C.: SANE, December 1978).

134. Quote from Nicholas Georgescu-Roegen in hearings before the Joint Economic Committee, "Long-Term Economic Growth," November 9, 1976, p. 15.

135. Henry Adams, *The Degradation of the Democratic Dogma* (New York: Macmillan, 1949).

136. Source: U.S. Department of Commerce, Industry and Trade Administration estimate that in 1979 advertising expenditures will reach $47.23 billion (ITA press release 79-1, January 3, 1979).

137. Jerry Mander, *Four Arguments for the Elimination of Television* (New York: Morrow Quill, 1978).

138. Vincent E. Giuliano, "The Mechanization of Office Work," in *The Information Technology Revolution,* ed. Tom Forester (Cambridge: MIT Press, 1985), p. 301. Some experts have estimated that by 1988 nearly 60 percent of the American work force will be linked to electronic work stations. Presently there are more than 350,000 computers in the

nation's schools, and at any given moment on Wall Street there are five times as many computers communicating with each other as people. See Craig Brod, *Technostress* (Reading, Mass.: Addison-Wesley, 1984), pp. 1–5.

139. Peter Schrag, *Mind Control* (New York: Pantheon, 1978), pp. 33–34.

140. Ibid., p. 33.

141. Ibid., p. 43.

142. Personal Communication, Subcommittee on Labor, Health and Human Services, Education and Related Agencies of the Appropriations Committee of the United States House of Representatives, October, 1988.

143. "Is Anyone Out There Listening?," a CBS News Report, Parts I and II, August 22–23, 1978.

144. Ibid.

145. Ibid.

146. Ibid.

147. Ibid.

148. Ibid.

149. Martin V. Melosi, *Garbage in the Cities: Refuse, Reform, and the Environment, 1880–1980* (College Station, Tex.: Texas A & M University Press, 1981).

150. National Research Council, *Causes and Effects of Changes in Stratospheric Ozone: Update 1983* (Washington, D.C.: National Academy Press, 1984).

151. "The Trashing of America," *Omni*, February, 1988, p. 40.

152. "The Trashing of America," *Omni*, February, 1988, p. 40.

153. "The Sudden Rise of the Red-Bag Business," *New York Times,* March 27, 1988.

154. National Solid Wastes Management Association Survey, quoted in ibid.

155. Environmental Task Force, "Temik Follow-Up" (Washington, D.C., 1985), p. 4.

156. *Pesticides: Need to Enhance FDA's Ability to Protect the Public From Illegal Residues* (Washington, D.C.: U.S. General Accounting Office, October 1986), p. 47.

157. *Pesticides: EPA's Formidable Task to Assess and Regulate Their Risks* (Washington, D.C., October 1983).

158. *A Congressional Agenda to Prevent Groundwater Contamination: Building Capacity to Meet Protection Needs* (Washington, D.C.: Environmental and Energy Study Institute, 1986), p. 46.

159. Ibid.

160. *Pesticides,* op. cit.

161. *Lead and Your Drinking Water* (Washington, D.C.: Environmental Protection Agency, Office of Water, April 1987).

162. Ibid.

163. "State Asbestos Programs Related to Asbestos Hazard Emergency Response Act," National Conference of State Legislatures (January 1988).

164. Scott Ridley, *The State of the States, 1988* (Washington, D.C.: Renew America Project—Fund for Renewable Energy and the Environment 1988), p. 2.

165. "Ozone Pollution Is Found at Peak in Summer Heat," *New York Times,* July 31, 1988.

166. Ibid.

167. Anatasia Toufenis, "The Dirty Seas," *Time,* August 1, 1988, pp. 44–46.

168. Ibid., p. 46.

169. Ibid.

170. Ibid., pp. 46–47.

171. Ibid., p 47.

172. "Don't Go Near the Water," *Newsweek,* August 1, 1988, p. 43.

173. Toufenis, op. cit., p. 48.

174. Ibid.

175. Ridley, op. cit., p. 2.

176. Thomas McKeown, "A Historical Appraisal of the Medical Task," in *Medical History and Medical Care,* ed. Gordon McLachlan and Thomas McKeown (London: Oxford University Press, 1971), p. 36.

177. *United States Chartbook: Health* (Washington, D.C.: HEW, National Center for Health Statistics, 1976–77), pp. 1–5.

178. Bernard Dixon, *Beyond the Magic Bullet* (New York: Harper & Row, 1978), p. 3.

179. Personal Communication, Subcommittee on Labor, Health and Human Services, op. cit.

180. Dixon, op. cit., p. 226.

181. Ivan Illich, *Medical Nemesis* (New York: Bantam, 1977), pp. 18–19.

182. Dixon, op. cit., pp. 72–74.

183. Ted Howard and Jeremy Rifkin, *Who Should Play God?* (New York: Delacorte, 1977), p. 199.

184. Milton Silverman and Philip Lee, *Pills, Profits and Politics* (Berkeley: University of California Press, 1974).

185. Ibid.

186. Illich, op. cit., p. 23.

187. House Subcommittee on Oversight and Investigations, 1976, as reported in the *Washington Star,* April 1977.

188. John B. McKinlay and Sonja M. McKinlay, "The Questionable Contribution of Medical Measures to the Decline of Mortality in the U.S. in the Twentieth Century," *Milbank Memorial Fund Quarterly: Health and Society,* Summer 1977, p. 425.

189. John B. McKinlay and Sonja M. McKinlay, "A Refutation of the Thesis That the Health of the Nation Is Improving," a study report as part of a research project supported by grants from Milbank Memorial Fund (to Boston University) and the Carnegie Fund (to Radcliffe Institute), pp. 412–14.

190. Michael J. Canlon, "EPA Cites U.S. Environment as a Leading Death Cause," *Washington Post,* August 27, 1978.

191. Emile Benoit, "A Dynamic Equilibrium Economy," *Bulletin of the Atomic Scientists,* Feburary 1976.

192. *East West Journal,* August 1977, p. 13.

193. Ralph C. Dougherty et al., "Sperm Density and Toxic Substances: A Potential Key to Environmental Health Hazards," in J. D. McKinney, *Environmental Health Chemistry— The Chemistry of Environmental Agents as Potential Human Hazards* (Ann Arbor, Michigan: Ann Arbor Science Publishers, Inc., 1980).

194. Ophuls, op. cit., pp. 78–79.

195. Daly, op. cit., pp. 193–94.

196. Douglas M. Costle, Administrator, "Defense by Disaster:

Proving the Value of Environmental Protection," EPA Speech, Washington, D.C., March 29, 1979.

197. Stewart T. Herman, *The Health Costs of Air Pollution* (Fairfax, Va.: American Lung Association, 1977).

198. U.S. Congress, Office of Technology Assessment (OTA), Acid Rain and Transported Air Pollutants: Implications for Public Policy (Washington, D.C.: U.S. Government Printing Office, 1984).

PART SIX
ENTROPY: A NEW WORLD VIEW

1. World Conference, *The Changing Atmosphere: Implications for Global Security* (Toronto, Canada: Conference Statement, June 1988), p. 10.
2. "The Endless Summer?" *Newsweek,* July 11, 1988, p. 20.
3. Ibid.
4. Lester R. Brown, *State of the World, 1987: A Worldwatch Institute Report on Progress Toward a Sustainable Society* (New York: Norton, 1987), p. 182.
5. J. Darmstadler, *How Industrial Societies Use Energy: A Comparative Analysis* (Baltimore: Johns Hopkins University Press, 1977).
6. Bill Keepin, "Greenhouse Warming: A Rationale for Nuclear Power?" Testimony before the House Committee on Science, Space and Technology Subcommittee on Natural Resources, Agriculture Research and Environment and Subcommittee on Science, Research and Technology, June 29, 1988.
7. B. J. Friedan and K. Baker, "The Market Needs Help: The Disappointing Record of Home Energy Conservation," 2 *Journal of Policy Analysis and Management* 432–48 (1983).
8. David B. Goldstein, "Refrigerator Reform: Guidelines for Energy Gluttons," 86(2) *Technology Review* 36–46 (1983).
9. Ibid.
10. Ibid.
11. Eric Hirst, *Evaluation of Utility Home Energy Audit (RCS) Programs* (Oak Ridge, Tenn.: Oak Ridge National Laboratory, Feb. 1984).

12. Goldstein, op. cit., pp. 36–46.
13. Elizabeth Tucker, "Energy—Standard Veto: No One Won, Groups Say," *Washington Post,* November 5, 1986.
14. U.S. Department of Energy, *Residential Energy Consumption Survey: Consumption and Expenditures* (Washington, D.C.: U.S. Government Printing Office, 1982).
15. Testimony of Claudine Schneider before the House Committee on Science, Space and Technology Subcommittee on Natural Resources, Agriculture Research and Environment and Subcommittee on Science, Research and Technology, June 29, 1988.
16. Federal Highway Administration, Office of Traffic Operations, *Ridesharing Statistics, 1987* (Washington, D.C.: U.S. Government Printing Office, 1987).
17. Schneider, op. cit.
18. Report on Building a Sustainable Future (SERI), Committee on Energy and Commerce (Washington, D.C.: U.S. Government Printing Office, April 1981), vol. 1.
19. Keepin, op. cit.
20. American Council for an Energy Efficient Economy, *The Role of Federal Research and Development in Advancing Energy Efficiency: A Multi-Million Dollar Contribution to the U.S. Economy* (Washington, D.C., September 1987), p. 3.
21. Schneider, op. cit.
22. Milgram, quoted in Charles Papke, "Plastics Recycling As a Business," *Resource Recycling,* September/October 1986; Robert C. Letcher and Mary T. Sheil, "Source Separation and Citizen Recycling," ed. William D. Robinson, *The Solid Waste Handbook* (New York: John Wiley and Sons, 1986).
23. Letcher and Sheil, op. cit.
24. S. L. Blum, "Tapping Resources in Municipal Solid Waste," *Science,* 191 (1976): 669–75.
25. David Morris, "A National Resource Recovery Policy Emerging," *Building Economic Alternatives* (Washington, D.C.: Co-op America, 1985).
26. Walter Liong-Ting Hang and Steven A. Romalewski, *The*

Burning Question: Garbage Incineration Versus Total Recycling in New York City (New York: New York Public Interest Research Center, 1986).

27. Aluminum Association, *Statistical Review for 1985;* "Reynolds Aluminum Will Close Its New Jersey Recycling Centers," *New York Times,* May 20, 1984.

28. Richard Keller, "Purchases of Recycled Paper: An Important Tool for Market Development," *Resource Recycling,* July/August 1983; Clifford Case and Richard Keller, "Buying Recycled Paper: The Story Continues," *Resource Recycling,* July/August, 1985.

29. Shigeo Egusa, "A Second Life for Wastepaper," 6 *Journal of Japanese Trade and Industry* (1985).

30. Organization for Economic Co-operation and Development (OECD), *Household Waste: Separate Collection and Recycling* (Paris, France: 1983); William U. Chandler, *Materials Recycling: The Virtue of Necessity,* Worldwatch Paper 56 (Washington, D.C.: Worldwatch Institute, October 1983).

31. Dennis Hayes, *Rays of Hope* (New York: Norton, 1977), p. 139.

32. Schneider, op. cit.

33. Philip H. Abelson, "Electric Power from the North," *Science,* June 28, 1988.

34. Gever, *Beyond Oil,* p. 127 (Cambridge, Mass.: Ballinger Publishing Co., 1986).

35. Gever, Ibid., p. 132, Figure 4-11.

36. *Newsweek,* July, 1988, "A Gaping Hole in the Sky," p. 21.

37. USDA, ERS, *China: Outlook and Situation Report;* Perry and Wong, *Reform in Post-Mao China;* Vaclav Smil, *The Bad Earth: Environmental Degradation in China* (Armonk, N.Y.: M.E. Sharpe Inc., 1984); Liu Dizhong, "Tree Target for 1986 Planted in Six Months," China Daily, July 9, 1986.

38. Keepin, op. cit.

39. Ibid.

40. "Public Citizen Condemns Nuclear Provisions of Johnston-Wirth Global Warming Bill," Press Release, July 28, 1988.

41. Keepin, op. cit.
42. Ibid.
43. For information on various solar techniques, see: Denis Hayes, *Rays of Hope* (New York: Norton, 1977) and Stephen Lyons, ed., *Sun: A Handbook for the Solar Decade* (San Francisco: Friends of the Earth, 1978).
44. Ibid.
45. Source: Resources for the Future, Washington, D.C., June 1979.
46. W. Jackson Davis, *The Seventh Year: Industrial Civilization in Transition* (New York: Norton, 1979), p. 69.
47. Wilson Clark, *Energy for Survival* (Garden City, N.Y.: Doubleday/Anchor Books, 1975), p. 115.
48. Tristram Coffin, "Conversion, the Answer to Inflation and Recession," *Washington Spectator,* February 1, 1979.
49. E. F. Schumacher, *Good Work* (New York: Harper & Row, 1979), p. 18.
50. Murray Bookchin, "Technology for Life," in Lyons, op. cit.
51. William Ophuls, *Ecology and the Politics of Scarcity* (San Francisco: Freeman, 1977).
52. Howard Odum, "Net Energy from the Sun," in Lyons, op. cit.
53. Richard Munson, "Ripping off the Sun," *The Progressive,* September 1979, p. 13.
54. Hayes, op. cit., p. 20.
55. Donald C. Winston, "There Goes the Sun," *Newsweek,* December 3, 1979, p. 35.
56. Nicholas Georgescu-Roegen, "Technology Assessment: The Case of the Direct Use of Solar Energy," *Atlantic Economic Journal* 6 (December 1978): 20.
57. Munson, op. cit., p. 12.
58. Ibid., p. 13.
59. Ibid., p. 14.
60. Lawrence A. Mayer, "Climbing Back from Negative Growth," *Fortune,* August 1975.
61. Emile Benoit, "The Coming Age of Shortages, Part I," *Bulletin of the Atomic Scientists,* January 1976, p. 14.
62. The Hunger Project, San Francisco, California, 1978.

63. Anil Agarwal, "New Strategy for World Health," *New Scientist,* June 22, 1978, p. 821.

64. C.T. Kurien, "A Just, Participatory and Sustainable Society: A Third World Perspective," paper presented at the Conference on Faith, Science and the Future, World Council of Churches, Boston, Mass., July 12–24, 1979.

65. Herman Daly, "The Ecological and Moral Necessity for Limiting Economic Growth," paper presented at the Conference on Faith, Science and the Future, World Council of Churches, Boston, Mass., July 12–24, 1979.

66. Graham Hovey, "More Crowding Forecast in World's Poorer Cities," *New York Times,* August 16, 1979, p. D1.

67. Boyce Rensberger, "Expert Says Only Hope to Feed World Is with Food Production Unlike That in U.S.," *New York Times,* December 8, 1976, p. A19.

68. O. A. El Kholy, "Science, Technology and the Future: An Arab Perspective," paper presented at the Conference on Faith, Science and the Future, World Council of Churches, Boston, Mass., July 12–24, 1979.

69. Robert L. Heilbroner, *An Inquiry into the Human Prospect* (New York: Norton, 1974), p. 86.

70. Schumacher, op. cit., p. 123.

71. All quotes in this paragraph from *Less Is More,* ed. Goldian Vanden Broeck (New York: Harper & Row, 1978).

72. Ibid.

73. E. F. Schumacher, *Small Is Beautiful* (New York: Perennial, 1973), p. 54.

74. Hazel Henderson, *Creating Alternative Futures* (Berkeley: Windhover, 1978), p. 394.

75. C. W. Hollister, "Twilight in the West," in *The Transformation of the Roman World,* ed. L. White, Jr. (Berkeley: University of California Press, 1966), p. 204.

76. Barry Commoner, *The Poverty of Power* (New York: Bantam Books, 1977), p. 163.

77. Howard S. Gellor, "Progress in the Energy Efficiency of Residential Appliances and Space Conditioning Equipment," in *Energy Sources: Conservation and Renewables* (New York: American Institute of Physics, 1985).

78. Ibid.
79. Ibid.
80. Keith Schneider, "Scientists Trying to Give Crops an Edge Over Nature's Forces," *New York Times,* August 1, 1988.
81. Jonathon B. Tucker, "Amaranth: The Once and Future Crop," *Bioscience,* January, 1986.
82. Ibid.
83. Sam Love, "The New Look of the Future," *The Futurist,* April 1977, p. 78.
84. Schumacher, *Small Is Beautiful,* op. cit., p. 54.
85. Davis, op. cit., pp. 217–18.
86. Nicholas Wade, "Nicholas Georgescu-Roegen: Entropy: the Measure of Economic Man," *Science,* October 31, 1975.
87. Bertrand Russell, *The Scientific Outlook* (New York: Norton, 1962), p. 85.
88. John Lukacs, *The Passing of the Modern Age* (New York: Harper Torchbooks, 1970), p. 152.
89. Russell, op. cit., pp. 92–93.
90. Ibid.
91. Max Born, *The Restless Universe* (New York: Harper, 1936), p. 277.
92. Will Lepkowski, "The Social Thermodynamics of Ilya Prigogine," *Chemical & Engineering News,* April 16, 1979, p. 33.
93. George Vecsey, "Buddhism in America," *New York Times Magazine,* June 3, 1979, p. 30.
94. The Gallup Opinion Index, "Religion in America," 1977–78.
95. Richard Quebedeaux, *The Young Evangelicals* (New York, Harper & Row, 1974), pp. 127–28.
96. Henlee H. Barnett, *The Church and the Ecological Crisis* (Grand Rapids, Mich: Erdmans, 1972), p. 69. Also, Francis A. Schaeffer, *Pollution and the Death of Man: The Christian View of Ecology* (Wheaton, Ill.: Tyndale House, 1970), p. 37.
97. Barnett, ibid., pp. 78–79.
98. Schaeffer, op. cit., pp. 91–92.
99. Barnett, op. cit., p. 81.
100. Schaeffer, op. cit., pp. 49–50.

101. Francis A. Schaeffer, *How Should We Then Live?* (Old Tappan, N.J.: Fleming Revell, 1976).
102. Ibid., p. 227.
103. Wendell Berry, *The Unsettling of America* (New York: Avon, 1977), p. 20.
104. "Entropy Concept in Philosophy," in *Entropy and Information in Science and Philosophy*, ed. Libor Kubat and Jiri Zeman (New York: Elsevier, 1975), p. 240.

Bibliography

PART ONE
WORLD VIEWS

Adams, Henry. *The Degradation of the Democratic Dogma*. New York: Macmillan, 1919.

Bacon, Francis. *Novum Organum*. Book 1, Aphorisms, 2, 71.

Barrett, William. *The Illusion of Technique*. Garden City,. N.Y.: Doubleday/Anchor, 1976.

Bluhm, William. *Ideologies and Attitudes*. Englewood Cliffs, N.J.: Prentice-Hall, 1974.

Boulding, Kenneth. *The Meaning of the Twentieth Century*. New York: Harper & Row, 1965.

Brinton, Crane. *The Shaping of Modern Thought*. Englewood Cliffs, N.J.: Prentice-Hall, 1963.

Bury, J. B. *The Idea of Progress: An Inquiry into its Origin and Growth*. New York: Macmillan, 1932.

Descartes, René. *Discoursean Method*. Part 6.

Ferkiss Victor. *The Future of Technological Civilization*. New York: Braziller, 1974.

Gardiner, Patrick (ed.). *Theories of History*. New York: Free Press, 1959.

Germino, Dante L. *Modern Western Political Thought*. Chicago: Rand McNally, 1972.

Girvetz, Harry K. *The Evolution of Liberalism*. New York: Collier, 1967.

Himmelfarb, Gertrude. *Darwin and the Darwinian Revolution*. New York: Norton, 1968.

Hofstadter, Richard. *Social Darwinisn in American Thought*. Boston: Beacon, 1955.

Holton, Gerald. *Thematic Origins of Scientific Thought: Kepler to Einstein*. Cambridge, Mass.: Harvard University Press, 1973.

Humpshire, Stuart. *The Age of Reason: The 17th Century Philosophers*. New York: New American Library, 1956.

Kuhn, Thomas S. *The Structure of Scientific Revolutions*. Chicago: University of Chicago Press, 1970.

Lewis, Elwart (ed.). *Medieval Political Ideas*. New York: Knopf, 1954.

Lindsay, Robert Bruce. *The Role of Science in Civilization*. New York: Harper & Row, 1963.

Lukacs, John. *The Passing of the Modern Age*. New York: Harper, 1970.

Marty, Martin. *A Short History of Christianity*. New York: Collins, World, 1959.

Mumford, Lewis. *Technics and Civilization*. New York: Harcourt, Brace, 1934.

Nisbet, Robert. *Twilight of Authority*. New York: Oxford University Press, 1975.

Pollard, Sidney. *The Idea of Progress*. New York: Basic Books, 1968.

Pynchon, Thomas. "Entropy." *Kenyon Review* 22 (Spring 1960).

Randall, John Herman. *The Making of the Modern Mind*. New York: Columbia University Press, 1940.

Roszak, Theodore. *Where the Wasteland Ends*. Garden City, N.Y.: Doubleday/Anchor Books, 1973.

Rousseau, Jean Jacques. *The Social Contract*. Hardmondsworth. Middlesex, England: Penguin Books, 1968.

Schrag, Peter. *The End of the American Future*. New York: Simon & Schuster, 1973.

Stent, Gunther S. *The Coming of the Golden Age: A View of the End of Progress*. Garden City, N.Y.: Natural History Press, 1969.

Bibliography

Tawney, R. H. *Religion and the Rise of Capitalism*. New York: Harcourt, Brace, 1926.

Tillinghast, Pardon E. (ed.). *Approaches to History*. Englewood Cliffs, N.J.: Prentice-Hall, 1963.

Whitehead, Alfred North. *Science and the Modern World*. New York: Macmillan, 1925.

PART TWO
THE ENTROPY LAW

Angrist, Stanley W. and Loren G. Hepler. "Demons, Poetry and Life: A Thermodynamic View." *Texas Quarterly* 10 (September 1967).

Asimov, Isaac. *A Short History of Biology*. Garden City, Natural History Press, 1964.

Asimov, Isaac. "In the Game of Energy and Thermodynamics You Can't Even Break Even." *Smithsonian,* August 1970.

Asimov, Isaac. "What Is Entropy?" *Science Digest* 73 (January 1973).

Berry, R. Stephen. "Recycling, Thermodynamics and Environmental Thrift." *Bulletin of Atomic Scientists* 28 (May 1972).

Blum, Harold F. *Time's Arrow and Evolution*. Princeton, N.J.: Princeton University Press, 1968.

Brillouin, L. "Life, Thermodynamics and Cybernetics." *American Scientist* 37 (October 1949).

Capek, Milic. *The Philosophical Impact of Contemporary Physics*. New York: Van Nostrand, 1961.

Daly, Herman E. *Toward a Steady State Economy*. San Francisco: Freeman, 1973.

Davies, Paul. *The Runaway Universe*. New York: Harper & Row, 1978.

Ditta, Mahadev. "A Hundred Years of Entropy." *Physics Today* 21 (January 1968).

Dobzhansky, Theodosius. *The Biological Basis of Human Freedom*. New York: Columbia University Press, 1956.

Eddington, Sir Arthur. *The Nature of the Physical World*. Ann Arbor: Ann Arbor Paperbacks, University of Michigan Press, 1958.

Georgescu-Roegen, Nicholas. *Energy and Economic Myths.* Elmsford, N.Y.: Pergamon Press, 1977.

Georgescu-Roegen, Nicholas. *The Entropy Law and the Economic Process.* Cambridge, Mass.: Harvard University Press, 1971.

Georgescu-Roegen, Nicholas. *Analytical Economics: Issues and Problems.* Cambridge, Mass.: Harvard University Press, 1966.

Georgescu-Roegen, Nicholas. "The Steady State and Ecological Salvation: A Thermodynamic Analysis." *Bioscience* 27 (April 1977).

Heilbroner, Robert L. *An Inquiry into the Human Prospect.* New York: Norton, 1974.

Hiebert, Erwin N. "The Uses and Abuses of Thermodynamics in Religion." *Daedalus* 95 (Fall 1966).

Houston, Jean. "Prometheus Rebound: An Inquiry into Technological Growth and Psychological Change." In *Alternatives to Growth I.* Edited by Dennis L. Meadows. Cambridge, Mass.: Ballinger, 1977.

Kelley, Hillary Jay. "Entropy of Knowledge." *Philosophy of Science* 36 (June 1969).

Kubat, Libor, and Jiri Zeman (eds.). *Entropy and Information in Science and Philosophy.* New York: Elsevier, 1975.

Lindsay, R. B. "Entropy Consumption and Values in Physical Science." *American Scientist* 47 (Autumn-September 1959).

Lindsay, Robert Bruce. *The Role of Science in Civilization.* New York: Harper & Row, 1963.

Lotka, Alfred J. "Contribution to the Energetics of Evolution." *Proceedings of the National Academy of Sciences* 8 (1922).

Lotka, Alfred J. "The Law of Evolution as a Maximal Principle." *Human Biology: A Record of Research* 17 (September 1945).

Mayr, Ernst. "Evolution." *Scientific American,* September 1978.

Miller, G. Tyler, Jr. *Energetics, Kinetics and Life: An Ecological Approach.* Belmont, Calif.: Wadsworth, 1971.

Morowitz, Harold J. *Energy Flow in Biology.* New York: Academic Press, 1968.

O'Manique, John. *Energy in Evolution.* New York: Humanities Press, 1969.

Parsegian, V. L. "Biological Trends within Cosmic Processes." *Zygon* 8 (September–December 1973).

Polgar, Steven. "Evolution and the Thermodynamic Imperative." In *Human Biology*, vol. 33. Detroit, Mich.: Wayne State University Press, 1961.

Porter, George. "The Laws of Disorder." *Chemistry*. Reprint 85. Vol. 41 (May–December 1968); vol. 42 (January–February 1969).

Prigogine, Ilya, Gregoire Nicolis, and Agnes Babloyantz. "Thermodynamics of Evolution." *Physics Today*, November 1972.

Rodgers, Donald W. "An Informal History of the First Law of Thermodynamics." *Chemistry* 49 (December 1976).

Russell, Bertrand. *The Scientific Outlook*. New York: Norton, 1962.

Schrodinger, Erwin. *What Is Life? The Physical Aspect of the Living Cell*. New York: Macmillan, 1947.

Schumacher, E. F. *A Guide for the Perplexed*. New York: Harper & Row, 1977.

Seifert, H. S. "Can We Decrease Our Entropy." *American Scientist* 49 (Summer–June 1961).

Simpson, George Gaylord. *The Meaning of Evolution*. New Haven: Yale University Press, 1949.

Stebbing, L. Susan. "Entropy and Becoming." *Philosophy and the Physicists*, New York: Dover, 1958.

Wagner, Vern. *The Suspension of Henry Adams: A Study of Manner and Matter*. Detroit: Wayne State University Press, 1969.

Warshofsky, Fred. *Doomsday: The Science of Catastrophe*. New York: Pocket Books, 1979.

Watanabe, Satosi. "The Concept of Time in Modern Physics and Bergson's Pure Duration." In *Bergson and the Evolution of Physics*. Edited by D. A. Y. Gunter. Knoxville, Tenn.: University of Tennessee Press, 1977.

White, Leslie A. "Tools, Techniques and Energy." In *Cultural and Social Anthropology*. Edited by P. Hamond. New York: Macmillan, 1964.

Wiener, Philip P. (ed.). "Entropy." In *The Dictionary of the History of Ideas*. Vol. 2. New York: Scribner's, 1973.

PART THREE
ENTROPY: A NEW HISTORICAL FRAME

Adams, Brooks. *The Law of Civilization and Decay*. Freeport, N.Y.: Books for Libraries, 1971.

Adams, Richard Newbold. *Energy and Structure*. Austin, Texas: University of Texas Press, 1975.

Ayres, Eugene. "The Age of Fossil Fuels." In *Man's Role in Changing the Face of the Earth*. Edited by William L. Thomas, Jr. Chicago: University of Chicago Press, 1956.

Barrett, William. *The Illusion of Technique*. Garden City, N.Y.: Doubleday/Anchor Books, 1978.

Bates, Marston. "Process." In *Man's Role in Changing the Face of the Earth*. Edited by William L. Thomas, Jr. Chicago: University of Chicago Press, 1956.

Bluhm, William T. *Ideologies and Attitudes: Modern Political Culture*. Englewood Cliffs, N.J.: Prentice-Hall, 1974.

Boulding, Kenneth. "The Interplay of Technology and Values: The Emerging Superculture." In *Values and the Future: The Impact of Technological Change on American Values*. Edited by Kurt Bauer and Nicholas Rescher. New York: Free Press, 1969.

Boulding, Kenneth. *The Meaning of the Twentieth Century*. New York: Harper & Row, 1965.

Childe, V. Gordon. *Man Makes Himself*. New York: New American Library, 1951.

Congress of the United States, Joint Economic Committee. "Productivity and Technological Change." In *U.S. Long-Term Economic Growth Prospects: Entering a New Era*. Washington, D.C.: U.S. Government Printing Office, January 25, 1978.

Daly, Herman E. *Steady-State Economics*. San Francisco: Freeman, 1977.

Darby, H. C. "The Cleaning of the Woodland." In *Man's Role in Changing the Face of the Earth*. Edited by William L. Thomas, Jr. Chicago: University of Chicago Press, 1956.

Douglas, Jack D. (ed.). *The Technological Threat*. Englewood Cliffs, N.J.: Prentice-Hall, 1971.

Dubos, René. *The Torch of Life*. New York: Simon & Schuster, 1962.

Ellul, Jacques. *The Technological Society*. New York: Random House/Vintage Books, 1964.

Environmental Quality Council. Executive Office of the President. *Environmental Quality, Ninth Annual Report*. Washington, D.C.: U.S. Government Printing Office, December 1978.

Farb, Peter. *Humankind*. Boston: Houghton Mifflin, 1978.

Ferkiss, Victor. *The Future of Technological Civilization*. New York: Braziller, 1974.

Gall, John. *Systemantics: How Systems Work and Especially How They Fail*. New York: Pocket Books, 1975.

Georgescu-Roegen, Nicholas. *Analytical Economics*. Cambridge, Mass.: Harvard University Press, 1966.

Georgescu-Roegen, Nicholas. *The Entropy Law and the Economic Process*. Cambridge, Mass.: Harvard University Press, 1971.

Giarini, Orio, and Henri Louberge. *The Diminishing Returns of Technology*. Oxford: Pergamon Press, 1978.

Harmon, Willis W. "The Coming Transformation II." *The Futurist* 11 (April 1977).

Heilbroner, Robert L. *An Inquiry into the Human Prospect*. New York: Norton, 1974.

Heilbroner, Robert L. "Do Machines Make History?" In *Technology and Culture*. Chicago: University of Chicago Press, 1967.

Hirsch, Fred. *Social Limits to Growth*. Cambridge, Mass.: Harvard University Press, 1978.

Houston, Jean. "Prometheus Rebound: An Inquiry into Technological Growth and Psychological Change." In *Alternatives to Growth I*. Edited by Dennis L. Meadows. Cambridge, Mass.: Ballinger, 1977.

Hoyt, Robert S. *Europe in the Middle Ages*. New York: Harcourt, Brace & World, 1966.

Kariel, Henry S. *Beyond Liberalism, Where Relations Grow*. New York: Harper & Row, 1978.

Kranzberg, Melvin, and Carroll W. Pruell, Jr. *Technology in Western Civilization*. New York: Oxford University Press, 1967.

Lewontin, Richard C. "Adaptation." *Scientific American*, September 1968.

Lindsay, Robert B. *The Role of Science in Civilization*. New York: Harper & Row, 1963.

Lukacs, John. *The Passing of the Modern Age*. New York: Harper, 1970.

Meadows, Donella. "Limits to Growth Revisited." In *Finite Resources and the Human Future*. Edited by Ian G. Barbour. Minneapolis: Augsburg, 1976.

Mesthene, Emmanuel G. *Technological Change*. New York: New American Library, 1970.

Miles, Rufus, E., Jr. *Awakening from the American Dream*. New York: Universe, 1976.

Mishan, E. J. *The Economic Growth Debate*. London: George Allan & Unwin, 1977.

Morison, Elting E. *Men, Machines and Modern Times*. Cambridge, Mass.: MIT Press, 1966.

Mumford, Lewis. *Technics and Civilization*. New York: Harcourt, Brace, 1934.

Nichols, Roy F. "The Dynamic Interpretation of History." *New England Quarterly*, June 1935.

Oltmans, Willem L. *On Growth*. New York: Capricorn Books, 1974.

Ophuls, William. *Ecology and the Politics of Scarcity*. San Francisco: Freeman, 1977.

Ortega y Gasset, José. *The Revolt of the Masses*. New York: Norton, 1932.

Randall, John, Jr. *The Making of the Modern Mind*. Cambridge, Mass.: Houghton Mifflin, Riverside Press, 1940.

Renshaw, Edward F. "Productivity." In *U.S. Economic Growth from 1976 to 1986: Prospects, Problems and Patterns*. Vol. 1. Studies for the Joint Economic Committee. Washington, D.C.: U.S. Government Printing Office, 1976.

Roszak, Theodore, *Where the Wasteland Ends*. Garden City, N.Y.: Doubleday/Anchor Books, 1972.

Rothman, Harry. *Murderous Providence: A Study of Pollution in Industrial Societies*. New York: Bobbs-Merrill, 1972.

Sauer, Carl O. "The Agency of Man on the Earth." In *Man's Role in Changing the Face of the Earth*. Edited by William L. Thomas, Jr. Chicago: University of Chicago Press, 1956.

Schwartz, Eugene S. *Overskill: The Decline of Technology in Modern Civilization*. Chicago: Quadrangle, 1971.

Sears, Paul B. "The Processes of Environmental Change by Man." In *Man's Role in Changing the Face of the Earth*. Edited by William L. Thomas, Jr. Chicago: University of Chicago Press, 1956.

Slater, Philip. *The Pursuit of Loneliness: American Culture at the Breaking Point*. Boston: Beacon, 1976.

Spengler, Oswald. *The Decline of the West*. Vol. 1. New York: Knopf, 1926.

Spoehr, Alexander. "Cultural Differences in the Interpretation of Natural Resources." In *Man's Role in Changing the Face of the Earth*. Edited by William L. Thomas, Jr. Chicago: University of Chicago Press, 1956.

Stent, Gunther S. *The Coming of the Golden Age: A View of the End of Progress*. Garden City, N.Y.: Natural History Press, 1969.

Teich, Albert H. *Technology and Man's Future*. New York: St. Martin's Press, 1972.

Toynbee, Arnold. *A Study of History*. New York: Oxford University Press, 1961.

White, Leslie A. "Tools, Techniques and Energy." In *Cultural and Social Anthropology*. Edited by P. Hamond. New York: Macmillan, 1964.

White, Lynn, Jr. "The Historical Roots of Our Ecological Crisis." *Science,* March 10, 1967.

Wilkinson, Richard G. *Poverty and Progress*. New York: Praeger, 1973.

Wittfogel, Earl A. "The Hydraulic Civilizations." In *Man's Role in Changing the Face of the Earth*. Edited by William L. Thomas, Jr. Chicago: University of Chicago Press, 1956.

PART FOUR
NONRENEWABLE ENERGY AND THE APPROACHING ENTROPY WATERSHED

Clark, Wilson. *Energy for Survival*. New York: Doubleday/Anchor Books, 1975.

Commoner, Barry. *The Poverty of Power*. New York: Bantam, 1977.

Davis, W. Jackson. *The Seventh Year: Industrial Civilization in Transition*. New York: Norton, 1979.

Gever, John, Robert Kaufmann, David Stole, and Charles Vorosmarty, "Beyond Oil: The Threat to Food and Fuel in the Coming Decades," by Carrying Capacity, Inc. Ballinger Publishing Company, Cambridge, Massachusetts, 1986.

Hayes, Dennis. *Rays of Hope*. New York: Norton, 1977.

Lovins, Amory. *Soft Energy Paths*. New York: Ballinger, 1977.

Lyons, Stephen (ed.). *Sun: A Handbook for the Solar Decade*. San Francisco: Friends of the Earth, 1978.

Meadows, Donella, Dennis Meadows, et al. *The Limits to Growth*. New York: Universe Books, 1972.

Nash, Hugh (ed.). *Progress As If Survival Mattered*. San Francisco: Friends of the Earth, 1978.

Odum, Howard T. and Elisabeth C. Odum. *Energy Basis for Man and Nature*. New York: McGraw-Hill, 1976.

Ophuls, William. *Ecology and the Politics of Scarcity*. San Francisco: Freeman, 1977.

PART FIVE
ENTROPY AND THE INDUSTRIAL AGE

Adams, Richard Newbold. *Energy and Structure*. Austin, Texas: University of Texas Press, 1975.

Baker, Thelma S. (ed.). *The Urbanization of Man*. Berkeley, Calif.: McCutchan, 1972.

Barber, William J. *A History of Economic Thought*. New York Penguin Books, 1967.

Barbour, Ian G. (ed.) *Finite Resources and the Human Future*. Minneapolis: Augsburg, 1976.

Benoit, Emile. "The Coming Age of Shortages, Part I." *Bulletin of the Atomic Scientists*, January 1976.

Berry, R. Stephen. "Recycling, Thermodynamics and Environmental Thrift." *Bulletin of the Atomic Scientists*, May 1972.

Berry, Wendell. *The Unsettling of America: Culture and Agriculture*. New York: Avon, 1977.

Bookchin, Murray. *The Limits of the City*. New York: Harper & Row, 1974.

Boulding, Kenneth. *Beyond Economics*. Ann Arbor, Mich.: Ann Arbor Paperbacks, 1960.

Broun, Hon. George E., Jr. "Transportation and the Energy Crisis." *Congressional Record*, July 30, 1973.

Brown, Lester R. *The Twenty-ninth Day*. New York: Norton, 1978.

Brown, Lester R. "State of the World, 1988," by Worldwatch Institute, Penguin Books Canada Ltd., Ontario, 1988.

Caldwell, Malcolm. *The Wealth of Some Nations*. 2nd edition. London: Zed Press Ltd., 1977.

Clark, Wilson. *Energy for Survival*. Garden City, N.Y.: Doubleday/Anchor Books, 1975.

Commoner, Barry. *The Poverty of Power*. New York: Bantam Books, 1976.

Daly, Herman E. "On Economics as a Life Science." *Journal of Political Economy* 76 (May–June 1968).

Daly, Herman E. *Steady State Economics*. San Francisco: Freeman, 1977.

Davis, W. Jackson. *The Seventh Year: Industrial Civilization in Transition*. New York: Norton, 1979.

Deane, Phyllis. *The Evolution of Economic Ideas*. London: Cambridge University Press, 1978.

Dixon, Bernard. *Beyond the Magic Bullet*. New York: Harper & Row, 1978.

Dubos, René. "Promises and Hazards of Man's Adaptability." *Environmental Quality in a Growing Economy*. Essays from the 6th RFF Forum. Baltimore: Johns Hopkins Press, 1966.

Eckholm, Erik. "Disappearing Species: The Social Challenge." *Worldwatch Paper*, no. 22 (June 1978).

Environmental Quality Council. Executive Office of the President, *Environmental Quality, Ninth Annual Report*. Washington, D.C.: U.S. Government Printing Office, December 1978.

Farb, Peter. *Humankind*. Boston: Houghton Mifflin, 1978.

Georgescu-Roegen, Nicholas. *Analytical Economics*. Cambridge, Mass.: Harvard University Press, 1966.

Georgescu-Roegen, Nicholas. *Energy and Economic Myths*. Elmsford, N.Y.: Pergamon Press, 1977.

Georgescu-Roegen, Nicholas. "Energy and Economic Myths." *Southern Economic Journal* 41 (January 1975).

Georgescu-Roegen, Nicholas. *The Entropy Law and the Economic Process*. Cambridge, Mass.: Harvard University Press, 1971.

Georgescu-Roegen, Nicholas. "Inequality, Limits and Growth from a Bioeconomic Viewpoint." *Review of Social Economy* 35 (December 1977).

Georgescu-Roegen, Nicholas. "The Steady State and Ecological Salvation: A Thermodynamic Analysis." *Bioscience* 27 (April 1977).

Georgescu-Roegen, Nicholas. "Technology Assessment: The Case of the Direct Use of Solar Energy." *Atlantic Economic Journal* 6 (December 1978).

Goodman, Robert. *After the Planners*. New York: Simon & Schuster, 1971.

Harrington, Michael. *The Twilight of Capitalism*. New York: Simon & Schuster, 1976.

Heilbroner, Robert L. *The Economic Transformation of America*. New York: Harcourt Brace Jovanovich, 1977.

Heilbroner, Robert L. *The Worldly Philosophers*. New York: Simon & Schuster, 1953.

Henderson, Hazel. *Creating Alternative Futures: The End of Economics*. New York: Berkeley-Windhover, 1978.

Hoffer, Abram, and Morton Walker. *Ortho-Molecular Nutrition*. New Canaan, Conn.: Keats, 1978.

Illich, Ivan. *Medical Nemesis*. New York: Bantam, 1977.

Ise, John. "The Theory of Value as Applied to Natural Resources." *American Economic Review* (St. Albans, Vermont) 15 (June 1925).

Jacobs, Jane. *The Death and Life of Great American Cities*. New York: Random House/Vintage Books, 1961.

Jegen, Mary Evelyn, and Bruno Manno (eds.). *The Earth is the Lord's*. New York: Paulist Press, 1978.

Leavitt, Helen. *Super Highway: Superhoax*. New York: Ballantine Books, 1971.

Lekachman, Robert. *A History of Economic Ideas*. New York: McGraw-Hill, 1959.

McKinlay, John B., and Sonja M. McKinlay. "The Questionable Contribution of Medical Measures to the Decline of Mortality in the U.S. in the Twentieth Century." *Milbank Memorial Fund Quarterly: Health and Society,* Summer 1977.

McWhinney, Ian R. "Medical Knowledge and the Rise of Technology." *Journal of Medicine and Philosophy,* Vol. 3, no. 4 (1978).

Meadows, Donella. "The World Food Problem: Growth Models and Nongrowth Solutions." In *Alternatives to Growth I.* Edited by Dennis Meadows. Cambridge, Mass.: Ballinger, 1977.

Mesthene, Emmanuel G., *Technological Change.* New York: New *Australian Economic Papers,* June 1976.

Miles, Rufus. *Awakening from the American Dream.* New York: Universe, 1976.

Mishan, Ezra J. *The Costs of Economic Growth.* New York: Praeger, 1969.

Mowbray, A. Q. *Road to Ruin.* Philadelphia: Lippincott, 1969.

National Wildlife Federation. *The End of the Road.* Washington, D.C., 1977.

Office of Technology Assessment, U.S. Congress. *The Effects of Nuclear War.* Washington, D.C.: U.S. Government Printing Office, 1979.

Oltmans, Willem L. *On Growth.* New York: Capricorn, 1974.

Ophuls, William. *Ecology and the Politics of Scarcity.* San Francisco: Freeman, 1977.

Perelman, Michael. "Energy, Entropy and Economic Value." *Australian Economic Papers,* June 1976.

Powles, John. "The Effect of Health Services on Adult Male Mortality." In *Ethics in Science and Medicine.* Vol. 5. Elmsford, N.Y.: Pergamon Press, 1978.

Powles, John. "On the Limitations of Modern Medicine." In *Science, Medicine, and Man.* Vol. 1. Elmsford, N.Y.: Pergamon Press, 1973.

"The State of the States 1988," by the Renew America Project of the Fund for Renewable Energy and the Environment, Washington, D.C., 1988.

Rothschild, Emma. *Paradise Lost: The Decline of the Auto Industrial Age.* New York: Random House, 1973.

Schwartz, Eugene. *Overskill: The Decline of Technology in Modern Civilization*. Chicago: Quadrangle, 1971.

Turvey, Ralph. "Side Effects of Resource Use." *Environmental Quality in a Growing Economy*. Essays from the 6th RFF Forum, Baltimore: Johns Hopkins Press, 1966.

Ullman, Edward L. "The Role of Transportation and the Basis for Interaction." In *Man's Role in Changing the Face of the Earth*. Edited by William L. Thomas, Jr. Chicago: University of Chicago Press, 1956.

Wade, Nicholas. "Entropy, the Measure of Economic Man." *Science* 190 (October 31, 1975).

Ward, Barbara. *The Home of Man*. New York: Norton, 1976.

Wilkinson, Richard. *Poverty of Power*. New York: Praeger, 1973.

Wogaman, J. Philip. *The Great Economic Debate*. Philadelphia: Westminster Press, 1977.

PART SIX

ENTROPY—A NEW WORLD VIEW

Adams, Henry. "A Letter to American History Teachers." In *Degradation of the Democratic Dogma*. New York: Peter Smith, 1949.

Adams, Richard N. *Energy and Structure*. Austin: University of Texas Press, 1975.

Ahlstrom, Sydney E. *A Religious History of the American People*. New Haven: Yale University Press, 1972.

Barnett, Henlee H. *The Church and the Ecological Crisis*. Grand Rapids, Mich.: Eerdmans, 1972.

Bell, Daniel. *The Coming of Post Industrial Society*. New York: Basic Books, 1973.

Bellah, Robert N. *The Broken Covenant*. New York: Seabury Press, 1975.

Bellak, Leopold. *Overload: The New Human Condition*. New York: Human Sciences Press, 1975.

Berry, Wendell. *The Unsettling of America: Culture and Agriculture*. New York: Avon Books, 1977.

Bloesch, Donald G. *The Evangelical Renaissance*. Grand Rapids, Mich.: Eerdmans, 1973.

Blum, Harold F. "Order, Negentropy and Evolution." In *Time's Arrow and Evolution*. Princeton, N.J.: Princeton University Press, 1968.

Boulding, Kenneth. "The Entropy Trap." In *The Meaning of the Twentieth Century*. New York: Harper & Row, 1965.

Brillouin, L. "Life, Thermodynamics and Cybernetics." *American Scientists*, October 1949.

Brush, Stephen G. "Thermodynamics and History." *The Graduate Journal*, 1967.

Butler, Samuel. *Erewhon*. New York: Penguin Books, 1977.

CBS Reports. "Is Anyone Out There Learning?" Parts I, II, III. Religion." *Daedalus*, Vol. 95, no. 4 (1966).

Callenbach, Ernest. *Ecotopia*. New York: Bantam, 1975.

Capek, Milic. *The Philosophical Impact of Contemporary Physics*. New York: Van Nostrand, 1961.

Davis, W. Jackson. *The Seventh Year: Industrial Civilization in Transition*. New York: Norton, 1979.

Dayton, Donald. *Discovering an Evangelical Heritage*. New York: Harper & Row, 1976.

Eddington, Sir Arthur. *The Nature of the Physical World*. Ann Arbor, Mich.: Ann Arbor Paperbacks, University of Michigan Press, 1958.

Eisenstadt, S. N. *The Protestant Ethic and Modernization*. New York: Basic Books, 1968.

Ellul, Jacques. *The Technological Society*. New York: Random House/Vintage Books, 1964.

Esser, Aristide H. "Environment and Mental Health." *Science, Medicine and Man*. Vol. 1. Elmsford, N.Y.: Pergamon Press, 1973.

Geiser, Robert L. *Behavior Mod and the Managed Society*. Boston: Beacon, 1976.

Henderson, Hazel. *Creating Alternative Futures: The End of Economics*. New York: Berkley-Windhover, 1978.

Henry, Carl. *Contemporary Evangelical Thought: A Survey*. Grand Rapids, Mich.: Baker Book House, 1968.

Hiebert, Erwin N. "The Uses and Abuses of Thermodynamics in Religion." *Daedalus*, vol. 95, no. 4 (1966).

Holton, Gerald. *Thematic Origins of Scientific Thought*. Cambridge, Mass.: Harvard Universiy Press, 1973.

Hudson, Winthrop S. *Religion in America*. New York: Scribner's, 1973.

Huxley, Aldous. *The Perennial Philosophy*. New York: Harper, 1970.

Iyer, Raghavan. *The Moral and Political Thought of Mahatma Gandhi*. New York: Oxford University Press, 1973.

Jaki, Stanley L. *The Relevance of Physics*. Chicago: University of Chicago Press, 1966.

Jegen, Mary, and Bruno Manno. *The Earth Is the Lord's*. New York: Paulist Press, 1978.

Kelley, Hillary Jay. "Entropy of Knowledge." *Philosophy of Science* 36 (June 1969).

Kuhn, Thomas S. *The Structure of Scientific Revolutions*. Chicago: University of Chicago Press, 1962.

Lambert, Frank L. "Ontology of Evil." *Zygon* 3 (June 1968).

Lepkowski, Mil. "The Social Thermodynamics of Ilya Prigogine." *Chemical and Engineering News*, April 16, 1979.

Lindsay, Robert B. "Entropy, Consumption and Values." *American Scientist* 47 (Autumn–September 1959).

Lindsay, Robert B. "Science and Communication." In *The Role of Science in Civilization*. New York: Harper & Row, 1963.

Lipowski, Z. J. "Sensory and Information Inputs Overload." *Comprehensive Psychiatry* 16 (May–June 1975).

Lovins, Amory B. *Soft Energy Paths*. Cambridge, Mass.: Ballinger, 1977.

Lukacs, John. *The Passing of the Modern Age*. New York: Harper, 1970.

Marty, Martin E. *A Short History of Christianity*. New York: Collins World, 1959.

Miller, G. Tyler, Jr. "Entropy, Poetry and Literature." In *Energetics, Kinetics and Life*. Belmont, Calif.: Wadsworth, 1971.

Morowitz, Harold. "Order, Information and Entropy." In *Energy Flow in Biology*. New York: Academic Press, 1968.

Morris, David, and Karl Hess. *Neighborhood Power*. Boston: Beacon, 1975.

Mumford, Lewis. *Technics and Civilization*. New York: Harcourt, Brace, 1934.

O'Manique, John. *Energy in Evolution*. New York: Humanities Press, 1969.

Ostwald, Wilhelm. "Monism as the Goal of Civilization." Edited and published by the International Committee of Monism, Hamburg, Germany (1913).

Parsegian, V. L. "Biological Trends within Cosmic Processes." *Zygon* 8 (September–December 1973).

Perrin, Noel. *Giving Up the Gun*. Boston: Godine, 1975.

Prigogine, Ilya. "Thermodynamics of Evolution." *Physics Today* 25 (November 1972).

Quebedeaux, Richard. *The Young Evangelicals*. New York: Harper & Row, 1974.

Russell, Bertrand. *The Scientific Outlook*. New York: Norton, 1962.

Schaeffer, Francis A. *How Should We Then Live?* Old Tappan, N.J.: Revell, 1976.

Schaeffer, Francis A. *Pollution and the Death of Man: The Christian View of Ecology*. Wheaton, Ill.: Tyndale House, 1970.

Schrag, Peter. *Mind Control*. New York: Pantheon, 1978.

Schumacher, E. F. *A Guide for the Perplexed*. New York: Harper & Row, 1977.

Schumacher, E. F. *Good Work*. New York: Harper & Row, 1979.

Schumacher, E. F. *Small is Beautiful*. New York: Perennial, 1973.

Schwartz, Eugene. *Overskill: The Decline of Technology in Modern Civilization*. Chicago: Quadrangle, 1971.

Simpson, George G. "The Search for an Ethic." In *The Meaning of Evolution*. New Haven: Yale University Press, 1949.

Slossen, Edwin E. "Wilhelm Ostwald." In *Major Prophets of Today*. Freeport, N.Y.: Books for Libraries Press, 1914.

Spillmann, Betty E. *The Logic of Life*. New York: Pantheon, 1973.

Stebbing, L. Susan. "Entropy and Becoming." In *Philosophy and the Physicists*. New York: Dover, 1958.

Stent, Gunther S. *The Coming of the Golden Age: A View of the End of Progress*. Garden City, N.Y.: Natural History Press, 1969.

Strizenec, Michal. "Information and Mental Processes." In *Entropy and Information in Science and Philosophy*. Edited by Libor Kubat and Jiri Zeman. New York: Elsevier, 1975.

Szumilewicz, Irena. "The Entropy Concept in Philosophy." In *Entropy and Information in Science and Philosophy*. Edited by Libor Kubat and Jiri Zeman. New York: Elsevier, 1975.

Tawney, R. H. *Religion and the Rise of Capitalism*. New York: Harcourt, Brace, 1926.

Teich, Albert H. (ed.). *Technology and Man's Future*. New York: St. Martin's Press, 1972.

Tillich, Paul. *A History of Christian Thought*. New York: Simon & Schuster, 1967.

Toynbee, Arnold J. *A Study of History*. New York: Oxford University Press, 1961.

Vanden Broeck, Goldian (ed.). *Less is More*. New York: Harper, 1978.

Wade, Nicholas. "Science and Its Contours: Must Rationality Be Rational?" *Science,* September 13, 1974.

Wallis, Jim. *Agenda for a Biblical People*. New York: Harper & Row, 1976.

Weber, Max. *The Protestant Ethic and the Spirit of Capitalism*. New York: Scribner's, 1958.

White, Lynn, Jr. "The Historical Roots of Our Ecological Crisis." *Science,* March 10, 1967.

Zeman, Jiri. "Information, Knowledge and Time." In *Entropy and Information in Science and Philosophy*. Edited by Libor Kubat and Jiri Zeman. New York: Elsevier, 1975.

About the Author

Jeremy Rifkin is an author, activist, and philosopher.

His critically acclaimed books, including *Entropy; Time Wars; Algeny; Declaration of a Heretic; Who Should Play God?;* and *The Emerging Order* are wide-ranging and interdisciplinary, covering topics from politics to philosophy and science. His books have been translated into twelve languages and are used in hundreds of college courses.

In 1986, the *National Journal,* one of the nation's leading public policy journals, selected Mr. Rifkin as one of the 150 people in the United States who have the most influence in shaping federal government policy. Mr. Rifkin is President of the Foundation on Economic Trends in Washington, D.C.